TOMMY'S WAR
British Military Memorabilia
1914–1918

TOMMY'S WAR

British Military Memorabilia

1914–1918

PETER DOYLE

FOREWORD BY RICHARD HOLMES

THE CROWOOD PRESS

First published in 2008 by
The Crowood Press Ltd
Ramsbury, Marlborough
Wiltshire SN8 2HR

www.crowood.com

British Library Cataloguing-in-Publication Data
A catalogue record for this book is available from the British Library.

ISBN 978 1 86126 996 6

Dedication
In loving memory of Christopher Edward Spencer (1958–2007).

Frontispiece: The harvest of war: unexploded British shells on the Somme.

Typeset and designed by D & N Publishing
Lambourn Woodlands, Hungerford, Berkshire.

Printed and bound in Singapore by Craft Print International Ltd

Contents

Foreword by Professor Richard Holmes

THE British soldier of the First World War is all too often seen as the victim of war's brutality, clad in monotonous khaki, with his identity crushed by dour uniformity. In fact the army in which he served was a deeply tribal organization, its members distinguished by a variety of insignia that marked out both status in the hierarchy and function within the group; these were, in effect, his tribal markings.

Nervous study of the badges and brassard worn by an approaching lieutenant colonel would establish (long before he asked why the devil our transport was blocking his road) that he was the General Staff Officer Grade 1 of an infantry division, and thus rather an important chap. As his soldiers tramped by we could not only tell their rank from the stripes on their sleeves and badges on their cuffs or shoulders, but also identify the number of occasions on which they had been wounded, and the amount of time they had put in, from their wound and service stripes. Medal ribbons above the left breast pocket marked campaign service, or bravery that had been officially recognized. A long glance at a man would tell the canny observer a good deal about his background and past performance and thus, for a man's courage in one battle sometimes stands surety for his behaviour in another, point to his future conduct.

It might also tell us a good deal about his unit. Serious-minded adjutants ensured that their officers wore dark khaki shirts, while the more relaxed tolerated straw-coloured confections. Cavalry officers liked khaki stocks secured by a gold pin. Leather tunic buttons were *de rigueur* in some units but banned in others, and even those Foot Guards officers who were allowed leather buttons still wore them grouped according to regimental practice: singly for the Grenadier Guards, in pairs for the Coldstream, and so on. Cunning quartermasters (was there, indeed, any other sort?) did their best to ensure, by bribery, barter and sometimes simple theft, that their men all wore the same type of equipment, with no eye-jarring mix of webbing and leather.

At the beginning of the war, regiments could be identified by cap badges worn by all ranks, and brass shoulder titles pinned through the epaulette by all non-commissioned personnel. Even when, early in the summer of 1916, the steel helmet replaced the service cap, Glengarry or tam-o'-shanter for wear in the field, shoulder titles still survived. A young soldier recently exhumed from the cutting of the old Ypres to Roulers railway line near Tyne Cot cemetery was marked out, in death as in life, by his Lancashire Fusilier title.

For Territorial units and some of Kitchener's 'New Army' battalions, shoulder titles did more than identify a man's regiment. They also drew attention to a specific battalion, for example, the 'city battalions' of the King's Liverpool Regiment, raised through the patriotic energy of Lord Derby, or the sportsmen's battalions of the Royal Fusiliers. There were times when soldiers personalized even their shoulder titles. The T that topped Territorial titles was often filed down to make a 1, showing that the man who wore it was not just any Territorial, but one who had volunteered for foreign service and constituted the first-line battalion of his old unit. Badges were not confined to the army, but were worn by munitions workers and others on essential war service. 'Sweetheart badges', usually a brooch in the form of a regiment's cap badge, were worn by wives and girlfriends.

As Peter Doyle's wonderful book so graphically shows, the material culture of the war was not confined to the braid and brass that men wore on their uniforms. It spread in a myriad of ripples at the front, through the rear areas and back in Britain, with items such as photographs, postcards, posters, trench newspapers and journals all helping to bind the nation to the army that served it. This was a society that knew the difference between a brigadier and a bombardier, had some inkling what an officer might have done to wear the purple and white ribbon of his Military Cross, and understood a good deal about the iconography of the regimental system. This volume is as rich and varied as the culture it describes, and shows us Tommy, as he might have wished to be remembered, in colour and not in drab.

Richard Holmes

Preface and Acknowledgements

This book is intended to illustrate the average life of the British soldier of the Great War through an exploration of the surviving objects, artefacts as diverse as trench periscopes and bully beef tins, which together illustrate just what it was like to fight this most peculiar and intimate war. Other authors have successfully described the soldiers' war in intricate detail: Dennis Winter's *Death's Men*, Malcolm Brown's *Tommy Goes to War*, John Ellis's *Eye-Deep in Hell*, and, more recently, Richard Holmes' *Tommy* have all attempted to paint a canvas of the life of the soldier in the trenches, a picture that is sometimes at odds with the outpourings of the literary generation of soldier-poets in the post-war era of disillusionment. The soldiers themselves, writing in later life, also appear vividly to recall exact details of their everyday life – what they ate, smoked, drank and did – mundanities recalled perhaps to cover the deeper memories of the assault on the senses they encountered in the trenches.

What is missing from all these works, understandably, is an appreciation of what the objects so closely associated with four years of warfare 'in the trenches' really looked like, how they were used, and what they meant. This book attempts to fill this significant gap, providing a visual reference that is usually filled only by the contents of museum cases.

This book is not an exploration of Grand Strategy. It is not a discussion of the rights and wrongs of the war, the conduct of the generals, or the outcome of battles. It is about the mundanity of warfare, the life of the average soldier of the 'poor bloody infantry', or PBI – what he ate, where he slept, what he wore and how he endured. The cavalry also endured where it was deployed – either in the open conditions of the Middle East, or where deployed as supplementary infantry on the Western Front – but the Great War is seen primarily as a 'footslogger's' war. In this war, the engineer created the longest fortifications in history, and the artilleryman tried to break them, using latter-day siege engines in the form of howitzers and mortars. But, ultimately, the infantry would inevitably have to rise from the protection of the trenches to take by force of arms their enemies' version of the same fortress.

Through the objects of Tommy's life, this book tells the story of what it was really like to serve as an infantryman in the Great War, principally on the Western Front, but also in the other 'sideshows' across the world. Through an exploration of what anthropologists and archaeologists call 'material culture', it recounts this story – the story of holding the line and enduring – and creates a visual encyclopaedia of the time.

ACKNOWLEDGEMENTS

In writing this book I have drawn upon a wealth of experience gained from a lifetime's collecting, and I would like to thank all those who, through the years, have added to my knowledge and supported my interest. I am particularly indebted to Laurie Milner, who has generously opened up his collection to inspection by a wide-eyed enthusiast, and who has proved to be an effective sounding board for ideas. A number of the objects illustrated here are his; most of the others are mine.

Other people who have aided in this project, providing either ideas or access to material include: Richard Archer, Peter Barton, Bella Bennett, Martin Brown, Steve Chambers, Peter Chasseaud, Sheila Dellow (for details of her Auntie Win and Uncle Bert), Paul Evans, Adam Forster of Worldwide Arms (for permission to photograph his SMLEs), Steve Henderson, Malcolm Hole (for the photograph of his grandfather, Sapper John Ablitt MM, DCM), Kristof Jacobs, Alain Jacques, Simon Jones, Len Ray, Andy Robertshaw, Eric Robinson (for details of his father, J. T. Robinson), Nick Saunders, Libby Simpson, Jane Staff, Tom Stafford, Nigel Steel, Tom Tulloch-Marshall (for help with On War Service Badges), Johan Vandewalle, Julian Walker (for details of the service of his grandfather, Pte Frederick Walker, KOYLI), Stephen Wheeler and Nick Wright.

Finally, none of this would have been possible (for a life-long collector) without the love and support of my parents, now sadly passed, and the belief and love of my wife Julie and son James.

Peter Doyle

NOTE ON NOMENCLATURE AND CONTEMPORARY VALUES

Throughout this book, and to avoid repetition, the terms 'First World War' and 'Great War' are used interchangeably. Both were in use during and after the war, the former reflecting the first time that war had erupted with such a wide geographic spread, the latter reflecting the scale of the conflict. To most people of Tommy's generation, the term Great War was the most widely used – on posters, in magazines and on the reverse of the inter-Allied Victory Medal, for example. With the eruption of a second, arguably greater World War, the term fell out of favour, to be replaced by 'First World War'. Despite this, the term 'Great War' has since seen a revival among historians and researchers, its language perhaps in keeping with an event that demarcates the close of the Edwardian period.

A number of abbreviations are used throughout: AOC (Army Ordnance Corps); ASC (Army Service Corps); BEF (British Expeditionary Force); Lt (Lieutenant); Pte (Private); RAMC (Royal Army Medical Corps); RE (Royal Engineers); RFA (Royal Field Artillery); RFC (Royal Flying Corps); RGA (Royal Garrison Artillery); Sgt (Sergeant).

Monetary values are given throughout in their original pounds, shillings and pence (£ s. d.) denominations. Until Britain's currency was decimalized in 1971, one pound (£) was worth twenty shillings (s.) and each shilling was worth twelve pence (d.). Today, one shilling is the equivalent of five new pence (p.); however, in 1914, its buying power was almost equivalent to five pounds today (and probably more in real terms), a function of the rapid rise in inflation experienced throughout the twentieth century. Linear measurements were all in Imperial at the time: feet and inches, with twelve inches to a foot. One foot is equivalent to approximately one third of a metre; an inch, around two and a half centimetres. In the British sector, trenches were laid out in Imperial; in some cases, metric was also used, where, for example, original French or Belgian maps were employed.

1 Introducing Tommy's War

'TOMMY Atkins' – the time-honoured name for the British soldier, a shorthand for the average man in uniform – reputedly dates back to Wellington's day, when, in a different, but equally momentous war, an appropriate name was needed for the model enlistment forms. Although it was not always to the liking of the soldiery, the name stuck, and was used universally throughout the Great War as an affectionate moniker for the man in the trenches. Other names reflected regional origins – Scots were usually 'Jock' and Welshmen, 'Taff', for example – but, despite these variations, 'Tommy' was still a name applied to all British soldiers. The Germans used it in an even wider sense: for them, Canadians, Newfoundlanders, Australians, New Zealanders and South Africans were undoubtedly lumped together under the universal appellation of 'Tommy'.

DEAR TOMMY,

YOU ARE QUITE WELCOME TO WHAT WE ARE LEAVING. WHEN WE STOP WE SHALL STOP, AND STOP YOU IN A MANNER YOU WONT APPRECIATE.

FRITZ

ABOVE: *'Tommy' was the term used universally to describe the British soldier. Here, a propaganda leaflet, left behind in the last retreats of the German army in 1918, hands over possession of the once-occupied territories of France to 'Tommy', courtesy of 'Fritz'.*

RIGHT: *'Tommy Atkins' was the subject of popular songs in wartime but, as pointed out by Rudyard Kipling, his bawdy reputation in peacetime meant that he was less welcome.*

OPPOSITE: *Tommy's trenches: preserved British trenches in Sanctuary Wood, Belgium.*

THE BRITISH SOLDIER IN THE GREAT WAR

It is a common perception that the average British soldier of the Great War was a volunteer, often underage, who was swept up in the great patriotic fervour of August 1914, and who joined the army to fight for King and Country. Disillusionment was to set in. The truth is somewhat more complex. For a modern audience brought up on the poems of Wilfred Owen and Siegfried Sassoon, on *Oh! What a Lovely War* and, more recently, *Blackadder Goes Forth*, the war seems an object lesson in futility, with thousands gassed and blown apart, 'hanging on the old front line', all in order to 'move Douglas Haig's drinks cabinet closer to Berlin'. For a growing number of historians, this is a gross oversimplification, and for many, a distortion of the facts. Indeed, a recent book *Mud, Blood and Poppycock* set out to explode, laboriously, many of the long-held tenets of the war, from 'the lost generation' to the 'needless slaughter' of the Somme. The pendulum has swung, perhaps, too far.

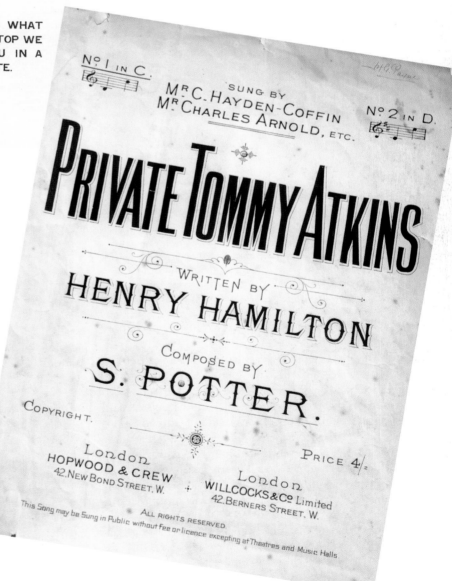

Tommy Atkins – a studio portrait of the typical British soldier of 1914–18, a gunner of the Royal Field Artillery in c.1917, with the 1903 pattern leather bandolier commonly used by mounted troops, and the 1917 pattern soft trench cap.

RIGHT: *The Battle of the Somme, July–November 1916, has often been portrayed as the graveyard of innocence, following the heavy casualties taken by the British volunteer battalions (the 'Pals'). Like Passchendaele in 1917, the Somme has become a byword for the suffering of the Great War, but some historians now see it as a necessary test in the development of the British 'art of attack', which was to win the war in the west in 1918. This book, written by John Buchan in 1917 when he was Director of Information for the British Government under Lord Beaverbrook, was intended to explain the battle for an American audience.*

Field Marshal Sir Douglas Haig, Commander-in-Chief of the British Expeditionary Force in France and Flanders from 1915, and the subject of much controversy. Haig has been portrayed in the past either as a 'butcher and bungler' or an 'educated soldier'. Military historians now mostly accept that he was the architect of victory in the west in 1918.

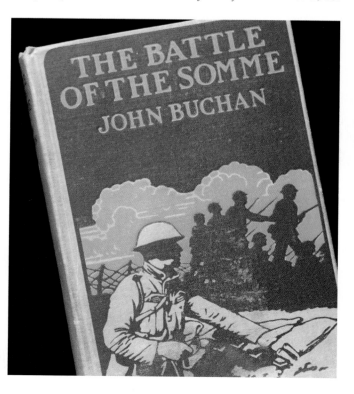

Much ink has been spilt in both attacking and defending the actions of the Generals – the 'donkeys' or 'butchers and bunglers' of popular historians – and many more pages will be written on the subject. For British and Commonwealth readers, books on major operations such as Gallipoli (1915), the Somme (1916), Vimy Ridge (1917), Passchendaele (Third Ypres 1917) or even the 'Forgotten Victory' of 1918 continue to flow from the presses as the anniversaries – and the last survivors – pass. Questions of whether the Somme was a catastrophe, or a phase of the 'learning curve' that ultimately led to Allied victory in 1918, or whether Passchendaele was a 'mincing machine' – an attritional battleground like that of Verdun – or a series of more or less successful bite-and-hold battles under difficult conditions, are typical of the accounts that line the shelves of most booksellers today.

BRITAIN DECLARED WAR AGAINST GERMANY
Wednesday, August 5, 1914.

"God Save the King."

Oh, the
bonnie,
bonnie Heather.
Let it bring
to you my friend all
the Gladness
and the Sunshine, and the
Joy that has no end.

But for the 'average' soldier, these issues were above the parapet or behind the lines. Often, Tommy had to write home for some indication of how the war was going (or read it in out-of-date newsprint sent to the front), as the routine of trench warfare was such that concentrating on that patch of sky observable from a six-foot, six-inch deep slit in the ground was all that was possible. These soldiers joined the army in the early war period for their own reasons – to escape, for adventure, from a sense of duty or from peer pressure. Later, from January 1916, they were compelled to join. Volunteer or conscript, all endured; most wrote home at some point or other to say that they were OK, 'in the pink' in the language of the day, and waiting for the war to end. In 1918–19 they came home, to get on with their lives and to forget. While the soldier-poets were putting pen to paper in the post-war period of 'disillusionment', the old soldiers were attempting to rebuild their lives.

LEFT: *The British declaration of war came on 4 August 1914, following the German violation of Belgian neutrality. This postcard, sent to the United States from Britain, trusts to the luck bestowed by a sprig of Scottish heather.*

BELOW: *The currency of the day: shillings and pence. The average British Tommy would be paid a shilling a day, plus allowances, but minus stoppages; pay would be issued at a formal parade, with the amount being recorded in his pay book.*

ABOVE: *Typical cap badges of the regular British Army. The King's Own (Royal Lancaster) Regiment had the unique distinction of bearing the lion of England on its head dress. This infantry regiment was typical in having two regular battalions; the Duke of Cambridge's Own (Middlesex) Regiment had four. The Royal Regiment of Artillery, distinguished by its distinctive gun, was one of the largest military units, its badge carrying the battle honour Ubique, meaning 'everywhere'.*

RIGHT: *Cap badges of Territorial regiments. Rural Cambridgeshire and Hertfordshire were less populous than some counties, and had only Territorial regiments, both of which served with distinction in the Great War.*

THE BRITISH ARMY

When Britain went to war in 1914, it had a small but highly trained professional force. In 1881, the Army had been overhauled to create a distinctly regional feel. Reforms by Lord Cardwell, then Secretary of State for War, had created county (regional in Wales, Scotland and Ireland) regiments throughout the United Kingdom; in some of the more populous areas of England, there was often more than one county regiment. Before Cardwell, there were 108 regular infantry regiments, and separate militia and volunteer battalions. After the reforms, there were sixty-one regiments, each allied directly with a county or region, and each given a home depot, and two regular battalions per regiment — although, following the Boer War, a few were to raise four regular battalions. All recruited locally, and the basic system of two regular battalions meant that one stayed at home while the other was away forming the Garrison of Empire, from Guernsey to India and far-flung Burma. A recruit could be expected to serve the first two years of his five-year term of service with the Home Battalion (generally understrength), the last five being with the overseas battalion; this meant that the home-service battalions had less experienced troops overall.

Following a further set of reforms in 1908, instigated by a new Secretary of State for War, Lord Haldane, in addition to the Regulars, each regiment gained a third Special Reserve Battalion, whose purpose was to gather recruits for the regular battalions. This was not a force that was deployed in the field. In fact, Special Reserve Battalions replaced the Militia that had served the same purpose prior to the Cardwell reforms. Men joining this battalion could enlist, receive six months' training, and be released to their civilian occupation on reduced pay, to be called to the colours in time of war. The fourth, fifth and sixth battalions of a regiment were territorial battalions, locally raised and under the control of county Territorial Associations, who were to manage recruitment through drill halls set up in different parts of the county. Irish regiments (the whole of Ireland was then part of the United Kingdom) were never to have territorial battalions, given the concerns simmering over home rule throughout the period. In addition, there were to be five all-territorial regiments, the multi-battalion County of London Regiment (distinct from the Royal Fusiliers, or City of London Regiment), and the Hereford-shire, Hertfordshire, Monmouthshire and Cambridgeshire regiments – these last four from counties whose population did not warrant a full-blown two-battalion regular infantry regiment.

Men serving as Territorials did so on the understanding that they were destined to serve as part-timers engaged on Home Defence, with no overseas commitment. The cavalry had its own equivalent, the Yeomanry, but, rather than battalions tied to regular cavalry units, these operated as separate regiments. When territorial recruits signed on, service was restricted to regular attendance at their local drill hall – earning them the not altogether flattering title of 'Saturday night soldiers' – and a regular field encampment. There were territorial gunners, engineers, RAMC, ASC, and so on. Although part-timers, the 'terriers' were liable for full-time service on the outbreak of war, the implication being that they would serve at home, while the Regulars proceeded overseas. However, on the outbreak of war, the vast majority of Territorials volunteered for overseas service.

Field Marshal Earl Kitchener of Khartoum – not a man to be trifled with – took over as Secretary of State for War in August 1914, replacing Haldane, who was widely suspected to have some German sympathies. Kitchener had little time for the Territorials, an organization that sat outside his direct line of control. He understood that the war would be costly in manpower, and that the eighty-four regular infantry battalions available at home – with seventy-three overseas – would be inadequate in a developing situation that he expected to last for at least three years. He therefore set in train a process whereby a direct appeal to the public would lead to the recruitment of enough men to support the war effort. Initially, these men would be recruited via the Special Reserve system but, following a request from the City of London to raise a whole battalion of stockbrokers, a plethora of 'City' and 'Pals' battalions were to be raised of men with similar backgrounds and circumstances. These new battalions started life with unofficial titles such as the 'Sportsman's Battalion', the 'Liverpool Pals' and the 'Grimsby Chums', but were soon assimilated into the military machine as additional battalions, numbered after the regular Special Reserve and territorial battalions of a county regiment – 23rd Royal Fusiliers, the 17th–20th King's (Liverpool) Regiment and the 11th Lincolnshire Regiment, respectively. In this way, recruitment avalanched in the early weeks of the war, with 300,000 men enlisting in August 1914 alone; by the end of the year that number had risen to 1,186,357.

The regular battalions available at home in 1914 were to form six infantry divisions; each division was to have

Field Marshal Earl Kitchener of Khartoum, Britain's most famous soldier, and a man not to be trifled with. Called to Government in 1914 as Secretary of State for War, he appealed for volunteers to what was to become known as 'Kitchener's Army'. He was lost at sea when HMS Hampshire, a cruiser en route to Russia, hit a mine off Orkney.

three infantry brigades, and each brigade in turn composed of four infantry battalions (later reduced to three following the manpower shortage that began to bite in 1917). Brigades rarely had more than one battalion from a given regiment, and a typical division would have men wearing a very different cap badge, the traditional identifier of regimental identity of the British soldier, even today. The typical infantry division of 1914 would also have a significant artillery presence, and an attached cavalry squadron, as well as components from all the other arms and services required to keep the division operating in the field, a massive undertaking with around 15,000 men in a typical, full-strength British division. Of these, it has been estimated that around 40 per cent of the strength were young soldiers with no more than two years' service; the remaining 60 per cent would be recalled Reservists, men who had served their five years but who were liable to recall for a further seven years.

The six original divisions were to form the British Expeditionary Force (BEF) in 1914, the first four of them taking part in the Retreat from Mons in 1914, the other two being present in France by September 1914. The British Army was destined to grow in size to seventy-five Infantry

Divisions, sixty-five of which would serve overseas as an effective fighting force, distributed between the various Corps and Armies engaged on all fronts. Of these, twelve would be Regulars, one would be raised from Royal Naval Reservists (the Royal Naval, later 63rd Royal Naval Division), thirty would be 'New Army', raised originally from volunteers during Kitchener's direct appeal to the public in 1914–15, and the remainder would be Territorials.

The volunteer spirit declined as the war progressed; although still vibrant in 1915, by 1916 the Army was facing a shortfall in manpower, with the inevitable consequence that conscription was to loom on the horizon. An interim scheme introduced by Lord Derby, Director General of Recruiting, in October 1915, whereby men would 'attest their willingness to serve' before returning to their civilian occupation, was not sufficiently enticing. By the end of 1915, more than one million available men had failed to register. With casualties increasing, it was inevitable that conscription would be required if losses were to be sustained. In January 1916, all men between the ages of eighteen and forty-one were liable to call-up, single men first, followed by married men in March 1916. Conscripts were to serve in all Divisions by the end of the war, whether originally 'Regular', 'New Army' or 'Territorial'. Of the 7.5 million men of the right age available during the war, a third would volunteer in 1914–15, a third would be medically unfit or exempt from service, and a third would be conscripted. It was on the 'conscript armies' that the German hammer blows of 1918 would fall, and it was these men, and the survivors from the early war, that would drive the Advance to Victory, the 'Hundred-Day' battles, commencing with Amiens on 4 August 1918, that would finally end the war in the West.

THEATRES OF WAR

The Great War was a world war, with campaigns fought by British troops on three continents – Europe, Asia and Africa. For the most part, the Western Front, situated in Western Europe, was to both demand most attention and consume in ever-increasing numbers men and *matériel*. This front became a continuous line of trenches from Switzerland to the North Sea, 475 miles (285km) across varied terrain; and by the end of the war British and Commonwealth troops were to occupy 120 miles (190km) of the front, in the historically strategic zone that straddled the Belgo-French border, extending south, deep into Picardy. Engaged from August 1914 at the Battle of Mons, the

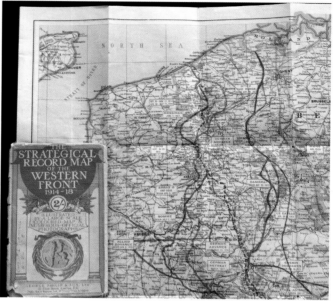

ABOVE: *Commercially available map, published by George Philip and Son, illustrating the British battle lines on the Western Front at the close of the Great War. Seven other maps, illustrating the battle fronts in all other theatres of war, were also published. This one belonged to Captain F. L. Turnbull of the American Corps of Engineers.*

LEFT: *Post-war cigarette cards illustrating some of the formation badges used by British Divisions in the Great War. From 1917 onwards these were used as uniform sleeve insignia, but were also painted on vehicles and used at headquarters to avoid writing out the name of the unit in full.*

'*V Beach', Gallipoli, taken from the line of the Ottoman defences in April 1915, with the Dardanelles in the distance. Here, the British 29th Division disembarked from the* River Clyde, *a collier converted as a landing ship, run aground. The Ottomans, in position at Sedd ul Bahir castle and in carefully prepared defences, pinned the experienced regular British troops on the beach until the following day.*

British Expeditionary Force was to grow in size and stature to become the backbone of the Allied effort in the closing months of 1918, in campaigns that defeated Imperial Germany – with 5,399,563 Empire troops employed on the Western Front alone, the vast majority from the UK. At Mons (1914), First and Second Ypres (1914), Loos (1915), The Somme (1916), Arras, Messines, Third Ypres and Cambrai (1917), the German offensives and Allied advance of 1918 were all to take their toll of casualties on the BEF – but, for the most part, the British soldier went about his business in the trenches never seeing his enemy.

Elsewhere, Tommy was engaged at Gallipoli, in a costly and unsuccessful attempt to defeat the Ottoman Empire on its home territory in European Turkey from April 1915–January 1916. That short period of time was none the less long enough to claim the second-biggest number of total British casualties, at 112,040 (still only a twentieth of the losses suffered in France and Belgium). Here, trench warfare was all too quickly established, and the drip-drip-drip of casualties and losses to disease contributed to the decision to beak the stalemate through ignominious withdrawal in December 1915–January 1916. The Ottomans were engaged across the Middle East – in Mesopotamia

(modern Iraq), which saw an initially successful advance past Basra lead to a crushing surrender at Kut-al-Armara in 1916. This would be reversed only in 1918. Palestine and the Arabian Peninsula – the scene of the exploits of 'Laurence of Arabia' – would be more successful, and the Ottomans were to sue for peace in late October 1918 after Allenby had taken Jerusalem.

At Salonika in mainland Greece, facing the Bulgarians and their German allies from 1916, more men were lost to disease than battle casualties, although here the Mediterranean Expeditionary Force (MEF) was to participate in the offensive that would see the first of the Central Powers capitulate (Bulgaria, in September 1918). There were numerous other theatres – in South West Africa, for example, and to bolster the hard-pressed Italians in the valley of the Isonzo. Farther afield, in the opening days of the war, there was Tsingtao, in China; and, at its close, Archangel, in northern Russia. Tommy would go wherever he was needed. In all, the UK would suffer 3,058,985 casualties out of 5,704,416 soldiers enlisted, comprising 724,407 killed, 2,064,451 wounded and 270,117 missing or prisoners of war. Not surprisingly, the total figure for the whole of the British Empire was much higher.

RIGHT: Daily Mail war postcard showing British soldiers in a captured German trench on the Somme. Based on one of the most famous pictures of the war, this tinted photograph gives some idea of the depth of the trench systems in 1916. The Daily Mail postcards, which proved very popular, were published in colour, black and white and sepia formats from 1916.

.

LOWER RIGHT: Preserved trenches at Sanctuary Wood, in the Ypres Salient, Belgium. These trenches, based on the British lines, have been in private hands since the end of the war, and have been repaired many times. Nevertheless, they still provide something close to the feel of the originals.

TRENCH WARFARE

Trench warfare came as a surprise to High Command, who in 1914 had expected a war of movement. The battle plans of the major powers, based on the experience of other European conflicts, such as the Franco-Prussian War of 1870–71, predicted a rapid deployment of troops that would over-run their enemies. At the heart of German plans for a coming war was a similarly rapid deployment of troops westwards, exploiting the rail network, an operational necessity in view of the might of the Russian 'steamroller', a vast potential of manpower that could engulf the German armies in the east. The effectiveness of the Schlieffen Plan in the west – intended to engulf the French quickly and capture Paris using a pivoting 'closing-door' movement with its army – was compromised by operational issues and indecisiveness, and, although the French and their British allies were to reel back, the line was to hold.

Yet, after fighting in open fields during the first desperate battles of 1914, for the British retreat from Mons to the Aisne, the establishment of entrenched positions was determined, in the British Sector at least, following Sir John French's order in late 1914. Running snake-like through Europe, this simple line of entrenched positions would eventually extend from the Swiss frontier to the Belgian coast. Desperately, both sides fought to gain the advantage by outflanking movements in the so-called 'race to the sea'; the flooding of line of the Yser from Dixmuide to Nieuport ordered by Albert, King of the Belgians, would do much to stem the invasion. From the winter of 1914–15, the war took on the flavour of that already seen at Petersburg, Virginia in 1864, and at Port Arthur in the Russo-Japanese War of 1902: an extended siege. For the British, this siege was to be played out in a Salient around the Belgian town of Ypres, in French Flanders, and south to Picardy and the Somme.

Trench warfare has assumed an almost mythical status today, the phrase 'in the trenches' being almost synonymous with service in the First World War. For most British and Commonwealth (then Empire) soldiers, trench warfare was to be the norm, even in far-flung theatres such as Gallipoli and Salonika. Despised by the High Command as a 'phase of warfare' that would soon be transformed into open warfare, 'the trenches' would exist from their first inception in September 1914 through to the opening of the Battle of Amiens in August 1918, and the final Advance to Victory. The Western Front became an entity once the opposing forces had entrenched across northern Europe, in late 1914, and it was on the Western Front that trenches became the dominant feature of warfare. Trenches varied according to use, and their construction became more sophisticated as the war dragged on. In Flanders, the construction of trenches was mostly a battle with the prevailing geological conditions.

The combination of water-repelling clay and overlying water-retaining sands meant that, when it rained, the heavily shelled ground became the muddy quagmire that is associated with the Great War today. Elsewhere, such as on the Somme, trenches could be founded in startlingly white chalks, overlain by sticky clays and silts, which would dry to a choking dust in summer and would be churned to a cloying mud in winter.

The simple purpose of the trenches was, of course, to provide protection to the front-line troops and their supporting arms in the face of small-arms fire (rifles, machine guns and the like) and artillery. Once the trench lines reached practically unbroken from the sea to the fortress of Belfort on the Swiss border, outflanking movements were

I WONDER WHEN THE BLINKIN' TIDE GOES OUT TED.

TOP: *The French fortress town of Belfort, situated at a natural gap between the Jura mountains and the Rhone Valley, was effectively the southern end of the Western Front.*

ABOVE: *Geology had much to do with the conditions in the trenches. The Ypres clay, similar in all ways to the clay on which London is built, throws off water, leading to waterlogged conditions, particularly in the rainy season. Here, a contemporary postcard makes light of the miserable conditions.*

ABOVE RIGHT: *Archaeological investigations in Flanders in 2005, at the site of the British front line of 1915–17 on Pilkem Ridge. Here, the trenches were constructed using inverted 'A' frames, with the cross-piece of the 'A' forming the support for duckboards. This type of construction raised the trench floor above the saturated ground level.*

no longer an option, and the stalemate of 'the trenches' became the norm for four long years of war. In their simplest sense, trenches were linear excavations of variable depth that were mostly open to the sky. Sometimes (but rarely) they were roofed for the purposes of concealment, usually with close-boarded timber. For the most part, they were between six and eight feet deep; the prescribed depth, according to High Command, was five feet nine inches in dry soil, with a further nine inches of soil built up as a parapet.

In some places it was impossible to dig down more than a foot or so before reaching water-saturated ground, especially in the Ypres Salient, with its underlying foundation of water-repelling clay. There, the trenches were built up rather than dug down, creating what was known as 'High Command' or 'Parapet' trenches, usually with walls of the ubiquitous sandbags filled with whatever was closest to hand – preferably clay. In other situations, boxes or gabions were used as the basis for the parapet. In order to achieve this, specially constructed, inverted 'A' frames were manufactured to support both the sloping walls of the trenches and the duckboard flooring.

LEFT: *Corrugated sheeting used as a revetment of the slopes (sides) in the reconstructed trenches at Sanctuary Wood, in Belgium. Corrugated sheeting was combined with other materials, such as wattle and expanded metal (xpm) sheets. In reality, duckboards would have formed the original trench flooring, as long planks were favoured by the Germans.*

BELOW: *Fire bays in the British front-line trenches excavated in 2005 at Pilkem Ridge. These were intended to limit the effect of exploding shells and grenades, as well as to prevent the possibility of an enemy firing his weapon the length of the trench, known as 'enfilade fire'.*

Most trenches were 'floored' with wooden duckboards, which were built up to allow drainage beneath – in fact, it was common for successive levels of duckboards to be laid one on top of another to combat the difficult conditions encountered. In rare cases, bricks and rubble were used, when trench lines snaked through destroyed villages and houses. Trench sides (known as slopes) were supported or revetted with whatever was available: sometimes wattle, often corrugated sheeting and expanded metal (xpm), sometimes chicken wire. Timber was universally used to hold these materials in place, and layers of bonded sandbags strengthened the whole. Recent archaeology in Flanders has uncovered the remains of these *in situ*, and has supported the notion of a constant battle between man and nature in keeping the trenches in some kind of order – essential for the maintenance of morale.

The function of trenches varied. In the main there were two consistent types: fire trenches, which formed the front lines, and communication trenches, which joined them. Fire trenches (in other words, fighting trenches) were divided into a regular pattern of fire bays and traverses, which meant that no soldier could walk in a straight line for long, without having to switch back on himself. This was intended to limit the effects of shellfire, or the possibility of rifle and machine gun fire along the length of a trench – with inevitable consequences. British and German fire trenches were alike in this respect; the French version often had a more leisurely, curved zigzag. The spoil removed in digging a trench was used to form a parapet (a mound of earth in front of the trench on the enemy side) and a parados (a slightly higher mound at the rear). In areas where groundwater was close to the surface, 'borrow pits' were dug on either side of the trench to supply the extra earth needed to build up a sufficient height to protect the troops. Each fire trench was equipped with a fire step, ideally of the regulation

two feet high and eighteen inches wide, which made it high enough to raise an average man's head above the protection of the parapet, when he was required to do so.

Fire trenches were usually arranged in successive parallel rows, with the front line, support line and reserve line all connected by the communication trenches, which were the main thoroughfares of trench warfare. In well-established trench systems the front line consisted of a fire trench and ancillary support trench, with deeper dugouts providing accommodation for the troops. Throughout the war, dugouts were to evolve from simple scrapes in the trench slopes, providing little more than limited cover – and often requiring the occupant to stretch his legs out into the main trench line – to deeper affairs, dug or 'mined' to provide protection from the attentions of howitzer shells and trench mortars.

Visé Paris 763

F. Mackain

*Sketches
of Tommy's life
Up the line — N° 3*

We marched into the Trenches, late in the evening, going across fields on « duck boards ». There is nothing to be seen but shell-holes, and wintry looking tres.

Bystander copyright.
WHEN ONE WOULD LIKE TO START AN OFFENSIVE ON ONE'S OWN
Recipe for Feeling Like This—Bully, biscuits, no coke, and leave just cancelled.

ABOVE: *Contemporary Mackain postcard depicting movement up the line; starting with duckboard tracks in some cases, troops would enter the line through communication trenches, or CTs. This card was sent home from a soldier in France.*

LEFT: *The miserable conditions – and inadequate cover – of a typical early British trench dugout, as depicted by cartoonist Bruce Bairnsfather. Later on, dugouts would be deeper, to escape the intense artillery fire. Like his contemporary, Fergus Mackain, Bairnsfather had experienced front-line life and was able to comment on its conditions. Both illustrators were admired by the average Tommy.*

Due to the complexities of the growing trench systems, it was possible to get hopelessly lost, and trench signboards had to be fixed up to allow newcomers to a particular stretch to get oriented. Trenches were named or numbered, according to the preference of the commanders in charge, and were often themed. This complex system would grow throughout the war, and would be recorded on equally complex trench maps. The purpose of communication trenches (or 'CTs') was to link the forward or fire trenches, and to allow men, munitions and supplies to travel up to the line. They also had to allow wounded soldiers to come out of the line and, for this reason, they were wide enough for stretcher-bearers to carry out their duties. Very often these long trenches bore names such as 'alley', 'lane' or 'street', indicating their intended purpose. Running from the rear areas and connecting all the forward trenches up to the front line, they offered protection for supply and troop movements from the rear. They were usually dug in a zig-zag or wavy pattern and in Flanders, where the geological conditions meant that revetment was essential, they had similar dimensions to a fire trench. In some cases (as at Arras, and Nieuport on the Belgian coast), CTs were replaced by underground subways, which provided much more protection from the searching of enemy artillery.

ABOVE: *A roll of German barbed wire found on the Somme. German wire was a formidable obstacle.*

BELOW: *Mackain postcard, illustrating the life of a trench sentry at night.*

*Sketches
of Tommy's life
Up the line — Nº 6*

On Sentry Go at Night.

F. Mackain

Visé Paris 763

Between the front lines of the opposing trenches was 'no man's land', a strip of contested ground that varied in width from a few feet to tens of yards. The forward trenches on both sides were protected by belts of barbed wire, an American invention that had seen some limited use in earlier wars, but which was to reach the apex of its achievement in the Great War. No man's land was crossed when soldiers went 'over the top', climbing out over the parapet to face the enemy. For the most part, no man's land was observed by day through trench periscopes set up for the purpose; putting his head above the trench was virtually suicidal for a soldier, and head injuries were common in tall soldiers and the curious, especially before the advent of the steel helmet in 1915–16. By night, sentries were expected to look out through no man's land, and working parties were also to move forward into the contested zone, to repair barbed wire, carry out patrols, and so on. They had to be vigilant – star shells and opportunistic bursts of fixed machine guns were a threat, as were nervous sentries on their own side. Forward extensions of the trench systems were also created, with saps digging out a short way into no man's land in order to give advance warning of impending attack.

THE ROUTINE OF TRENCH WARFARE

From the advent of trench warfare in late 1914, there emerged a routine that would come to encompass the world of the average soldier. It was a routine that would provide some order to the otherwise bizarre experience of living in a ditch, during which time the normal civilized code of activity during the day and rest during the night would become reversed. Soldiers inhabiting the trenches were expected to wear their equipment at all times, night and day, so it was hardly a comfortable existence.

For both sides, there was a trench routine that usually commenced with 'stand-to' (from stand to arms) at one hour before dawn, when all troops in the front line would stand upon the fire step armed and ready to confront an attacker – the theory being that most attacks would take place at dawn. Stand-to would last at least an hour and a half, and would finish when the enemy parapet could be seen through the periscopes set up along the line of the trenches. Following stand-to, most men were stood down, but sentries were left on duty, one per platoon, to man the fixed box periscopes. With stand-down, a tot of rum would be issued to each man, a welcome respite from the often freezing conditions.

Breakfast would follow, a meal comprising rations that had been brought up at night, which were meant to last a forty-eight-hour period. Tea, bacon and bread were the staples, but often it could be simply bully-beef and biscuits. After breakfast, it was time for platoon commanders to make their inspection of rifles, which the men had cleaned during their meal. Attention was given particularly to the breech and chamber, the parts of the gun that were most liable to fouling from mud and dirt. Such fouling would put paid to the delicate mechanism of the Canadian Ross Rifle, replaced from 1916 by the Lee Enfield. Those men not on 'sentry-go' were detailed for fatigues to repair trenches and engage in similar activities that went on throughout the day, breaking for lunch at midday and an evening meal at around 6pm.

Bairnsfather postcard, illustrating the sensation felt by the average sentry in putting his head above the parapet at night – a suicidal action during the day.

The night routine would commence with another 'stand-to' before dusk, and another officers' inspection. The trenches then came alive to a routine of repair, supply and patrol, with men engaged on endless trench improvement. Patrols and wiring parties ventured out into no man's land, keeping an eye open for star shells that could catch them starkly silhouetted against the sky, targets for watchful sentries and searching machine guns. Night sentries, with a round in the chamber ready for an alert, were detailed to look over the parapet – dangerous when the enemy had his guns trained at head height for the same reason. Sleep on sentry duty was a capital offence; experienced NCOs made it their business to visit their charges every fifteen minutes, and officers would also be vigilant in their duties. Other men would sleep, if they were lucky, or be detailed to go on endless carrying details, bringing up supplies from the rear along communication trenches.

On average, men spent a period of four to eight days in the front-line trenches, but this depended very much on circumstances, with some battalions spending longer in hard-pressed areas. While some were in the front fire trenches, others would occupy the support lines behind, ready to provide reinforcement when hard pressed in an attack or raid. There was to be a rhythm to trench warfare,

BRITISH INFANTRY PRACTISING AN ATTACK.

with, typically, five days in the front line, five in reserve, five at the front again and, finally, five days in reserve. Relief when it came saw the battalion removed from the front-line trenches and taken to the rear areas, where they were billeted in farm buildings. There, they received their pay and were able to buy such comforts as egg and chips, *café au lait* and beer. During this period, reinforcements and replacements for losses sustained would arrive, and men would be trained in the use of new weapons, gas procedures, and so on.

Going over the top – or 'over the bags' – was quite a rare occurrence in the life of an average soldier. Major attacks were relatively scarce; larger artillery-supported trench raids were uncommon and, in most cases, getting to grips with the enemy meant small-scale stealthy raids with pistol, knife and club. These were intended to keep the enemy

TOP LEFT: *Sepia* Daily Mail *war card, depicting a practice attack by British soldiers.*

ABOVE: *Bullets and Billets,* Bruce Bairnsfather's *celebrated war memoirs, published while the war was still in progress. It outlines the birth of his war cartoons, and his role as an infantry officer in Belgium.*

LEFT: *Envelopes for Bruce Bairnsfather's* Fragments from France *postcards. First published by* The Bystander, Bairnsfather's *cartoons were an instant hit and were published in collected* Fragments from France *magazines, and as postcards.*

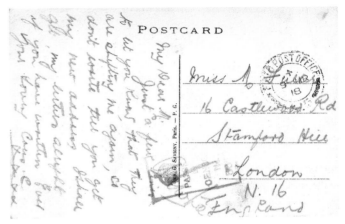

Metal shoulder title from the 23rd Battalion, Royal Fusiliers (1st Sportsman's). This battalion was one of the first volunteer battalions of what became known as the 'Pals', raised from ex-public school 'sportsmen'. Artist Fergus Mackain, chronicler of Tommy's life in a series of postcards published in France, was to serve in its ranks for much of the war, before being transferred to the ASC.

BELOW: Reverse of the Mackain postcard of 'movement up the line' (see page 19). Mackain's cards were, perhaps uniquely, drawn by a soldier artist and published in France; as such, they were often sent home by soldiers using them as a shorthand to describe aspects of their trench life.

on his toes, and to provide information on who was occupying the trenches across no man's land through the capture of prisoners, or the removal of identifying insignia, such as shoulder straps, from enemy dead. The value of these raids still remains a controversial question today.

SKETCHES FROM TOMMY'S LIFE

Throughout this book, illustrations of the life of the average British soldier are taken from contemporary publications and postcards. The ubiquitous postcard, which was in its heyday in 1914, was widely used worldwide by everyone, from the lowliest private soldier to the loftiest general officer. Many tend to display mawkish sentimentality, particularly those that date from early in the war, and those from the other belligerent nations; for Britons, comic cards and photographic cards nestled against Bamforth song cards with their Victorian emotions. Military themes were popular, and those that 'told it as it was' were particularly popular with the average Tommy.

Bruce Bairnsfather's cards are a case in point. Bairnsfather was a soldier, a subaltern, who left for war in the autumn of 1914 with his men of the 1st Battalion of the Royal Warwickshire Regiment. Destined to serve his time in the mud of the southern part of the Ypres Salient, close to Ploegsteert ('Plugstreet') Wood, Bairnsfather was to use a skill that had been honed at Hassell's school of commercial art in London in drawing cartoons illustrative of the life of the soldier in the trenches of 1914–15. According to legend – and as described in his account of this time, *Bullets and Billets* – his first cartoons were drawn on the walls of the ruined rural buildings in the area. Published in Britain by the popular illustrated magazine *The Bystander*, Bairnsfather's *Fragments from France* would be an immediate hit with the public, popular with civilian and soldier alike for depicting aspects of life in the trenches that were difficult to discern from the more purple accounts of the press. Bairnsfather became a celebrity, and the power of his work was enough for him to be promoted to captain, and to be withdrawn from the front line to take on the role of 'officer cartoonist'. His creation, 'Old Bill' – a wise Old Contemptible, 'out since Mons' – was also to attain celebrity status. Bairnsfather's *Fragments from France* books and postcards were mostly obtained and sent by men on leave.

The drawings produced by another soldier, Fergus Mackain, were less famous than those produced by Bairnsfather; they were published in France as postcards called *Sketches from Tommy's Life*, first in Boulogne by Imprimérie P. Gaulthier and then by the Paris firm of Visé. 2049 Private Fergus H.E. Mackain served with the 23rd (1st Sportsman's) Battalion Royal Fusiliers, which was raised by Mrs Cunliffe-Owen in the autumn of 1914. Mrs Cunliffe-Owen was a society lady sufficiently well connected to be able to telegraph Lord Kitchener with the question, 'Will you accept complete battalion of upper- and middle-class men, physically fit, able to shoot and ride, up to the age of 45?' The answer was clear: 'Lord Kitchener gratefully accepts complete battalion.' The influential lady remained in the driving seat until she handed over the battalion to the army in April 1915. The 23rd Battalion was to serve in the 99th Brigade throughout the war, with 4,987 officers and men serving, and 3,241 as casualties – killed, wounded and missing. Mackain served with the battalion as a private, and was transferred to the Army Service Corps later in the war – usual with men who had suffered wounds and illness.

Mackain's story is not unusual, and his life as a private soldier was undistinguished. His cards are unique, however, not simply because they illustrate the life of the average 'Tommy' in extraordinary detail – many other artists, like Bairnsfather, can claim that too – but because they were published in Boulogne, and were therefore sent home by ordinary soldiers on active service. His cards often have Field Post Office stamps, and messages that draw attention to the similarities between the soldiers depicted on the cards and the soldier sending the cards home. In this way, Mackain's cards act as window on what life must be like for the average soldier at the Front, and are authentic documents of life in the Great War.

DON'T IMAGINE YOU ARE NOT WANTED

EVERY MAN between 19 and 38 years of age is WANTED!

Ex-Soldiers up to 45 years of age

"YOUR COUNTRY NEEDS **YOU**"

MEN CAN ENLIST IN THE NEW ARMY FOR THE DURATION OF THE WAR

RATE OF PAY: Lowest Scale 7s. per week with Food, Clothing &c., in addition

1. Separation Allowance for Wives and Children of Married Men when separated from their Families (Inclusive of the allotment required from the Soldier's pay of a maximum of 6d. a day in the case of a private)

For a Wife **without** Children	- -	12s. 6d. per week
For Wife with One Child	- -	15s. 0d. per week
For Wife with Two Children	- -	17s. 6d. per week
For Wife with Three Children	- -	20s. 0d. per week
For Wife with Four Children	- -	22s. 0d per week

and so on, with an addition of 2s. for each additional child.
Motherless children 3s. a week each, exclusive of allotment from Soldier's pay

2. Separation Allowance for Dependants of Unmarried Men.

Provided the Soldier does his share, the Government will assist liberally in keeping up, within the limits of Separation Allowance for Families, any regular contribution made before enlistment by unmarried Soldiers or Widowers to other dependants such as mothers, fathers, sisters, etc.

YOUR COUNTRY IS STILL CALLING. FIGHTING MEN! FALL IN!!

Full Particulars can be obtained at any Recruiting Office or Post Office.

2 Joining Up

For many people today, the image of the volunteers of the Great War queuing to join the army and 'have a bash at the Boche' (a term derived, it seems, from an obscure French dialect version of *Allemand*, similar verbally to *cochon*, or 'pig') seems remote and peculiar. With jaundiced eyes born from the visual assault provided by decades of warfare on our television screens, this seems madness. Why would ordinary decent men 'join the colours' to fight a war, the reasons for which seem now remote and detached? Who started the war, and why? These are reasonable questions; yet they are questions that seem inadequately served by answers of petty jealousies from prickly Imperial neighbours on the continent of Europe. These seem slim enough reasons for a man to risk his life in the 'hell of the trenches', particularly from the perspective of a more cynical age, where casualties in war of any type are unacceptable, and where images of the mud of Flanders and the trenches of the Somme have become icons of futility.

Yet the 'futility' of the First World War is a modern invention born from the outpouring of literature and the interpretation of surviving images. To the men and, latterly, women of the Great War generation, joining up was a reasonable response to a perceived threat to the security of the British Empire. It is rare for the last handful of surviving veterans – there are still a few – to talk of the futility. They knew what they were fighting for – at least, at first. Home, country, family and King underpinned more incidental reasons: boredom, excitement, the chance to escape, or the sheer desperation of difficult home circumstances, were all typical. As the war drew on, the main driver for the average soldier was 'not letting his mates down', what Australian commentators call 'mateship', which held for all troops who served in the many theatres of the Great War.

It is possible to track many different phases of enlistment and types of soldier: in the pre-war Regular Army, it was the 'old sweats' serving in the tradition-rich regiments of the army throughout the Empire; in the Territorial Army, the 'Saturday night soldiers' joined to serve at home, but many also signed up for service overseas; Kitchener's Army was made up of the volunteers of 1914–15, who, after training, were to serve *en masse* in the Somme and after; finally, there were the conscript armies of 1917–18, men who were to stem the tide of the German breakthroughs of 1918 and, eventually, lead the Allies to victory in 1918. Each man had his own reason for joining.

For all of these men, enlistment meant being kitted out as a soldier, the discomfort of the transition from civilian life, and intensive training before travelling overseas for the long trail to the front.

RIGHT: Pte Fergus Mackain's postcards capture the spirit of Tommy Atkins.

OPPOSITE: A rare original of Lord Kitchener's famous recruiting poster, 'Your Country Needs You'. There were to be many variants.

JOINING UP

In the early stages of the war – indeed, within hours of its declaration – there was a flurry of activity in military circles. Regular soldiers were recalled from leave, Reservists were recalled to duty, Territorials were called to the colours, and the ordinary civilian inspired by the spirit of the nation was urged to join his country's forces. Within the first month of war, and following Lord Kitchener's widely publicized appeal for 100,000 men, volunteers flocked to the colours to enlist, overwhelming the authorities. This flow was to continue almost unabated throughout 1914 and into 1915. The pressure was maintained by the recruitment posters that began to appear everywhere, using all kinds of devices to appeal to a myriad of emotions: 'Women of Britain say Go!', 'Daddy, what did you do in the Great War?', 'Britons, Your Country Needs You!' Spirited public figures raised whole battalions of men to serve with the colours – these were more or less private armies, clothed, fed and equipped from the purses of wealthy and influential people – before the War Office was prepared to take over the establishment as Service Battalions of His Majesty's Regular Army.

The initial volunteers would serve in the Regular battalions and see action soon enough; the locally raised units would be trained together and be deployed *en masse* in the great offensive on the Somme in July 1916, where the losses were to shock a nation already in mourning from the toll of 1915. These men would serve on all battle fronts and, by the end of the war, the few survivors would form the core of 'old sweats', reinforced by the conscripts of 1916 onwards.

Anti-German Propaganda

In the early days of the war, anti-German feeling was stirred up by the stories of atrocities in Belgium. Some were greatly exaggerated, from the mutilation of nuns to the bayoneting of babies, but it is clear that there were some terrible actions carried out. One savage incident saw the sacking of the university city of Louvain, where civilians were summarily shot, suspected as acting as francs-tireurs, *and where the ancient city, its university and library were sacked and burned. These and other acts were to add to the patriotic fervour whipped up by the popular press, with references to 'Remembering Belgium' appearing on recruiting posters and postcards. The graphic political cartoons of Dutchman Louis Raemaekers, published in Britain in the magazine* Land and Water, *made the point particularly strongly.*

Another feature of the anti-German propaganda drive was the issue of 'commemorative' medals that mocked the pomposity of the German military. A series of simple iron crosses, mimicking the German award for gallantry, were produced, bearing the slogan 'For Kultur' and listing the Belgian cities where the atrocities had taken place. Whether these were given away in a recruitment drive, or sold for charity, is not known. This kind of propaganda continued to be developed throughout 1914–15, the best-known example being the issue of a facsimile of a German bronze medal to commemorate the sinking of the RMS Lusitania in 1915 – an act that was to have far-reaching repercussions, with the eventual entry of the United States into the war. All would add to the hothouse atmosphere of 1914–15.

Please do not destroy this

When you have read it carefully through kindly pass it on to a friend.

A German Naval Victory

"With joyful pride we contemplate this latest deed of our navy. . . ."
Kölnische Volkszeitung, 10th May, 1915.

This ... ck in Germany with the object of keeping alive in
Germa... of the glorious achievemen... ...on Navy
in ... ...ed passenger shi... ...non-
...

...nd "No co... ...y sinking, ...
... United ... ...has c... ...he d... ... ...ess ... ...ber ... ...ce of the ... ...nd gives ... to the warning against submarines ... apparently to propound the theory that ... ...tention, the guilt of the crime will rest with ...

...e medal are issued by the Lusitania Souvenir
...ommittee, 32, Duke Street, Manchester Square W. 1.
... profits accruing to this Committee will be handed to
St. Dunstan's Blinded Soldiers and Sailors Hostel.

Recruitment Posters

With the abrupt arrival of war, in August 1914, it was clear that, if Britain was to honour her commitments to her allies by fielding an army on the continent of Europe, something more than the 300,000 or so men of the regular armies would be needed to see it through to the end. Kitchener was clear that the war would last at least three years, and he required more men to bolster the ranks of the Regulars. It is well known that he mistrusted the Territorials, with their local focus and home-service commitment. He preferred instead to appeal directly to the man in the street to join the New Army, an appeal that would delve deeply into the sense of duty and patriotism that was prevalent at this potent time of Britain's history. In the days before wireless and mass media, this appeal for manpower was made via the newspapers and, most effectively, through the use of posters. These were to be seen in every public space, from large billboards to more intimate corners on public transport, in post offices and the like – anywhere they were likely to reach their target audience, as depicted by Mackain in one of his cards.

The Parliamentary Recruiting Committee, an all-party group that employed the local infra-structure of the political parties to distribute posters and circulars to those areas most likely to pro-duce recruits, approved most recruiting posters. In the Second World War, a number of artists were commissioned to produce posters, but in the First World War it was the printers who proposed ideas for designs. Once they had been approved by the committee, these were distributed, providing a sim-ple and direct appeal that was in tune with the time. Typically, recruiting posters played on an individual's sense of duty and wider responsibilities. Historical figures and heroes were widely used to portray this message, as were the image and words of Lord Kitchener himself. The most famous image – of the head and pointing finger of the Field Marshal – was produced by Alfred Leete. It was first published as a cover of the magazine London Opinion *in September 1914, and was used subsequently in a variety of posters with the slogan 'Your Country Needs You' – as in the rare orig-inal example illustrated. This slogan was reused in other posters, such as the small-format typo-graphical poster card that identifies the need for 'you and 300,000 men like you'. Other posters attacked the conscience of the average man: 'Are You in This?', 'Daddy, what did you do in the Great War?' and 'Be Honest with Yourself'.*

Other posters targeted specific groups, to exploit new recruitment possibilities. The Bantams recruiting poster is one example, which is extraordinarily patronizing to modern eyes. This was an experiment to recruit men whose height was below the statutory five feet three inches, which first started in the northern town of Birkenhead, before spreading across the country.

Despite the questionable tone of some of these posters, it is clear that they were effective, with 1.2 million men joining in the first months. However, their potency was to decrease as the war dragged on, and the Parliamentary Recruiting Committee ceased its work on the advent of conscription in 1916, having produced over six million posters in its term of office.

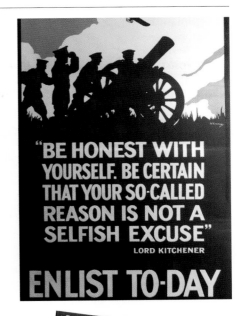

Sketches of Tommy's life

In Training. — N° 1

" That seems to mean me all right "

Recruitment Poster Cigarette Cards

If it was not enough simply to create recruiting posters, in 1915, tobacco company W. D. and H. O. Wills provided extra exposure for them by reproducing a series of the most colourful examples as cigarette cards. It is not certain whether they were intended to be a souvenir of the most popular posters, or whether they were to serve as another kind of recruiting vehicle. There were twelve in the series, and they reflect the diversity of the vehicle used to drive home the early war message: 'Britain must have more men.'

Music Hall Recruiters

The music hall was one of the most popular forms of entertainment in the pre-war and wartime years, and its stars, such as the impersonator Harry Tate, were household names. (Harry Tate also became associated, in rhyming slang, with the British RE8 reconnaissance aircraft used on the Western Front from 1917 onwards.) Several of the major stars used their stage appearances to create recruiting opportunities, often offering members of the audience the chance to join the army there and then, with recruiting sergeants ready to take the names of willing recruits in the foyer. Scotsman Harry Lauder – famous for Roamin' in the Gloamin' *– was knighted in 1919 for his services in the Great War, having toured the music halls on a recruitment drive in 1915, and having visited France to entertain the troops (an experience that was recounted in his 1918 book* A Minstrel in France*). His own son, Captain John Lauder of the 8th Argyll & Sutherland Highlanders, was killed at Pozieres on the Somme on 28 December 1916, and Sir Harry wrote the song* Keep Right on to the end of the Road *in the wake of his loss.*

Another music hall star, male impersonator Vesta Tilley, was also honoured in 1919, along with her husband, for services to recruitment and the promotion of war bonds. Vesta Tilley (born in 1864 as Matilda Alice Powles) was extraordinarily successful as a recruiter, earning the nickname 'Britain's best recruiting Sergeant', because of her ability to take on the male role, dressed in a variety of uniforms to put her point across (opposite), and performing songs such as Jolly Good Luck to the Girl who loves a Soldier*. Her act was to evolve as the war progressed, with the addition of the song* I've got a bit of a Blighty One *– a reference to the type of wound that was destined to get a soldier away from the front and back home to 'Blighty'. She retired in 1920 as Lady de Frece, moving to Monte Carlo with her husband in the post-war years.*

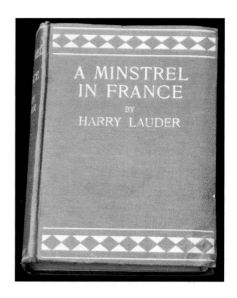

Recruiting Songs

Men in civilian garb were assaulted on all sides by messages compelling them to join the nation's armed forces. Posters, postcards, newspapers and even popular songs were deployed to maintain the recruitment drives of 1914–15 and supply the armies at the front with sufficient men (a need that was well understood by Kitchener and the War Cabinet). Images of women were used extensively: as the victims of war in Belgium, depicted on posters and in political cartoons; as the personification of nationhood, such as Britannia and Marianne; and in the role of sweethearts and mothers imploring their loved ones to join the fight. This was used in the Parliamentary Recruiting Committee poster by E. V. Kealey, 'Women of Britain say Go!', which depicts a small family group observing soldiers marching away. Another powerful use of women's imagery was in the 1914 Paul Ruben's 'women's recruiting' song Your King and Country Want You, with its verse, 'Oh! We don't want to lose you, but we think you ought to go', followed by the promise, 'We shall cheer you, thank you, kiss you, when you come back again.' In the face of this, and pushed by the fear of the white feather, many men had little option but to join. Having joined up, the same song was subject to merciless parody by the troops, the same lines being reworked as, 'Oh! We hate you; and I'll boo you and hiss you if you sing it again!'

Recruiting for Kitchener's Army Game, *c.*1914

The object of this game is to recruit as many able bodies as possible from the major cities of the United Kingdom (which included the whole of Ireland at the time). In its way, the existence of this game added to the pressure on the civilian to join, chiming with the popular Parliamentary Recruiting Committee poster, 'Daddy, What did you do in the Great War?' by Savile Lumley, in which a middle-aged man is asked this potent question by his daughter – the implication being that he had not played his part in the conflict. This game, played at home, would be a reminder to father to play his part in the conflict. Based on the principle of the traditional game of snakes and ladders, each player, having 'signed the pledge', would advance around the UK, picking up recruits from its major cities. The 'snakes' in this case were a variety of defects, such as 'under-development', 'drink', 'defective teeth' and 'smoker's heart'. The player with the highest number of counters (recruits) won the game.

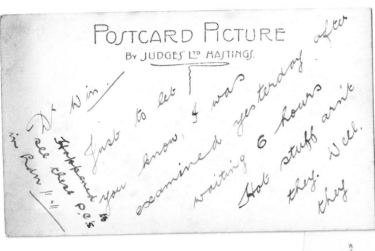

Recruiting Offices

Recruiting offices sprang up across the country as the demand for men increased. Existing facilities were unable to cope with the throughput of men, so local municipal buildings were soon pressed into service, usually bedecked with banners and posters. Mobile recruiting offices were also established, with buses and trams carrying the message 'Britain Needs More Men'. Recruiting sergeants and other military personnel would be on hand to give an impression of military efficiency, and to provide the necessary persuasion – a persuasion that was to intensify as the war passed into its second year. Denoted by a range of military badges, a red sash, or, as in this case, by cloth shoulder titles indicating 'Army Recruiter' (top), these men would help fill the ranks of Kitchener's Army. On arrival, recruits would be asked their age. Nineteen was the minimum, but it is well known that there were very many under-age soldiers; the army would later insist that such boys had been taken in good faith, having 'lied about their age'.

Would-be soldiers were given the briefest of medicals, based on their height (at first, above five feet three inches) and chest measurements (thirty-four-inch maximum expansion), the condition of their teeth (to handle the almost unbreakable ration biscuit; in fact, it has been estimated that 70 per cent of all recruits would require treatment) and their eyesight (to be able to sight a rifle effectively). As these cards to Win Dellow of Enfield indicate (above), not everyone was accepted – any one of the above could signify rejection. If they were found fit (categorized 'A1'), recruits would 'attest', swearing an oath of allegiance and signing their forms, and receive the 'King's Shilling', the symbolic issue of the first day's pay of their stint in the army – for three years or the duration ('I'm in for duration' was a usual statement from a wartime soldier). The card illustrated (left) shows the location of the recruiting office in Leeds, one of many that took in soldiers for Kitchener's Army, the 'Leeds Pals'.

King's Shilling

This shilling (dated 1915) was undoubtedly issued to a recruit on his enlistment into the army. On joining, each recruit would be given his first day's pay of a shilling, the daily rate of the average Tommy until 1917. The issue of the King's Shilling, and the repeat of the oath of allegiance to the crown, would bind the Great War recruit to service for 'the duration'. As Private Frederick Hodges of the Bedfordshire Regiment would later remember, 'We swore to defend with our lives King George V, and his heirs.' The full oath was as follows:

'I ...swear by Almighty God, that I will be faithful and bear true Allegiance to His Majesty King George the Fifth, His Heirs and Successors, and that I will, as in duty bound, honestly and faithfully defend His Majesty, His Heirs, and Successors, in Person, Crown and dignity against all enemies, and will observe and obey all orders of His Majesty, His Heirs and Successors, and of the Generals and Officers set over me. So help me God.'

Kept as a souvenir, this example of a King's Shilling has the King's head ground down (technically illegal) so that the date of the soldier's enlistment, 22 November 1915, could be engraved, while preserving the same date, 1915, on the reverse. Serving as a good luck charm, or fob token, this shilling survived the war, and was no doubt worn with pride by its owner.

The King's Commission

With so many men joining the army as private soldiers, there was to be a severe shortfall in officers to command them. Regular officers and NCOs would provide the backbone for the new battalions that were raised following Kitchener's call, but, with the demands of regular battalions to be met, manpower resources were tight. Other sources were men on the Reserve lists – usually just retired from service, but including more senior men 'dug out' of retirement – together with men on leave from the Indian Army, who were 'requisitioned' by Kitchener. Direct recruitment from public schools and universities was also tried, but many of the potential officers had already joined the ranks as private soldiers, and it would take some time to persuade them that they might have the skills to command. Among many others, men in Kitchener's Army units such as the Public Schools Battalion (16th Middlesex Regiment) and the University and Public Schools Battalions (18th–21st Royal Fusiliers) were targeted. All prospective officers underwent a period of training (hasty at first, but more considered as the war progressed) and, if successfully 'passing out', would receive their Commission. This document, in beautiful calligraphy, put trust in an officer to command and defend King and Country. This example belonged to 2nd Lieutenant Joe Clark, promoted from the ranks of the Leeds Pals, and recipient of the Military Medal in action. Photographs show him as a private soldier, and as a lieutenant with row of medal ribbon, at the end of the war.

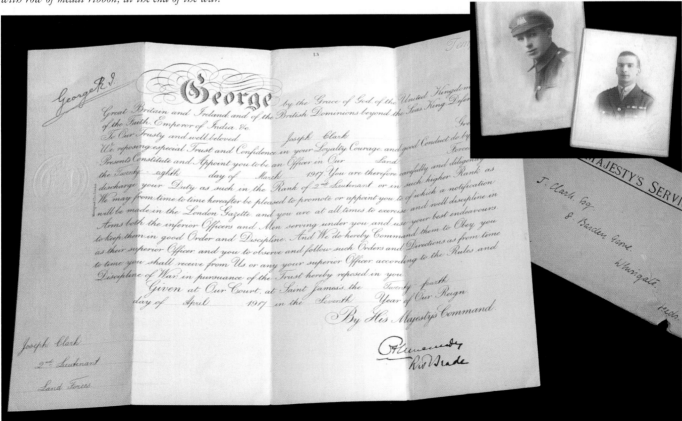

EXEMPTION AND CONSCRIPTION

Although there was a rush of men who wanted to join the colours in the early stages of the war, it was inevitable that there would be others who were less keen. Such men ran the risk while in civilian clothing of approbation from the female vigilantes of the 'Order of the White Feather'. Despite the actions of these women, and the activities of the relevant offices, recruitment experienced a sharp dip in fortune in 1915, declining month-on-month, particularly as news of casualties was published. If Britain was to preserve its role in the war, some action to stem the tide was urgently needed. Parliamentary Under-Secretary for War Lord Derby was appointed Director of Recruitment in October 1915, the additional responsibility reflecting his success in raising the Liverpool Pals. Balking at the outright introduction of conscription, Lord Derby introduced a registration or attestation scheme that would encourage ablebodied men to 'attest their willingness' to serve in His Majesty's Forces, and allow them to return to their civilian occupation before being called up. The scheme was not successful, however, with a poor turn-out overall. Ultimately, conscription had to be brought in, through the Military Service Acts of 1916. With the introduction of conscription came the need for exemption. Men engaged on vital war service were deemed to be exempt from military service, and carried a card to this effect, as well as wearing an official lapel badge in a variety of designs. The purpose of the badge was to show all and sundry why an able-bodied man was not in uniform, to distinguish war worker from an out-and-out 'shirker'.

The White Feather

Being given the white feather by a lady was a fear of many men not in uniform. The white flag was the universal emblem of surrender, and the white feather was to evoke an image of cowardice. This practice emerged early in the war when female vigilantes took it upon themselves to issue such feathers to any man not in uniform — including, in some cases, wounded, off-duty or on-leave soldiers. The use of the white feather as a symbol of cowardice has a long history, dating back at least a century before the Great War, and with the founding of the Order of the White Feather by Admiral Charles Fitzgerald and author Mary Ward in 1914, women were persuaded to present men who were not in uniform with the device. Other pressure was applied by the women of the Active Service League, established by author Baroness Orczy, who vowed never to be seen on the arm of a man not in uniform. The fear of receiving a feather was effective and led to the need for some way of denoting men on war service, but otherwise in civilian dress — the lapel badge was used extensively in both world wars. This and the Silver War Badge, instigated in 1916 and awarded to all those honourably discharged, would provide some protection from the white feather.

The Derby Scheme

With the flow of volunteers decreasing steadily month-on-month during 1914–15, Lord Kitchener and the War Cabinet were becoming increasingly concerned that the British Army would not be able to withstand its losses at the front, especially as the nation was now fighting on three continents and the war was expected to last at least three years. National Registration in 1915 had identified that there were at least 3.4 million men who were technically able to join the forces, but, by the autumn of 1915, the number joining was falling at an alarming rate, and was insufficient to fulfil the requirement of 35,000 men per week envisaged by Kitchener. Conscription was not an attractive proposition – it had never before been tried in Britain. In considering the issue, Director of Recruiting Lord Derby drew up the scheme that was to bear his name. This entailed the voluntary registration, or attestation (a legal undertaking) to join the colours when called to them, of all men between eighteen and forty, with men of the same age and marital status being grouped together in forty-six consecutive groups. Of the single men, Group 1 was made up of eighteen-year-olds, Group 23, the forty-year-olds, the intention being that these attested men would be called to the colours in batches. Married men, who would be last to go, were numbered from 24–46.

Attested men, like Frederick Walker of Stratford (whose enlistment forms are illustrated), were to serve one day in the colours – receiving their shilling – before transferring to a reserve until called up. They were entitled to wear an armband like those illustrated, in khaki for the Army, dark blue for the Navy. Lord Derby invited all eligible men to attest by 15 December 1915, but the experiment was a failure, with over 2 million of the 3.5 million men available for military service failing to attest. As a result, the Military Service Act of January 1916 – the first of five such acts through the war – announced the introduction of conscription. Single 'Derby Men' would be the first to be called to the colours. Conscripts would form much of the army that marched to victory in 1918.

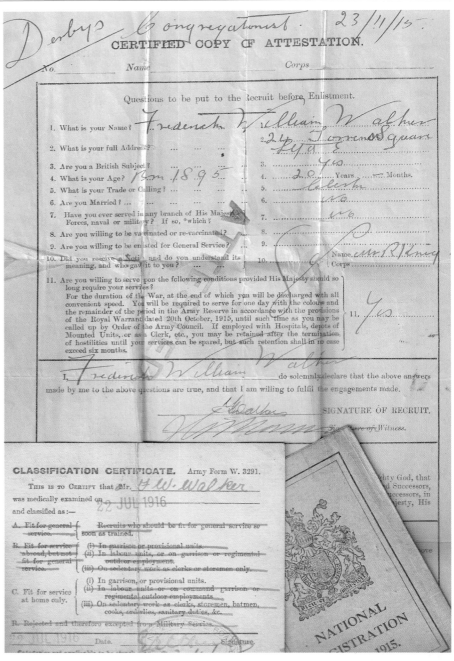

HELPING TO SWELL THE FIGURES 3.

'On War Service' Badges

On War Service badges were issued from 1914, in a variety of forms, to workers engaged on vital war work but not otherwise in uniform. Their prime purpose was to provide male war workers with protection from the attentions of the Order of the White Feather. Many unofficial versions are known, but recent research suggests that there are really only three official versions, all of which bear the title 'On War Service', with the dates 1914, 1915 and 1916, the last of which was issued only to women. The first to be produced was a circular blue enamel buttonhole badge bearing the Imperial Crown. The Admiralty issued this badge for all men whose work entailed building ships or providing armaments for the Navy. Originally, these badges were un-numbered, and there were fears that men not entitled to wear one might appropriate examples for their own use. In early 1915, the Ministry of Munitions issued its own version, an oval buttonhole badge with crown and date, but having a central device that resembled the cap badge of the Ordnance Corps – three cannons below three cannonballs. Early issues were enamelled and later ones were made simply from brass; both were worn from issue right through the war. The issue of these devices was strictly controlled by the Committee on War Service Badges, each having its own unique number (left), matching that recorded on a certificate. Both badge and certificate were issued only to men engaged in Certified Occupations – those deemed to be employed 'on the production of any commodity directly required for the fulfillment of any contract with the Ministry of Munitions, the War Office, or the Admiralty'. Not surprisingly, the issue of the badge was to have important implications for men of military age following the passing of the first Military Service Act in January 1916. From 1916 onwards, such badges would imply exemption from conscription; in mid-1916 alone there were 1,347,627 officially 'badged' men, many of whom worked in the metal industries. The 1915-dated badge would continue to be issued, and strictly controlled, throughout the war, the date implying when it was first issued. There were strict penalties for anyone misappropriating a badge for their own use.

Exemption Certificates

With the introduction of the Military Service Act, in January 1916, all fit single men between the ages of eighteen and forty-one were to be compelled to join the colours; married men were included in the second Military Service Act, in May 1916. Unfit men, like Mr Perrott of Clapton (C11, below), were exempted for the time being, but three other acts, in April 1917, January 1918 and April 1918, would find ways of 'combing out' more men for military service. The last reduced the recruitment age to seventeen, and increased it to fifty-five. The identification of men needed for the war effort on the Home Front was essential. The National Registration Act introduced in July 1915 required every citizen between the ages of fifteen and sixty-five to register their name, place of residence, nature of work and other details, and to be issued with a National Registration Card like that illustrated on page 174. The register in October 1915 had 21,627,596 names on it, of which 5,158,211 were men of military age. Of this large figure, 1,519,432 men were identified as being in reserved occupations; many of them were recipients of the 'On War Service' badges and certificates. Such men became known as 'starred', from the black star that was added against their names on the official records. Initially, in 1916, the engineering Trades Unions were made responsible for identifying and exempting skilled men from military service, and they would issue their member with a Trade Card, like that illustrated for George Sydney Daniel of Sheffield, an apprentice in the Sheffield steel industry. Despite his card, George Daniel was later to serve in the fledgling Royal Air Force in 1918. The Trade Card scheme was later abandoned as being unworkable.

'War Munitions Volunteers'

Skilled workers were required to help feed the guns, and, just as in the steelworks of Sheffield and the shipyards of the Mersey, Clyde, Tyne and Lagan, men were required to help manufacture munitions. With many skilled workers being tempted to join the forces, carried along by the patriotism of the day, maintaining the necessary level of expertise was no mean task. The driver for this was the need to maintain the flow and quality of munitions. This came into sharp focus during the shell-shortage scandals of May 1915, which led to inadequate artillery preparation before battle, and the prevalence of 'duds', or unexploded shells. The situation improved with the appointment of David Lloyd George as Minister for Munitions, in July 1915. Like other workers engaged on War Service, munitions workers deserved the issue of lapel badges, in order to escape the attentions of the white feather vigilantes. With the introduction of the Military Service Act of 1916, skilled men were encouraged to register as 'War Munitions Volunteers', a status that exempted them from military service – at least in the short run. Badges were produced to identify these men, with examples known in enamel and gilt finishes (like that illustrated). As with the 'On War Service' badges, each had a unique issue number, attributed to one person only. Over 2.5 million men worked in munitions factories during the war.

'Munitionettes'

Women also found their place in the Royal Ordnance Factories, as 'munitionettes', with an estimated 80 per cent of shells being produced by a female workforce of nearly a million in the latter stages of the war. An idealized scene is depicted in this postcard from 1918 (issued to promote the purchase of war bonds). While men were issued with 'On War Service' badges, women were not subject to the attentions of the 'white feather brigade', and remained unmarked – other than by the yellowing of their skin, the result of a toxic-jaundice. (It was this potentially fatal condition, derived from TNT poisoning, that earned them the nickname 'canaries'.) From May 1916, a triangular pin-backed 'On War Service' badge was issued for trained women 'engaged in the manufacture of munitions of war or other urgent war work'. These badges did not have the same significance, since in this war women would not be conscripted, so no certificates were issued with them, and they were simply allocated by the employer.

FOOD FOR THE GUNS.

The Non-Combatant Corps

Conscientious objectors – 'COs' or 'conchies' – were those who objected to military service due to their deeply held beliefs that war was wrong. Mostly deriving from religious observance, for some, particularly the pacifist Quaker Brethren, war was morally wrong, and the act of taking part in any way was to condone an evil. Widely misunderstood (and often abused), with the introduction of the Military Service Acts conscientious objectors had to sit before a tribunal to determine their case on an individual basis. Those holding the most fundamental objections refused to engage in any work, civilian or military, which might support the waging of what they considered to be a morally corrupt act. For these men, the alternative could be a long spell in prison 'with hard labour' for refusing to wear the King's uniform. Others, who objected to the bearing of arms but not to joining the army, would serve in the RAMC as medical orderlies, or, from 1915, in the Non-Combatant Corps. Members of this Corps wore the King's uniform, unadorned other than by the simple brass title 'NCC' illustrated, and were engaged as heavy labourers in the rear areas, well away from the front, yet still open to much abuse. In this they differed from the men of the Labour Corps, formed in 1917 from Category B men, mostly derived from those wounded and thereby downgraded in fitness from front-line troops. Men of the Labour Corps would once more be called to take up arms during the German offensives of spring 1918. Insignia from this corps is illustrated (below).

REGULARS AND TERRITORIALS

The Regular Army was to maintain its cachet throughout the war, and belonging to the first or second battalion of an infantry regiment was seen as a badge of honour. Regular battalions recruited in the same way as the other components of the army – through the recruiting office – and men who joined its ranks could quickly be added to the battalion, having first passed through the third (reserve) battalion that acted as the clearing house for new recruits. In many cases, regular soldiers would not have to wait as long as the men of Kitchener's Army to join the ranks of their regiments already serving in France and Flanders.

The pre-war Territorial Army had a long-standing relationship with its local regions, and drill halls were located in communities up and down the country. These provided a means for men to join up and engage in part-time soldiering, with the knowledge that this would mean a move to full-time home service in time of crisis. With the coming of war, most 'terriers' joined the colours for full-time service overseas, and territorial recruitment was placed on the same level as all the others. Battalions were organized into regular (1st–7th, 29th–41st) and territorial (42nd–56th) divisions that were readily recognizable, and distinguishable from their Kitchener Army counterparts by their names, having different regional descriptors. By the end of the war, and in practical terms, these distinctions would be blurred, with the influx of men compelled to their military service through conscription.

Regular Infantry Cap Badges

With the adoption of the Service Dress cap in 1905 to complement the 1902 Service Dress, the continued role of the cap badge – first introduced in the late nineteenth century (replacing a range of helmet plates) – was assured. The cap badge served in peace and war to distinguish the regiment. Regiments were regional organizations and their constituent battalions were tied to a home depot, thereby providing a mechanism for local recruitment. In most cases, Regulars, Territorials and Kitchener men would wear the same badge. Despite shared insignia, battalions of the same regiment rarely served with each other in the field. Traditional marks of the British soldier, cap badges were highly prized by their owners, and have been coveted by children as souvenirs throughout history. This was certainly the case when soldiers of the British Expeditionary Force first arrived in France.

Most badges were constructed from brass, others from 'white metal', or a combination of the two (bimetal), with bronze insignia generally the mark of the officer. In the trenches, badges were often removed to hinder identification, in case of capture. Those illustrated are typical. They include badges changed after the war, such as the 'tram conductor' badge of the Manchester Regiment, the undistinguished star of the Cheshire Regiment, the white Hanoverian horse of The King's (Liverpool) Regiment, and the figure of Britannia representing the Norfolk Regiment (top); badges of the regular Irish regiments disbanded in 1922 with the formation of the Irish Free State (left); and badges of Welsh regiments, whose titles were corrected from 'Welsh' to 'Welch' in peace time (below left).

In 1916, all-brass economy versions were produced of badges that had been traditionally bimetal, reducing the number of operations used in their manufacture. Some examples are illustrated (below).

The Guards

Unlike the other infantry battalions, the elite Guards had only Regulars, with no Territorial battalions and no Service battalions. At the outbreak of war, there were four regiments of foot guards: Grenadiers, Coldstream, Scots and Irish. The Welsh Guards were added to the list, by Royal Warrant, in 1915, in recognition of the contribution of Welsh soldiers in all previous wars. Joining the Guards was not without cost, as author Stephen Graham, a private in the Scots Guards, was to find out. The burden of maintaining the standards expected of a Guards battalion was significant. All five battalions were to have a distinct dress code, even in the trenches, with clean uniforms, polished brasses, Service Dress caps with down-turned peaks, white on red cloth shoulder titles (when most other battalions wore brass ones) and, as illustrated, restrained brass cap badges, mostly based on the Orders of Chivalry.

Regular Arms and Services

The Royal Regiment of Artillery and the Royal Corps of Engineers, with their all-encompassing motto and de facto battle honour Ubique ('everywhere') were destined to grow into the largest of the arms of the British Army. Men of these respected corps would be in the thick of battle, and wore badges that are largely unchanged today. Both arms had regular soldiers: Territorial gunners were distinguished by variants in the cap badge and different shoulder titles; Territorial sappers were denoted only by differing titles. The same was true of the other services, the Royal Army Medical Corps (RAMC), Army Service Corps (ASC) and Army Ordance Corps (AOC). Members of these distinguished arms and services of the British Army were proud of the diversity of tasks they had to undertake in war; some of these are listed (for the RE and ASC) in two postcards illustrated from the early war period. A range of other corps served to feed, supply and succour the regular army in the field. Arms and services badges were mostly all brass; 1916 economy versions of these were unvoided (below) and made of solid brass that dispensed the need for cutting out the central cipher devices of the RA, RE and ASC, an extra, unnecessary process.

Territorial Army Cap Badges: The London Regiment

The Territorial Army was raised as a function of the Haldane reforms of 1908, which created numerous battalions out of the volunteer militia, and tied them to their county regiment. Territorial battalions were usually spread between a number of locally based (and locally recruiting) drill halls throughout a region; most were to wear the badge of their home regiment. For some counties – Cambridgeshire and Hertfordshire, Herefordshire and Monmouthshire – there were to be no regional Regulars. These counties would have to make do with wholly territorial regiments. In London, already well served with the Royal Fusiliers (City of London Regiment), the vast size and population of the city was sufficient to supply men for a large number of separate battalions, all of them with a distinctive cap badge, yet gathered loosely into the County of London Regiment. With names reflecting either the location of their drill hall – for example, the 10th (Hackney) and 20th (Blackheath and Woolwich) battalions – or their recruiting origins – for example, the Civil Service Rifles (represented by the Fleur de Lys *badge illustrated top right) and*

the Post Office Rifles – the constituents of the London Regiment were diverse. Some, such as the 5th Battalion (London Rifle Brigade) or the 14th Battalion (London Scottish (far right)), demanded subscriptions from their men to ensure that they belonged to the right 'class' of person; others, such as the Honourable Artillery Company (HAC) (right), refused to join the London Regiment, preferring to remain aloof (befitting their status as the oldest-established unit of the British Army) throughout the war.

The Imperial Service Commitment

Soldiers of the pre-war Territorial Army had signed on for home service, which meant that, in time of war, while the regular troops were away at the front, the Territorials would be at hand to repel the invader. The onset of a world war, however, left large numbers of men more or less unemployed, guarding railway yards and bridges, much in the manner of 'Dad's Army' (or the Home Guard) in the Second World War. The Territorial Force was therefore asked if it would volunteer for overseas service – known as the Imperial Service Commitment – and it is to the credit of the vast majority of the 'Saturday night soldiers' that they stepped forward to meet the challenge. Over 17,000 men signed initially, and the remainder were given a second chance on 15 September 1914. In fact, many units had already volunteered for overseas service before the war. All those who signed were entitled to wear a special Imperial Service badge, issued in 'white metal' (although rarer brass versions are known); it was to be worn on the right breast pocket of all those who accepted liability for service outside the United Kingdom, part of what was to become known as the Overseas Service Obligation. An unknown territorial gunner is pictured proudly wearing his badge (left); another gunner, Bombardier Norman Tennant of the 11th West Riding Howitzer Battery, RGA (TF), received his on volunteering for service in August 1914. He served on the Western Front throughout the war, and was awarded the DCM in action.

The Royal Naval Division

The Royal Naval Division defies any attempt at military categorization. Neither regular nor territorial soldiers, the men of the RND were sailors. Formed in 1914 from Royal Naval Reservists, the RND was the brain-child of the then First Sea Lord, Winston Churchill. With mobilization on the outbreak of war, it soon became apparent that there would be too many Reservists called to the Navy, and not enough ships to accommodate them. As such, the RND was raised from these men to serve as soldiers. They retained their naval distinctions and ranks, but were commanded by a general. Originally, eight battalions were raised, each named after famous admirals, organized into two brigades. Four battalions of Royal Marines were also to serve alongside their sailor colleagues. The division served with distinction at Antwerp in 1914, at Gallipoli in 1915 and, later, as the 63rd (Royal Naval) Division on the Western Front. The RND at first wore naval blue and 'Nelson' caps with distinctive cap tallies; khaki and SD caps replaced naval blue in 1915. Original cap badges of the division (from the Drake, Hawke, Nelson and Anson battalions), all rare today, are illustrated.

KITCHENER'S ARMY

Kitchener's Army was the result of Lord Kitchener's direct appeal in 1914, when he made it known that he wished to recruit 100,000 men for the army, part of a plan to increase the force by 500,000. The 'First Hundred Thousand', or K1, were recruited within days of the appeal. Kitchener issued four further appeals through the late summer and early autumn of 1914, and the final 100,000, K5, were sanctioned by the government in October of that year. The raising of specific 'Pals Battalions' was largely due to the action of Lord Derby, who raised his Liverpool Pals in 1914. Lord Derby's intention was to raise battalions of 'commercial

classes' that could be offered wholesale to Lord Kitchener to help fulfil his manpower appeals. The concept spread like wildfire throughout the north of England and the Midlands. Becoming a matter of civic pride, each battalion was raised by local dignitaries, who fed, clothed and equipped the men until the unit was taken over by the War Office; it was only at this point that their costs were met by the government. The idea caught on through the desire of a number of men to join together, either out of camaraderie, or to avoid mixing with working men outside their class. The men who joined Kitchener's Army were intensely proud of the soubriquet.

Lapel Badges

In the early stages of the war, supply of arms, uniform and equipment to the enthusiastic recruits of Kitchener's Army was a difficult task; the Kitchener battalions were to be fed, housed and equipped at the initial expense of the authority that raised them. Sourcing uniforms from official and even commercial suppliers at such a demanding time was extremely difficult, and recruits were more often than not clothed in civilian garb. In addition, as training camps had not yet been formed or established, Kitchener's men found themselves still living at home. Fuelled by their pride in enlistment, and their fear of the white feather, recruits wanted to distinguish themselves from the average citizen with a lapel badge. Some of these were flimsy cardboard tags, like that illustrated, from the 'UPS', the University and Public Schools Battalions (four in all) of the Royal Fusiliers. A larger number – more durable – were produced commercially, and some were later to see service as 'sweetheart' jewellery. Privately purchased, those illustrated are for the Bradford Pals, the University and Public Schools Battalions of the Royal Fusiliers, the 20th Battalion King's (Liverpool) Regiment (4th Liverpool Pals) and the 16th Battalion Welsh Regiment (Cardiff City). These were to form the unofficial 'uniform' of many Kitchener recruits in 1914–15.

'Kitchener Blue'

The first recruits to join Kitchener's Army were forced to make compromises, with little in the way of equipment, no uniforms and no barracks. Lapel badges stood in for uniforms in the first instance, and men 'went to war' training in flat caps and tweed suits with broom handles. As a stopgap, simple uniforms were supplied in what has become known as 'Kitchener Blue' – blue serge in place of khaki. These uniforms varied in design, from the standard Service Dress made up in blue serge, complete with brass general service buttons, through to that most commonly seen in photographs from this time – a plain, pocketless tunic, with stand and fall collars, and no shoulder straps. Examples like that illustrated (right) were reputedly surplus to requirements from the General Post Office. Other options included miscellaneous obsolete uniforms, including the traditional red tunic of soldiers past. Issued with a field service forage cap, insignia was variable, from paper labels through to standard shoulder titles and buttons pressed into service as collar and cap badges. Supplied piecemeal, contemporary photographs of Kitchener men with quaint blue uniforms, khaki puttees and service boots are at odds with the images of men in the trenches we have come to associate with the First World War.

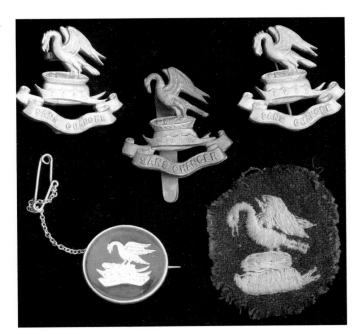

The Liverpool Pals

The first of the 'Pals' battalions, the Liverpool Pals – or, more properly, the 1st–4th City Battalions of the King's (Liverpool) Regiment – were born of the initiative of Lord Derby. The so-called 'King of Lancashire', through a letter published in the Liverpool press on 27 August 1914, had introduced the notion that men of the 'commercial classes' might wish to serve their country in a battalion of their comrades, or pals. At a public meeting held the next day, Lord Derby announced that he would be sending Lord Kitchener a telegram to say that not one, but two battalions of like-minded men would be offered to the nation. In fact, in just over a week, he had found enough men for three battalions, with a fourth being added within weeks. Lord Derby took a personal interest in his 'Pals', the example of which was emulated up and down the country. At his own expense he commissioned in silver a badge bearing his 'eagle and child' emblem, which was given out to each original member of the four Liverpool Pals battalions. Hallmarked to 1914, London and Chester, these badges were treasured and rarely, if ever, worn in the field. Brass and bronze versions of the distinctive badge were produced too, along with unique shoulder titles. Examples of the cap badges (including the coveted silver version), a sweetheart brooch and divisional sign for the 30th Division are illustrated (left), along with a shoulder title for the 1st City Battalion, the Liverpool Pals (right).

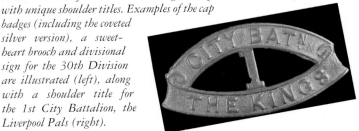

The Leeds Pals

Leeds was not slow in following Lord Derby's example, with letters appearing in the local Yorkshire press in late August 1914 calling for the raising of a 'friends' battalion. Again targeted at the middle classes of a prosperous city, the recruitment campaign in Leeds resulted in a battalion of the Prince of Wales' Own West Yorkshire Regiment – the 15th, otherwise known as the Leeds Pals – by early September 1914. Trained on the hard moors surrounding the city, the men of the Leeds Pals would wear the arms of the City of Leeds – as well as a distinctive shoulder title bearing the name of the city. Like that of the Liverpool Pals, the Leeds Pals cap badge was issued in brass and bronze, with rare silver versions (worn by officers) also known. The owner of this collection, 2Lt Tom Willey, was to be killed on the Somme on 1 July 1916.

The Tynesiders

The northeast of England raised two brigades (with four battalions each) of 'Pals', but not without some difficulties. The industrial centre of the Tyne was home to many workers from the far corners of the United Kingdom, and the idea was developed to raise battalions from men of Irish and Scottish descent. The idea proceeded apace in early September 1914, but was knocked back at first by the refusal of the War Office to allow a battalion of Tyneside Scots to wear the kilt, and then by the devastating news that, in fact, too many 'Pals' battalions had already been raised. However, with the fall-off in recruiting overall, this decision was overtaken by events and, in October, Lord Haldane (then Lord Chancellor) visited Tyne and Wear to welcome the raising of the Scots and Irish battalions. In fact, there was to be a brigade (comprising four battalions) each of Tyneside Scottish and Tyneside Irish. The Scots were never granted the right to wear the kilt, but they did sport the Glengarry, with four successive badge designs. The first, in 1914, was an unprepossessing circular 'garter' design; the three variants illustrated (top left), based on a larger St Andrew's cross, replaced it in 1915–16. The Tyneside Irish were not, however, destined to have a distinctive cap badge; instead, they made do with the badge illustrated (top), as a shoulder title, and a distinctive collar badge for officers. The Tyneside Scots would also have distinctive titles; the title illustrated (top right) is from the 1st Tyneside Scottish (20th Northumberland Fusiliers).

Kitchener's Army Books

The first rush to form Kitchener's Army led to a rash of books in 1914–15 that chronicled the raising of the New Army and followed it, in true boy scout fashion, to the crossing for France and its first engagements. Kitchener's Army, *written by Edgar Wallace and issued originally as a partwork, is full of the ideal of men engaged in Swedish drill and rifle practice. More rare is the final part of the work, its Roll of Honour, which was to form a sad postscript. At the battalion level, there are books that chronicle the raising, training and development of the unit, in the same fashion. The* University and Public Schools (UPS) Battalion *is typical of the genre. Finally, the most famous Kitchener's Army book has to be 'Ian Hay's' (John Hay Beith)* First Hundred Thousand, *chronicling a typical Scots pals battalion of K1, up to its first taste of action in the Battle of Loos in September 1915. Published in early 1916, in an illustrated first edition, this book was followed by a sequel in 1917.* The First Hundred Thousand *remains in print, and has weathered the passsage of time.*

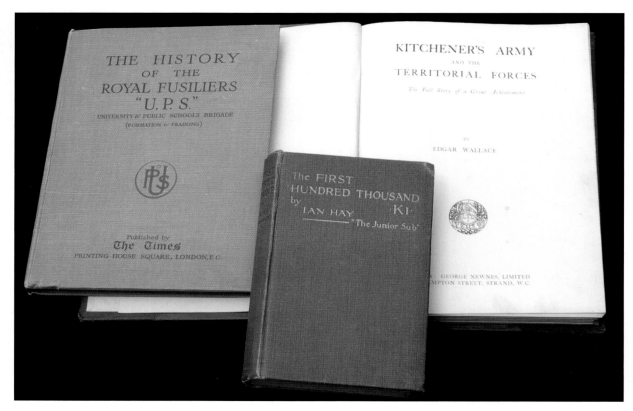

CAMP LIFE: IN TRAINING

For the regular soldier, mobilized for war, there was the usual budget of training: six months with the third battalion at the base depot before being deployed into the first or second battalion (or, in the case of larger units, like the Middlesex Regiment, its first four battalions). For the Territorials, there was the regular parade on a Saturday night, with a summer camp – in wartime, this was to be replaced with drafts in the normal manner. Finally, for the Kitchener's Army recruit, there would be a period in civilian dress, with gradual issue of uniform and equipment, and the establishment of camps up and down the country. All of them would spend time in the camps honing their skills in readiness for the 'great adventure'.

Camp Postcards

Camps were set up across the country to house the vast influx of new recruits to the armed forces. For the Leeds Pals, raised and funded by the Corporation and Mayor of Leeds, there was a need for a new camp, which was constructed on the Pennine fells that surrounded the city. Many other camps were erected around the country; becoming part of the local geography, with postcards like that above indicating their prominence in the landscape. Others postcards invariably stressed the camp routine or conditions – those illustrated are typical. For the occupants of this camp, the routine was one of early to rise, early to bed, with the imposition of communal living in bell tents (designed to hold at least eight men, feet to the centre pole), or, for the better off, timber-constructed huts. All would form the basis for the transition from civilian to soldier, prior to being named for a draft to the front line. As the war ground on, so these camps would be filled with conscripts, and with those soldiers unlucky enough to have been wounded and passed fit once again for front-line duty. Men of the camps would make their way to the Channel ports before being sent overseas, and undergoing a further period of acclimatization training closer to the actual theatres of war.

Camp Silhouette Series

Of all the postcards produced of camp life early in the war, none captures the exuberance of the men more effectively than the Camp Silhouette Series, produced by postcard publisher Photochrom Ltd. These cards illustrate uniquely the spirit of training in early-war Britain, from Reveille to Pay Day. Beautifully crafted, they express a time of innocent enthusiasm before the grim reality of the true casualties of the war began to be felt. They were to resurface in the early days of the Second World War, when old stocks became relevant again.

Church Parade

Church parade was an important component of camp life, involving an inordinate amount of preparation – 'bull' to the soldier – in terms of cleaning, polishing and sprucing up. Some soldiers were able to claim exemption from the parade on the grounds of alternative religious beliefs. The religions admitted by the army were numerous, and chaplains were appointed to administer the needs of the majority. For the most part, church parade would be for those men who were Church of England in faith, and others would be excused the outing, left to carry out other wholesome activities at camp. Parades such as that illustrated below were an event observed by the local population, who turned out in full to see the men marching – devoid of equipment other than a belt – to church.

Camp Photographers

As in earlier wars, new soldiers were keen to record their appearance in uniform through a visit to a photographer's studio. In the nineteenth century, small, multiple photographic prints known as cartes de visite were obtained for distribution among friends and family. In the First World War, photography had moved forward such that the process created a negative, from which multiple copies of postcard-sized photographs could be obtained. The standard studio set, where new soldiers would pose before setting off for the front, usually had an incongruous backdrop and piece of furniture for support. Often anonymous now, these images provide valuable insights into the life of the soldier in uniform. Two soldiers of Kitchener's Army serving with the Welsh Regiment pose with the same backdrop in Ye Olde Guildhall Studios in Winchester. At another, unknown studio, three photos of the same soldier of the Sherwood Foresters survived the war undistributed. Other photos were taken in the rest areas when the soldiers finally reached France, but many remained uncollected.

The Swagger Stick

Many an off-duty soldier would not be seen without his swagger stick, a piece of pure military nonsense. Swagger sticks come in a variety of shapes and forms; the best have silver ends with the regimental badge. Cheaper, non-silver versions are also known, like that for the Liverpool Scottish, illustrated. Purchased from local outfitters and suppliers eager to cash in on a new-found trade, these items appear in the soldier portraits produced by the photographic studios – more often than not provided as props by the establishment. Those men rash enough to splash out on them would leave them behind, consigned like the officer's sword to the storeroom, a vestige of nineteenth-century warfare.

Training

The army had a hard task ahead of it in creating an efficient fighting force attuned to discipline and steady under fire, and it took training seriously. For the most part, this included a simple diet of physical training, involving the application of the Swedish drill system of 'physical jerks', long runs and the use of route marches in full equipment. For those unused to such exercise, this was a new, challenging experience. For the average soldier, military instruction included the use of the bayonet and the proper use of a soldier's principal weapon, for the most part, the Short, Magazine, Lee Enfield (SMLE) rifle. Bayonet training, as described by Rifleman Groom of the London Rifle Brigade, involved charging sacks marked with discs denoting head, eyes and heart, yelling like maniacs as it struck home. Details of bayonet training were often graphic, as in these surviving training notes; many found the experience terrifying.

In Kitchener's New Army, valuable weapons such as the SMLE were in short supply, and trainees would have to make do with wooden stand-ins while learning how to carry out manoeuvres with appropriate military bearing. For later war recruits, such as Private Hodges of the Bedfordshire Regiment, weapons use was a significant component of the training, including the correct deployment of the Mills grenade – a function of the needs of trench warfare. For all, training on the rifle range, an activity depicted well by Mackain, provided the opportunity to fire live rounds. Officers too would be expected to gain proficiency, as this photograph illustrates. At late stages of the war, training also involved acclimatization to gas warfare – the correct fitting of the respirator was taught, and the trainees were then required to enter a gas chamber, in order to test both the equipment and the nerves of the wearer. Specialist training – for the coveted scout, signaller or expert marksman's badges, for example – was also offered to those of ability; in return, as well as the badge, there would be extra pay. Procedures varied in length, but the average recruit would receive at least two months of training at home before proceeding overseas.

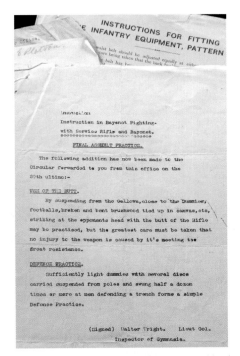

Going Overseas

A man proceeded overseas as a member of his battalion, or, as time passed in this long war, as a replacement to make up the losses sustained through casualties. Drafts invariably left the country through Dover or Folkestone, if their destination was France; if they were heading elsewhere, Southampton was their departure point. Leave was granted before proceeding overseas, but it was all too short, and there was many a heart-wrenching separation at rail termini. The regular soldiers of the BEF in August 1914 received a personal message from Lord Kitchener: 'Remember that the honour of the British Army depends on your individual conduct.' The slip of paper was to be kept in the pay book, and also included the firm reminder: 'You may find temptations both in wine and women. You must entirely resist both.' For most troops, arrival at their destination would involve a further period of training, to ensure battle-hardening and acclimatization to local conditions. In France, vast base camps were used and harsh training was carried out in so-called 'bull rings'. The most infamous was that at Etaples, a vast camp where training in the dune fields was presided over by 'canaries', physical training instructors distinguished by their yellow armbands and the crossed swords of the drill instructor – similar to those illustrated below. For some, this period would be uneventful; for others, it would have a dehumanizing influence – particularly the bayonet practice, In either case, when Tommy left in slow-moving trains, housed in trucks marked 'Hommes 8, Chevaux 40' (which led to some speculation if this was either/or, or if the horses were to join the forty men in the truck), it was at least a relief to know that finally, he was to go 'up the line'.

Sketches
of Tommy's life

At the Base. — Nº 1

Crossing the Channel was quite a thrilling thing. But an old B. E. F. man rather spoiled the trip by swanking without his life belt, and otherwise showing everybody the entire thing was far from new to him.

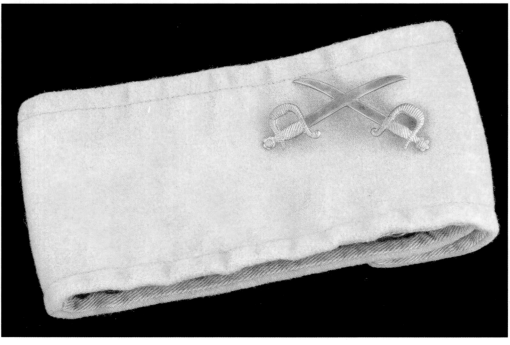

[*This paper is to be considered by each soldier as confidential, and to be kept in his Active Service Pay Book.*]

You are ordered abroad as a soldier of the King to help our French comrades against the invasion of a common Enemy. You have to perform a task which will need your courage, your energy, your patience. Remember that the honour of the British Army depends on your individual conduct. It will be your duty not only to set an example of discipline and perfect steadiness under fire but also to maintain the most friendly relations with those whom you are helping in this struggle. The operations in which you are engaged will, for the most part, take place in a friendly country, and you can do your own country no better service than in showing yourself in France and Belgium in the true character of a British soldier.

Be invariably courteous, considerate and kind. Never do anything likely to injure or destroy property,

200M 8/14 H W V

2

and always look upon looting as a disgraceful act. You are sure to meet with a welcome and to be trusted ; your conduct must justify that welcome and that trust. Your duty cannot be done unless your health is sound. So keep constantly on your guard against any excesses. In this new experience you may find temptations both in wine and women. You must entirely resist both temptations, and, while treating all women with perfect courtesy, you should avoid any intimacy.

Do your duty bravely.
Fear God.
Honour the King.

KITCHENER,
Field-Marshal.

Sketches of Tommy's life

At the Base. — Nº 8

But we also tried hard to kill ourselves, before we could get up the Line, by tearing like mad up and down a lot of sand hills in full fighting order.

Tommy's headgear: a selection of hats and helmets worn by the British soldier, including those of his Allies. German headgear such as the Pickelhaube (top) was eagerly sought after as souvenirs.

3 Tommy's Uniform and Equipment

The image of the British soldier in the First World War, like that of his allies and enemies, is iconic. As depicted in numerous official photographs, Tommy is a soldier burdened with his equipment, bent under its weight, and under that of his distinctive steel helmet, carrying the snub-nosed rifle that was to be one of the distinguishing features of the British infantryman for almost half a century. Such images from the Ypres Salient and the Somme epitomize the British soldier of the First World War. Understanding the composition of the soldier's uniform and equipment helps us to further understand the nature of this war. For the French and Germans, the silhouette of the *poilu*, with his archaic greatcoat and stylish Adrian helmet, and the *infanterie-man*, with his high boots and *Stahlhelm* are equally evocative of this most industrial of all wars. Together, these portraits of the principal combatants add a visual dimension to the outpouring of prose and poetry at the end of the war, soldiers depicted by official war artists, war photographers and cinematographers as they journeyed to and from battle, and in all attitudes stricken on the battlefield.

Although the images of the infantryman of 1914–18 portray a seemingly archaic combatant compared with today's laden and camouflaged soldier, the uniforms and equipment of the British Tommy were actually advanced for their time, more so in fact than those of his fellow combatants. His khaki wool serge uniform was designed to be warm in winter and relatively cool in winter; his carrying equipment constructed to distribute the weight of ammunition and accoutrements evenly; and his rifle was arguably the most advanced of its kind in the world. The British infantryman was well equipped to carry out his momentous task.

THE UNIFORM

The khaki uniform worn by the troops was first developed in 1902 as a replacement for the traditional red coat of the British infantryman. Red coats had seen battle in many theatres of war and over many centuries. A mythology surrounding its use arose, relating to its visibility on the battlefield, as well as its ability to hide the blood of its tattered warriors, the 'thin red line' of the Crimea. The fact that the red-coated British soldier could be easily seen from great distance was to become of major importance in the less formal wars of the late nineteenth and early twentieth centuries, and it was here that a universal service dress in a plain colour was needed. Although the red coat was still in service in action during the Zulu Wars of 1879, the need for something more suited to modern warfare was learned in India and the Afghan Wars, with the development of a uniform in a less conspicuous dun colour that became known as 'khaki' (derived from the Hindi-Urdu word for 'dust' or 'mud-covered'). A cotton Service Dress of khaki was in full use in the Boer War (1899–1902), and led to the development of the wool serge version used by Tommy in the First World War. This, together with an innovative set of load-bearing cotton-web equipment, and a world-class rifle, the 'Short, Magazine, Lee Enfield', established the British soldier of 1914–18 as one of the best clothed and best equipped of the day.

1902 Pattern Service Dress Tunic
The 1902 pattern Service Dress was the product of a basic military requirement to have a comfortable and serviceable uniform that would be suited for field conditions, in all weathers. Prior to the Boer Wars of 1899–1902 the British soldier had worn the red coat, which, coupled with the white, pipe-clayed, leather equipment of the time, made Tommy somewhat conspicuous. The need to blend into the veldt was recognized early on in South Africa, where the dun-coloured cotton khaki drill had been issued; this was seen to be inadequate, as it was not hard-wearing and was not warm enough in the cooler periods. As such, a wool serge version was produced that was to be embodied in Army Orders in 1902 as Service Dress. Service Dress went through several modifications in the 'Lists of Changes' issued periodically by the War Office, but by 1914 had settled down to a pattern that was used more or less throughout the war, issued from 1907 onwards, and illustrated by this group from different regiments (including Pte Frederick Walker of the Middlesex Regiment, far left).

It's funny how rotten your first uniform looks on you. You wonder how the other chaps manage to appear so smart.

Sketches of Tommy's life In Training. — N° 2

The wartime Service Dress tunic was characteristically loose-fitting (if it fitted at all; a fact not lost on contemporary cartoonists), with a turned-down collar, patches at the shoulder to bear the extra wear from the position of the rifle butt in action, and pleats to provide a good fit to the rear of the jacket. It had a pair of box-pleated patch pockets with button-down flaps at the upper chest, and a pair of deep pockets let into the tunic skirt, again with button-down flaps. A simple pocket was also sewn into the inside right skirt of the tunic to take the soldier's first field dressing. Two brass hooks, often removed or lost through use, were intended to support the belt in its correct position between the sixth and seventh tunic button. Shoulder straps bore regimental insignia in the form of brass shoulder titles, but a range of other insignia was also used, described below. Throughout the war, insignia were added to the sleeves, including rank badges, specialist 'trade' badges and divisional insignia.

In 1915, a 'utility' version was introduced, worn by Pte J.T. Robinson (left). It had none of the refinements of the original; it was even more shapeless, and it dispensed with the rifle patches at the shoulders, the pocket box pleats, the rear-fitting pleat to the tunic, the ornate GS buttons and the brass belt hooks. The utility version was never in favour and, although worn throughout the war, it was replaced with the standard 1902 pattern as soon as was practical. Post-war, the tunic was remodelled slightly. The 1902 Service Dress tunic can easily be distinguished from its post-war relative, the 1922 pattern Service Dress, by a number of features: a double pleat at the collar (the 1922 pattern had a single one); white tape 'lining' (that of the 1922 pattern was 'khaki', although some late-war 1902 pattern tunics are also known to have been issued with this colour lining); unlined pocket flaps (lined in 1922); and a paper sizing and manufacturer label, sewn into the right breast, but most often missing, for obvious reasons (the 1922 pattern has usually a cloth equivalent). These details are illustrated below.

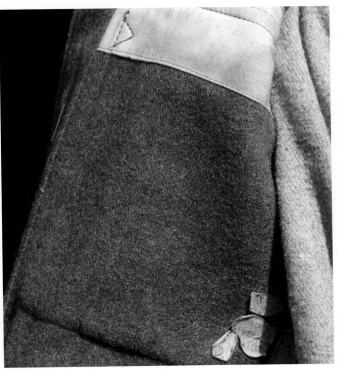

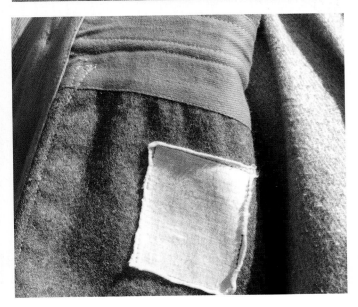

'Colonial' Variants

Although by 1918, men from across the Empire would be dressed in uniformity with the British Tommy (save for insignia), in the early stages of the war at least, there were significant differences between the dress of the British soldier and that of his comrades in arms. Head dress was one way of distinguishing the 'colonial' soldier: the 'lemon-squeezer' hat identified the New Zealand soldier (below), while the Australian soldier wore the characteristic 'slouch hat', adopted widely in 1916. The 1902 pattern tunic was often used by men of the Empire, but, initially at least, Canadians had their own version with two more buttons, and distinctive 'lancer' cuffs, as illustrated (right). Canadian head dress was similar to that of the British soldier. Australians, different to the core, adopted their own, distinctive tunic with pleats and an integral belt. It echoed the Norfolk jacket that was popular at the time, and is worn here by Sergeant Stenson of the 3rd Battalion AIF, illustrated in 1918. (Although wounded in action three times, Stenson survived the war.) The tunic illustrated below is actually an early version from the second war, broadly similar in cut to that of the first, and bearing the unique 'rising sun' badge (actually based on a decorative, fan-like array of bayonets in the commander's office) adopted by all Australian forces, and used to this day. Other nationalities within the Empire contented themselves with adopting distinctive insignia alone to identify their origin.

The SD Cap

In 1914, British soldiers – like all other combatants – went to war in headgear that contributed to their military smartness but was not designed to provide any kind of ballistic protection. That would come later. The French wore the kepi, and the Germans the ornate Pickelhaube; for Tommy it was the peaked cap (adopted in 1905), with stiffened rim and peak, and bearing the traditional cap badge of the British Army. The stiffness of this headgear made it awkward, and some soldiers clearly felt uncomfortable in it, when captured by the camera early in the war (top right). In late 1914, an answer to the impracticality of this headgear was the issue of the winter trench cap. Known universally as the 'gor'blimey', this soon became shapeless with wear, but it was a comfortable cap with flaps that could be fastened under the chin for extra warmth, or stowed on top of the cap – adding to its ungainly appearance (right). Examples are very rare today, and the 'gor'blimey', never a favourite with sergeant majors (hence its nickname), was to be replaced by the issue of the 1917 pattern cap (top). This cap was capable of being folded and stowed in the soldier's equipment, as it had no stiff components; a stitched peak – a unique feature of late-war 'trench' caps – was the only concession to smartness. The 1917 pattern cap had a black oilcloth or cotton khaki lining and was comfortable to wear – Tommy often personalized it by plaiting the leather strap, while parting the strap components was also popular (right). A final modification was the issue of a denim version in 1918, again with the same linings (above). Post-war, Service Dress caps returned to a stiffness that resembled in part their 1905 forebears.

Scottish Soldiers' Dress

Many Scottish regiments were kilted, a dress distinction that was always popular with onlookers, and which was worn with pride by the 'kilties' themselves. According to Private Dennis, transferred from an English rifle regiment to the Cameron Highlanders, the kilt was warm to wear, with its many folds of woollen tartan; the downside of the folds was their propensity to harbour lice, as well as their ability to soak up vast amounts of water, adding to the weight burden of the average soldier. The bright colours of some regimental tartans was also a problem, such that, by 1915, the kilt was covered by a simple apron of khaki cloth (opposite). The Scottish Service Dress tunic was also special – its front skirts were cut back in the manner of a traditional doublet to allow the wearing of the full-dress sporran; in Pte Dennis' case, this was carried out by the simple expedient of cutting the corners off his standard SD tunic. By 1916, the rather more prosaic gas helmet haversack would replace the sporran in the field. To complement the appearance of the Highland soldier, there was a range of caps and bonnets; in the early war years, the commonest was the Glengarry, but variations included the beret-like Balmoral bonnet, in a variety of patterns with diced borders (like that of the Liverpool Scottish, an English kilt-wearing Territorial battalion, illustrated), coloured pompoms (touries) and tartan backing for the usually flamboyant Scottish cap badge (those of the Highland Light Infantry, Argyll & Sutherland Highlanders, Cameron Highlander and Seaforths are illustrated). Later, Scots would adopt the khaki tam-o'-shanter, a large, circular but otherwise shapeless object that none the less clearly distinguished the Scot from others.

Shirt and Cardigan

The 'Grey-Back' wool flannel shirt – warm in winter, hot in summer – was the traditional accompaniment to Tommy's distinctive early nineteenth-century red coat. This shirt continued to be issued unchanged into the First World War, but was replaced in the post-war reorganization of the British Army and its uniforms by a rougher dark khaki version. It was mostly made up from light grey flannel (hence its nickname), but it did appear in different cloths – as illustrated in this contemporary camp photograph from c.1916 – including the dark grey flannel version from 1917 (illustrated opposite). 'Pullover' in style, the shirt had four buttons and a simple, collarless neckline – as the Service Dress tunic buttoned to the neck, a collar was not necessary. This shirt was worn over a set of cotton underwear – which often harboured lice in the closely confined conditions of the front line – and, for extra warmth, a coarsely knitted woollen cardigan (illustrated above) could be added to the complement of layers beneath the tunic.

Trousers and Puttees

Original Service Dress trousers of Great War vintage are rare today, since most pairs were worn out through overuse; they were, after all, more practical to wear in post-war conditions than the more conspicuous khaki Service Dress. The wartime pair illustrated survived only because they were never issued. Held up by braces or belt (various types were adopted by the soldier), Service Dress trousers were quite close-fitting, with a narrow leg intended to be worn with puttees to provide the required military silhouette. Puttees were derived, like the khaki Service Dress, from the British experience in India; 'puttee' coming from the Hindi word for 'bandage'. They were intended to provide a covering for the lower leg that would give greater support and protection. In fact, tying the puttee too tight could exacerbate the problem of 'trench foot', a condition akin to frostbite resulting from restricted blood circulation and prolonged water immersion. Puttees were used by most nations during the First World War, and represented a military fashion that was to stagger on in one or two armies in a second world conflict. Consisting of long wool serge strips provided with cotton tapes, puttees were wound around the leg from the ankle to the knee for the average infantryman. Mounted soldiers are distinguished by their practice of winding the puttee from the knee to the ankle, the tapes wound close to the ankle – as worn by the cavalry signalmen in a French studio shot (right). Finding ways of exerting their own personality, soldiers would also create, using judiciously applied folds, fancy patterns with their puttees – like this smartly turned out Sergeant from the Welsh Regiment (below). As depicted by Mackain, not all soldiers were as adept at tying their puttees.

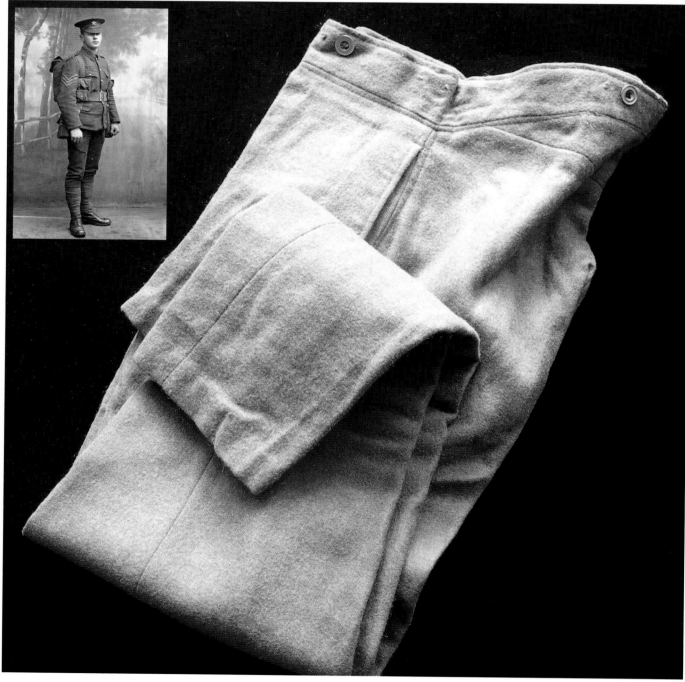

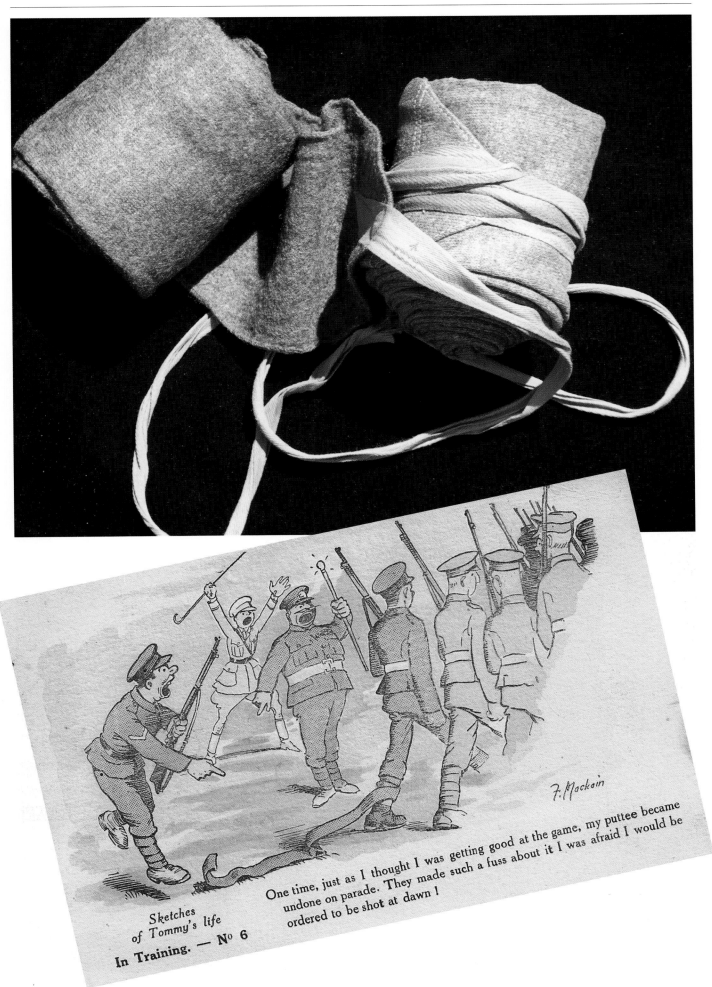

*Sketches
of Tommy's life*
In Training. — Nº 6

One time, just as I thought I was getting good at the game, my puttee became undone on parade. They made such a fuss about it I was afraid I would be ordered to be shot at dawn !

F. Mackain

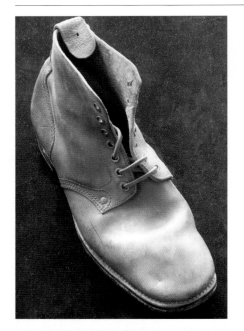

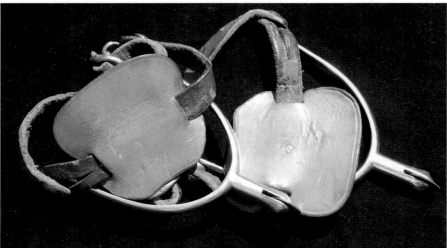

The Boots

According to the weekly Illustrated War News *of February 1916, the traditional centre of British shoemaking, Northampton, was stretched to capacity in supplying boots, not only for the British Army, but also for most of the Allies in the field, employed on all fronts. The 'Regulation' British field boot for most of the war was roughly square-toed, produced in thick hide with the rough side out, as illustrated in the* Illustrated War News *(top right). Soldiers issued with the boots for field use were instructed to pack them with dubbin in order to create a more water-resistant material, and this produced the tan colour that is so typical of the field boot. Pre- and post-war parade boots were, however, stained black for parade use. The soles of these boots were cleated with metal studs, which covered almost the whole of the sole in the standard infantryman's boot, or simply the toe area (as in the example illustrated) for mounted soldiers, who had to use stirrups. Detachable spurs were worn by mounted men, like the Canadian pair illustrated, which have been adapted by the addition of George V sixpences as improvised rowels.*

A lighter boot was also produced, the 'Standard Boot', which had seams of overlapping leather that could rub on the unwitting soldier's feet; a good worn example is illustrated (top). Although it was not intended for field use, this boot has been encountered in excavations on the Western Front.

The published photograph, and a boot fragment picked up from Flanders years ago, are also illustrated. Late war, a further boot pattern was introduced, with a distinctive crescent toe cap. Other footwear used by Tommy on the Western Front included the high boot of the mounted artilleryman, and the so-called 'trench waders', made by the North British Rubber Company in Scotland, and centrally held as 'trench stores'.

Cold-Weather Protection

The standard cold-weather protection issued to the average soldier was the greatcoat, a cumbersome wool serge coat, with a single row of brass GS buttons. Weighing in at around 6lb, it represented a considerable burden, even when dry. The greatcoat was bulky and long, difficult to wear with equipment, and prone to fouling with mud and water, which made it even heavier. The mounted pattern was shorter, and much preferred by the soldiers; indeed, the average Tommy in the winter trenches was tempted to cut down his coat accordingly, to prevent its skirts trailing in the mud. Officers, providing their own uniform, had more choice, and adopted the short, double-breasted wool 'British Warm' and the lightweight Burberry 'Trench Coat'. In fact, greatcoats were more often left with the large pack or 'valise' with the Battalion transport. There were a number of other means of keeping the body core warm. The first of these was the outlandish (and multicoloured) goatskin sleeveless jerkin issued in late 1914 that was to see action well into 1916; worn with the fur out, this garment may have been malodorous, but it was one way of keeping the trunk warm. Goatskins were replaced in 1915 onwards with hard-wearing sleeveless leather jerkins, lined with wool serge and with leather 'football' buttons, like the venerable example illustrated below. Worn both over and under the tunic, these provided warmth and protection, and were much favoured. A similar version was re-issued in the Second World War. The later models differed in construction, with a more irregular patching (Great War examples generally had four panels, like that illustrated) and simple plastic buttons (rather than leather). Protection from the wet weather of Flanders was, at first, provided through the groundsheet, and, from 1917 onwards, by the innovation of a groundsheet that could be buttoned up to the neck to provide a cape. These useful garments saw much use post-war, and few survive today from the Great War.

Warm-Weather Uniforms

Khaki Drill or 'KDs' was the standard uniform issued for warm climates. It consisted broadly of a cotton version of the standard serge Service Dress, but there were nevertheless some significant differences. KDs were of a lighter khaki colour than the serge Service Dress, had breast pockets alone, and in many cases had a stand-up collar (although the rise and fall collar was the norm). The tunic was fastened by five GS buttons, which were attached by loops to facilitate removal for laundry purposes. Three sets were issued, to cover the likely losses. Trousers were issued, but often shorts were worn with socks and puttees; unofficial cutdown serge SD trousers were used as shorts in the summer months on the Western Front. KDs were usually worn with the Wolseley pattern cork sun helmet, the solar topee, which provided protection only from the sun – this protection was enhanced by the use of additional neck flaps. Pte Robert Wheatley of the 6th Yorkshire Regiment is pictured at Mudros Harbour in 1915; he was to die in Gallipoli. An officer's private purchase helmet (its leather rim distinguishing it from that of the other ranks, which were in KD) is also illustrated. Khaki Drill and Wolseley helmets were used in all warm-weather climates – the Mediterranean, Middle East, Africa and India – although in some cases, as in Gallipoli and Salonika, there was to be a mixture of serge and KD worn. In many cases, shirts alone were worn, in shirtsleeve order like that reconstructed below. In the hottest climates, as in Mesopotamia, 'spinepads' were also issued, a vain provision to prevent the sun beating down on the spine, and a supposed preventive for sunstroke. This particular innovation, which actually added to the heat exhaustion of the average soldier, was fortunately not to last long.

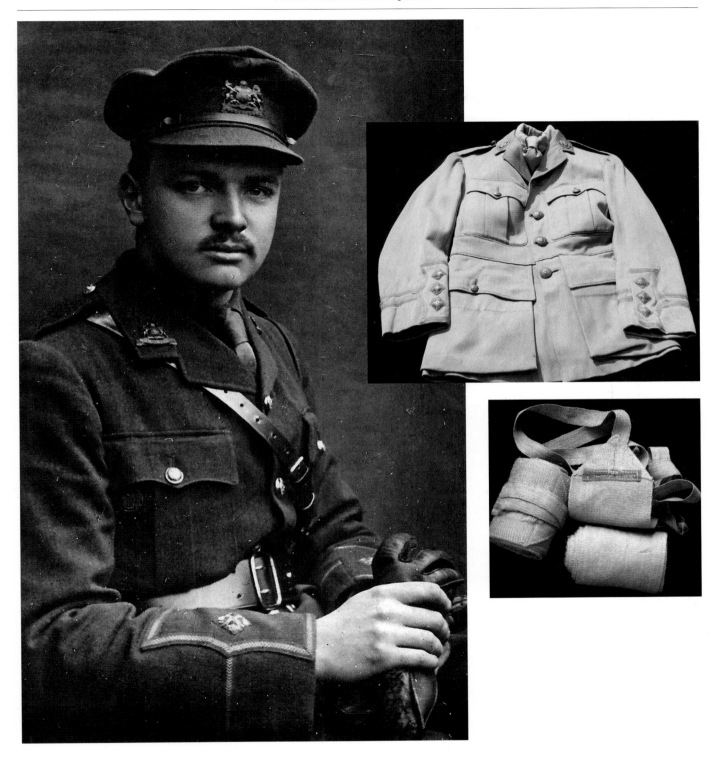

The Officer's Uniform

Officers' Service Dress, here illustrated in a wartime character study, was to distinguish the rank of the wearer easily — so easily, in fact, that it was to provide enemy snipers with something clear to aim at. Tailored to the needs of the individual officer, the Service Dress tunic nevertheless had to conform to the standard sealed pattern, having four buttons of regimental, rather than GS, pattern, an open step-down collar to be worn with regulation shirt and tie (the original 1902 pattern specification was for a closed stand and fall collar, sometimes used in the war), and a wide skirt with voluminous patch pockets. The collar bore pairs of distinctive collar badges, usually bronzed; cap badges were also bronzed. Badges of rank were generally applied to the cuffs of the tunic in a distinctive manner; these were easily spotted by the discerning sniper. Some officers took it upon themselves to move these badges to the shoulder straps, an affectation that had always been used by the Guards. Known as 'wind-up' tunics, the implication of this name was the reasonable fact that the alteration was made in order to make the tunic less conspicuous. Later in the war, many tunics were tailored like this from scratch. The version illustrated above, belonging to an unknown captain of the Loyal North Lancashire Regiment (5th Division, 116th Brigade), employs another method; brass buttons, cuff rank stars and lace have all been blackened to reduce their prominence in the field. The officer's SD tunic was worn with breeches of Bedford cord and a variety, according to personal taste, of footwear — from polished riding top boots and high-laced 'trench boots' to simple brown ankle boots and puttees. Officer's puttees (above), almost invariably made by Fox's, were distinguished by a small button marked 'L' or 'R' applied to each puttee, to identify left and right. The officers' cap had a leather peak, and 'trench' versions had a fold-down flap against poor weather.

STANDARD WEAPONS AND LOAD-BEARING EQUIPMENT

The training of the infantryman, then and now, instils the belief that a soldier's best friend is his (or, today, her) rifle. The soldier of the Great War was expected to keep his weapon clean, in working order and ready to be used; it would be inspected daily. From the latter part of the nineteenth century, the British Army had adopted a short rifle, the Short, Magazine, Lee Enfield (or SMLE), which could be used by both mounted and dismounted troops. This weapon was to become one of many trademarks of the British and Empire troops until well into the Second World War.

The question of appropriate load-bearing equipment has taxed the military mind every since the infantryman was first conceived. For centuries, the design of equipments – to include ammunition carriers, haversacks for accoutrements, ration carriers, and so on – has centred on the belt, with shoulder straps and braces designed to spread the weight. Both German and French equipments were founded in an archaic design, with the belt supporting much of the weight of the ammunition. British equipment was founded on a principal of weight distribution, a collaboration of military ideas and manufacturing innovation. It was to be much admired; although the post-war after-the-fact controversy of the laden infantryman continues to be a point of discussion in accounts of battles such as the Somme, in 1916.

The SMLE (Short, Magazine, Lee Enfield)

The principal weapon of the British soldier from 1902 was designated the Short, Magazine, Lee Enfield rifle, SMLE, or 'Smelly' to most soldiers. It was based on its predecessor, now known as the Long Lee Enfield, and the intention had been to build on the reliability of the arm (which had seen distinguished service in the Boer War), but to shorten it, lighten it, and provide the means of loading through a charger-fed magazine system. The resulting rifle, with its characteristic snub nose, appeared on 23 December 1902, and was to undergo several modifications through to its last model, the Mark VI, in 1926. It continues to be produced today. The SMLE Mark I (redesignated Rifle Number 1, Mark I in 1926) was developed following experience in the Boer War, which indicated that a lighter, more easily handled, better-sighting and quicker-loading weapon was needed. The charger system designed allowed for five rounds to be loaded at a time, and the magazine held ten altogether. The early Mark I rifles have the provision for a long-range volley sight – inaccurate, but capable in the right hands of putting down a volley with an effective range of 1,500–2,000 yards. The weapon in wartime service was the SMLE Mark I***, introduced on 22 April 1914 in order to take the new Mark VII bullet, which required alteration to the sights. In addition, the SMLE Mark III, introduced in January 1907 with changes to its sights and charger loading system, was also used; from January 1916, simplifications to this rifle (SMLE Mark III*) were made in order to speed up production for the New Army. Among other things, the volley sights, no longer needed in trench warfare with the decline in musketry skills, were omitted. Both Mark III and Mark III* versions are illustrated – both are popular and sought-after purchases at militaria shows. Details of the muzzle, rifle stock, breech (with magazine cut-off plate in this instance) and butt (with concealed compartment for the oil bottle) are shown. Other rifles were used, such as the American P14 rifle, and the obsolete long Lee Enfield; but none was admired as much as the SMLE.

Sketches of Tommy's life Up the line — N° 4

The only time I ever saw a man cry was when one of our chaps dropped his rifle in the mud after spending exactly two hours cleaning it.

Pull-Through, 'Four-be-Two' and Oil Bottle

As a 'soldier's best friend', the rifle had to be kept clean. This was not just part of the military obsession with 'bull'; it was essential if the principal weapon was to be effective, and not to jam when it was needed most. As such, in and out of the trenches, rifles would be subject to mandatory inspection. The breech and barrel were examined carefully for any sign of dirt, which would render a weapon unserviceable, with a round jammed irretrievably in the barrel. In order to clean his rifle, each soldier was provided with four-inch-wide flannel strips marked out in two-inch portions — 'four-be-two' in the language of the day — which would be passed through the barrel with the aid of a brass-tipped, and therefore weighted cord known as a 'pull-through'. To lubricate this action a brass bottle of machine oil was provided, stored, along with the pull-through, in the stock of the rifle itself. As illustrated by Mackain, keeping a rifle clean under trench conditions could be a trying task.

SAA and Cotton Bandoliers

In the trenches, soldiers had to carry 150 rounds of small arms ammunition (SAA) in their pouches, forming their reserve – and their primary source of ammunition when in action. The standard bullet was the .303in calibre Mark VII infantry bullet (pointed and thus distinguished from the older Mark VI, which was used by the Navy and Territorial battalions still using the long Lee Enfield pattern rifle. The rounds were issued in cotton bandoliers holding five chargers of five rounds each (below), and the bandoliers were packed in ammunition boxes. An open box of ammunition was kept in each fire bay (although the authorities frowned upon the draping of bandoliers from appropriate points in the trenches, considering this practice to be untidy). Both empties and live rounds were lost in their millions, and this is evidenced by the large numbers that turn up in farmers' fields and archaeological sites. This handful (right) from the fields of Flanders bears makers' marks for the laboratories of the Royal Arsenal (RL), as well as private manufacturers Kynoch (K), and Birmingham M & M Ltd (J). These examples are safely deactivated.

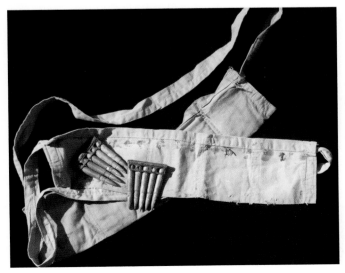

1907 Pattern Bayonet

With the development of a new, shorter rifle came the need for a longer bayonet, since the likely enemy of the British soldier would be equipped with the longer Mauser-type rifle; as a result, the British could find himself at a disadvantage in a lunging bayonet fight. The original bayonet issued with the SMLE, the 1903 pattern, was only twelve inches long, and this was inadequate to counter the threat of German blades. As such, the 1907 pattern bayonet – always referred to as a 'sword' in British rifle regiments – was five inches longer than its predecessor, to provide a reach comparable with any other existing weapons. The 1907 pattern bayonet attached to the SMLE by the use of a boss on the snub nose of the SMLE (beneath the muzzle) and a bayonet bar, connecting with the mortise groove on the pommel of the bayonet. Early versions had hooked quillons; by 1914, this had been superseded by the simpler version with an uncomplicated crosspiece illustrated, in mint and relic condition. (The relic bayonet was recovered by a farmer in Passchendaele village.) Both versions had simple leather scabbards with steel top-mounts and tips (chapes) that were carried suspended from the belt by simple frogs.

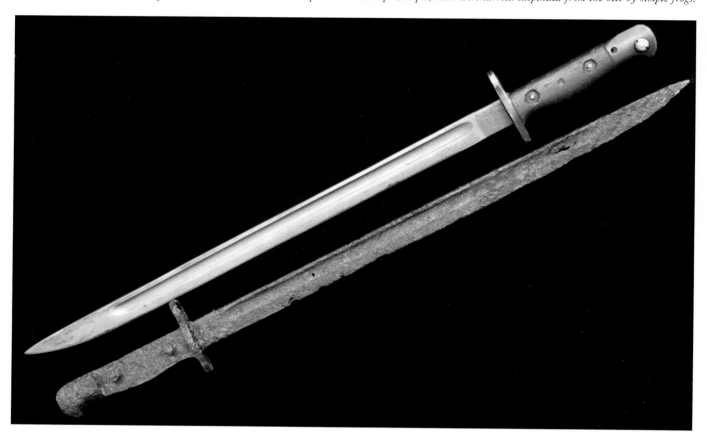

1903 Bandolier Equipment

The 1903 pattern leather bandolier equipment was developed, like many other items of military equipment, in the early part of the twentieth century, following the outcome of the Boer War. This equipment set, produced in brown leather, was intended to free the infantryman from the burden of its predecessor, the 1888 Slade Wallace Valise equipment, which was, some alleged, cumbersome and unbalanced. The 1903 pattern dispensed entirely with the need for a valise, or large pack; instead it comprised the following: a plain leather waist belt with two pairs of cartridge pouches of different pattern (as illustrated right), designed to take ten and fifteen rounds; an ammunition bandolier with five ten-round pockets worn over the chest (the cavalry version had an additional four pockets worn at the rear); a canvas haversack with webbing strap; a water bottle and leather strap; the mess tin and cover, designed to slip over the rear of the belt; and a greatcoat carrier, consisting of straps that connected with a D-ring on the mess tin cover, and similar rings on the waist-belt cartridge pouches. This equipment set was destined to be replaced by the far superior 1908 pattern webbing; it was clearly inadequate in load-bearing terms, had little stowage, and the cross straps of bandolier, haversack and water bottle constricted the chest of its wearer (opposite). Despite this, the bandolier, belt and water bottle saw much service with mounted troops of the Royal Regiment of Artillery in the Great War, as seen in the detailed wartime photograph of Royal Field Artillerymen on parade (opposite).

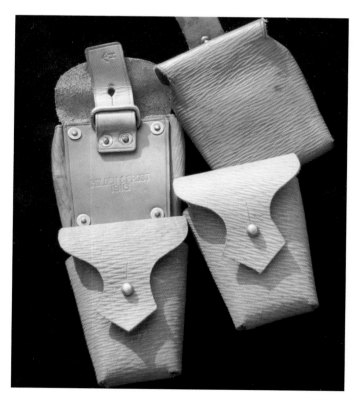

1908 Webbing Equipment

One of the greatest innovations in soldier's load-bearing equipment was the discovery and use of thick woven-cotton strapping, known as webbing, which was invented by the Mills Equipment Company in the United States during the late nineteenth century. This material was identified as being a suitable replacement for the leather Slade-Wallace equipment then in use in the British Army. Difficult to keep clean, and cumbersome when wet, leather has its disadvantages as the basis for a soldier's equipment set. The webbing equipment that entered service as the 1908 pattern was innovative; designed by Major Burrowes of the Royal Irish Fusiliers in 1906, it was a complete 'system', the various straps, pouches and haversacks being perfectly balanced. Unlike many of its contemporary systems, which tended to load the belt and put strain on the lower back of the soldier, there were additional straps behind the cartridge carriers that helped distribute their weight more evenly, with some of the weight being taken up by the shoulder straps. The 1908 set consisted of belt, cross straps, left and right cartridge carriers (designed to carry 150 rounds in ten pouches, each holding three five-round chargers), water bottle, entrenching tool head carrier and bayonet frog. One innovation was the helve for the entrenching tool being strapped to the scabbard of the bayonet – the small webbing strap for this is the rarest of all Great War webbing items. In addition, there was a small haversack and a large pack (otherwise known as the valise), with cross straps to keep the pack in place and balanced. The equipment could be taken off like a jacket (an idea that was to give rise to the 'battle jerkin' of the Second World War), and, on the march, the three-inch-wide belt could be unbuckled for comfort. Originally, the stud fastenings for the ammunition pouches matched on both left- and right-hand carriers; this was soon changed, in 1914, when it was found that ammunition was being lost from the left-hand version, and additional straps were added. Later in the war, and as an economy measure, the press-studs were replaced by post and hole fasteners, as in the additional set illustrated below.

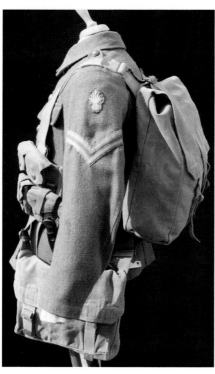

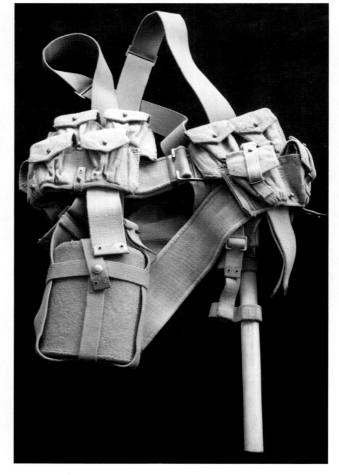

It was mandatory that web equipment be worn in the trenches; it could only be removed, temporarily, when visiting the latrine. Despite the rules, it was rare indeed that the full equipment set would be worn; instead, the large pack (containing greatcoat and a range of other items) would often be sent back with the battalion transport. The full equipment set was known as 'marching order' (opposite); when in the front line, the small pack would be transferred to the back, redistributing the weight of the set, in what became known as 'battle order' (right), shown here with respirator in 'alert' position.

Much has been made of the weight of a soldier's equipment, and contemporary postcards frequently illustrate this aspect of a soldier's life. This is not unusual – all combat infantrymen from the dawn of time have been encumbered with equipment. In fact, of the sixty-one pounds of equipment known to be carried by the average soldier (as indicated by the officer's Field Service Pocket Book), at least a third of this total was represented by the clothes he stood up in, and his rifle. In action, a soldier was issued with two extra cotton bandoliers of ammunition; the weight of these was offset by the loss of the large pack and its contents. Other items were issued of course, including GS spades and picks to help 'turn' or convert captured trenches, but the oft-depicted image of the soldier encumbered by equipment rising with difficulty from the trench, or 'drowning in mud from the weight of his pack', are likely to be an oversimplification of the facts.

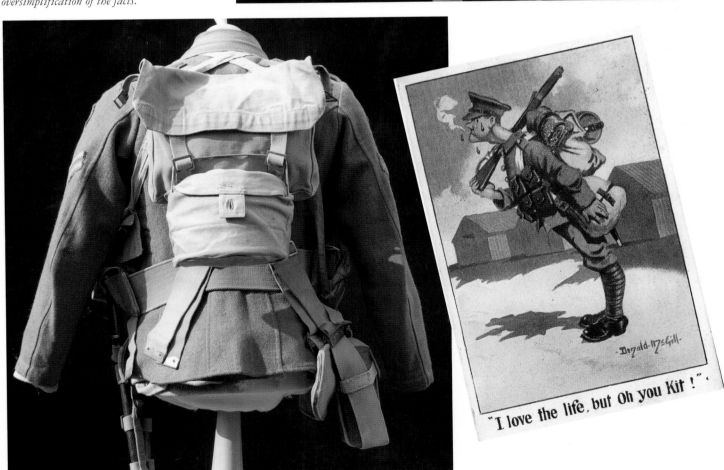

"I love the life, but Oh you Kit!"

1914 Leather Equipment

With the influx of a huge number of men into the armed forces at the beginning of the Great War, the Mills Equipment Company became seriously overstretched – it simply could not meet the demand placed upon it to supply regular, territorial and service battalions with sufficient webbing equipment sets. As such, a stopgap was needed, one that would do the same job, but which could be manufactured from leather, which was freely available. In 1914, a set of equipment based on the Mills-Burrowes webbing was issued; this, although using webbing for haversack (opposite) and large pack, used leather for waist belt, cross straps, cartridge carriers, entrenching tool holder, bayonet frog, water bottle cradle and so on. The belt used a snake and hook fastener, inherited from nineteenth-century belt patterns; a convenient hole in the leather backing to this fastener allowed the belt to be extended on the march. This fastening, and the presence of tabs and buckles, distinguish it from the earlier Slade-Wallace belt, which was still used by some rear echelon units such as the RAMC. Both are illustrated for comparison opposite.

The 1914 pattern cartridge carriers were simple pouches, designed to take a cotton bandolier holding fifty cartridges in five-round chargers – one hundred rounds in all (fifty rounds fewer than the 1908 pattern). The resulting set was serviceable, but less efficient at distributing weight than the original webbing set, and was almost exclusively issued to Service Battalions of Kitchener's Army. The sets were manufactured in the UK and in the United States, with varying quality, and consist of brown grained leather, in some cases dyed green. In some battalions, the leather equipment was discarded in favour of webbing salvaged from the battlefield, or from field hospitals, which explains the somewhat motley appearance of these battalions in period photographs. Since few examples survived the war, 1914 pattern equipment is rare and much sought-after today.

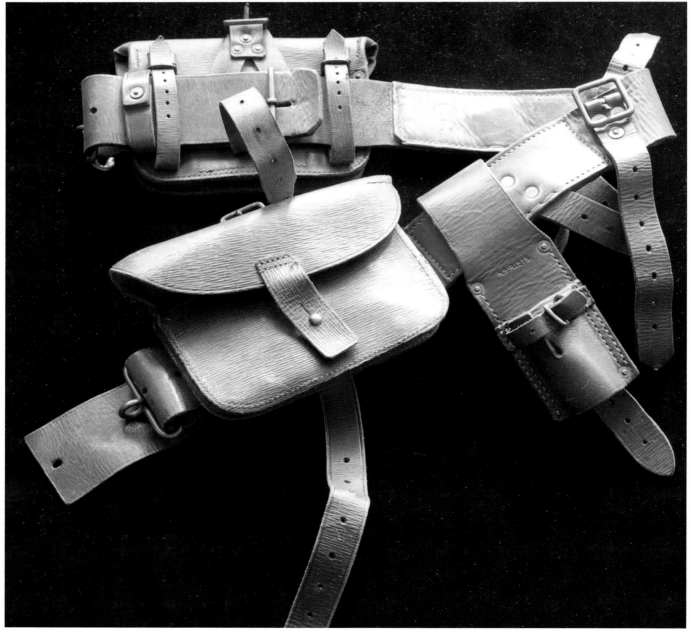

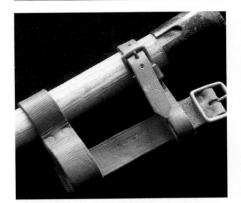

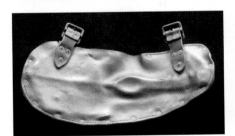

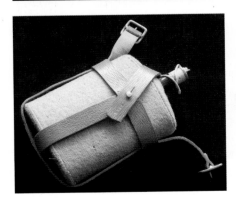

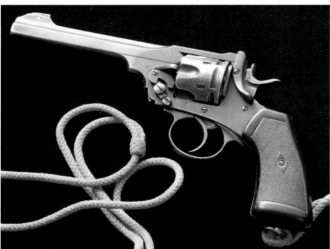

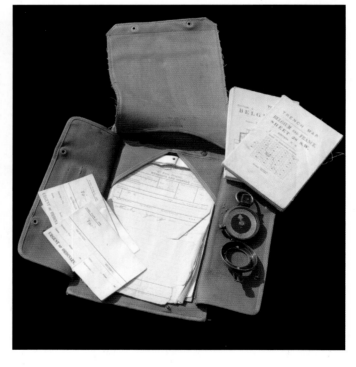

Officer's Equipment

As with the kit of all officers, load-bearing equipment was privately purchased, although it did have to conform to regulations. Based around the Sam Browne belt – usually with a single cross strap, but sometimes with double straps – the belt usually supported, in the early war period, the sword frog (soon discarded), the service revolver in a leather holster, an ammunition pouch, a canvas haversack and waterproof cotton map case and message pad. The example (right) carries the remnants of an original pad from October 1916, with the message 'Attack going on' still discernible. Separate from these, carried by a fully laden officer using leather cross straps, was a vernier compass in leather case, water bottle and binoculars – the latter notoriously difficult to source, since most were made in Germany pre-war. A walking stick ('ash plant') was also de rigueur. A typical set is illustrated above, assembled with all the most important items present. The usual side arm carried by an officer was a .455 calibre Webley revolver. The Mark VI was first introduced in May 1915, and became the most common service revolver used by the end of the war. An example dated 1917, complete with lanyard to be worn around the neck, is illustrated.

PERSONAL EQUIPMENT

Each soldier had to be self-sufficient in equipment to keep himself clean, tidy and presentable, even when in the trenches, and was issued with a set list of 'necessaries' under King's Regulations. Unless he was lucky enough to be a member of a rifle regiment – traditionally wearing black buttons and blackened insignia – he had to ensure that his brass fittings and insignia were burnished bright while out of the front line, and that his uniform was kept clean and in good repair. In the front line, of course, a more pragmatic approach had to be taken. It was expected that brasses would become dulled with exposure to the elements, and this would have the advantage of reducing the possibility of reflection leading to detection; besides, the troops had more than enough to do simply keeping body and soul together. Nevertheless, soldiers were expected to attend to their own personal cleanliness as far as was possible; regular shaving (often in the dregs of tea left in their tin cup or mess tin, the resulting suds tainting the next cup) represented one attempt to maintain morale. For some soldiers, the squalor of the trenches was to be one of the most clearly remembered 'horrors of war'.

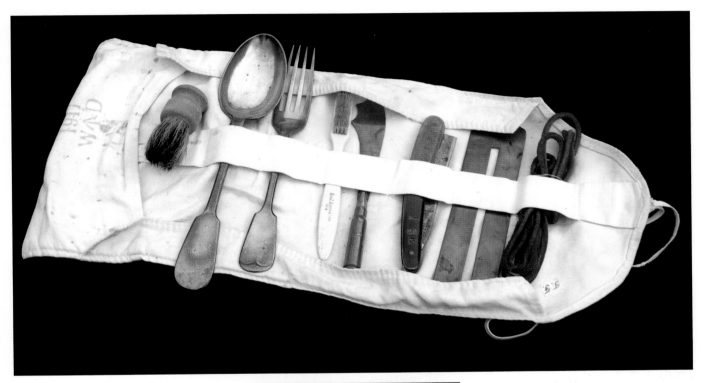

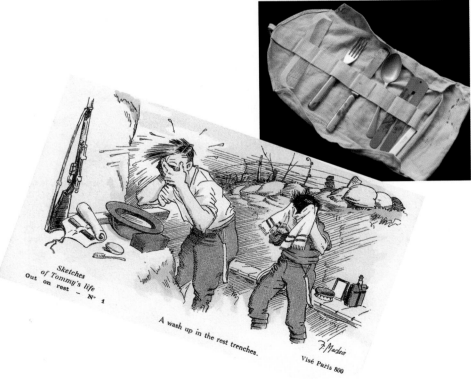

Sketches of Tommy's life Out on rest – Nº 1

A wash up in the rest trenches.

Visé Paris 800

The 'Holdall'

The holdall was a cloth roll, with a central strap of loops that were intended to hold a variety of objects of value to the everyday life of the soldier: knife (often discarded), fork and spoon; cut-throat razor, shaving brush, toothbrush and comb; button stick; and sundry other items, including bootlaces. In accordance with clothing regulations, soldiers were expected to mark these small items of equipment, using a punch for metal objects (or an engraving tool), or ink for cloth, with their regimental number (or the last four digits) and their regiment or corps. The holdall had a convenient pocket for holding additional items, including a shaving mirror, privately purchased, as well as soap, shaving requisites and the 'hussif' (housewife). The roll provided a convenient means of keeping objects together – although for the front-line soldier, fork and spoon could conveniently be carried tucked into the puttees. Most early examples are of a canvas material; later ones were made of less substantial cotton material. Both are illustrated above. The holdall would always be carried by the soldier, even in the front line. Mackain's contemporary postcard shows perfectly how it would be used.

Shaving Kit

For many young soldiers, shaving was a new experience, and their downy cheeks required attention little more than once a week. Army regulations insisted on a clean chin – and, although the pre-war army had expected that soldiers would maintain a moustache, the upper lip was also kept cleanly shaven. The standard issue was a Sheffield-produced cut-throat razor – usually with horn fittings, but often of black plastic, like those illustrated – upon which the soldier was expected to punch his regimental number and unit. Safety razors, a relatively new invention by the American K.C. Gillette, had been available from 1904 (the US Army was to be issued exclusively with these during the First World War), and many soldiers unused to the open blade bought their own, together with a wide variety of shaving soaps, provided in tins like those illustrated. Shaving in the dregs of cold tea from mess tins was common, although the soap was difficult to remove, tainting further tea issues, as Private Groom of the LRB was to find out at his cost. Steel mirrors, useful for both shaving and as impromptu signalling aids or periscopes, were also available.

The 'Hussif'

The housewife – or 'hussif' – was an essential piece of kit that held sewing materials, thread, needles, a thimble, wool, buttons and so on. The ravages of army life meant that some repair would be necessary and the housewife provided a means of keeping the uniform in at least some semblance of order; by 1917–18, with the proliferation of badges and patches, it also allowed the soldier to add insignia to his tunic. The 'hussif' was simple in construction, as illustrated – a pocket of cotton material with a piece of serge for patching (and holding needles), closed by a flap.

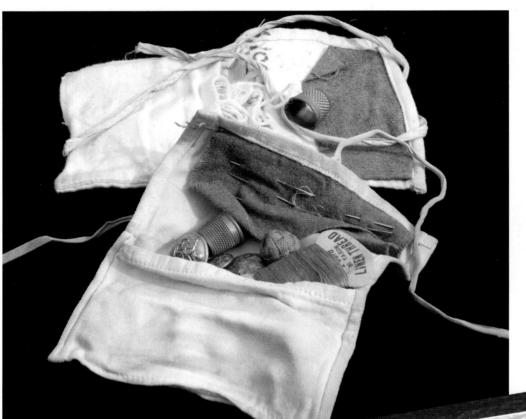

Brushes

Brushes were essential pieces of soldier's kit. Clothing Regulations from 1914 specified, in addition to shaving and toothbrushes, at least five other brushes issued as part of the soldier's 'necessaries': a hair brush; a brush for cleaning the serge uniform; a polishing brush for brass; a brush for cleaning web equipment (applying the patent Blanco cleaner made by the manufacturer Pickerings); a boot brush for applying dubbin; and another for providing a shine to the army boot while out of the front line. Clothes, boot and Blanco brushes are illustrated. Clothes brushes typically had white and black bristles; boot brushes had plain bristles; and equipment brushes were rectangular in shape, to avoid confusion. All these brushes added to the weight of the front-line soldier's equipment, and they would be consigned to storage with the large pack while Tommy was in the front line, to reappear while he was out on rest.

Button Stick and Polish

One of the first chores for a new soldier to learn was keeping his buttons bright, through the use of a button stick and a tin of Soldier's Friend (below right; for many, though, the concept of this tin of paste being 'a friend' was entirely alien). For those fortunate enough to wear the black buttons of a rifle regiment, such as Rifleman Dennis of the KRRC, polishing was restricted to the brass components of the webbing equipment; some keen types did use boot polish to give them a shine (Cherry Blossom was one of many brands available). The button stick, a simple plate of brass with a slot, was a device for keeping polish away from the uniform, and thus preventing staining. The normal button stick was found, however, to be unsuitable for protecting the brass fitments on the 1908 webbing, since the webbing straps could not be passed through easily. As a result, by 1917, at least two patents were placed for 'equipment protectors'. One, patented in 1917 (right), was destined to see service only after the war; another, commercially available version ('The Pioneer'), was more sophisticated, but only available for purchase by the discerning soldier from 1918–19 onwards.

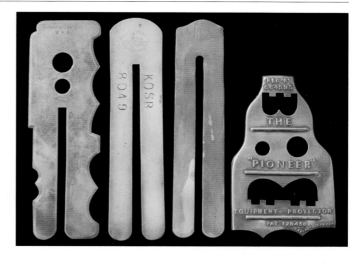

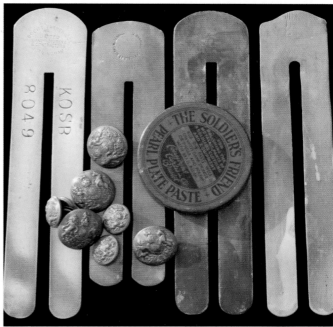

Clasp Knife

The clasp knife was one of the most important pieces of personal kit, used for duties as diverse as trench repair, tin opening and eating – the more dainty knife from the holdall being jettisoned or lost as the war dragged on. First World War versions are substantial; distinguished by their simple tin opener and copper loop. Worn on a lanyard around the body, this knife was the workhorse of the army, as depicted in the classic postcard image by Mackain.

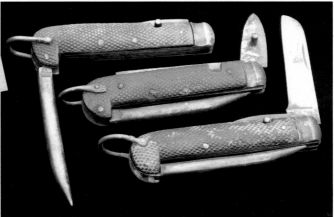

Identity Discs

Identity discs, known as 'dog tags' because of their obvious similarity to the small pieces of metal worn on the collar of a dog, have not always been part of the soldier's traditional accoutrements. In the American Civil War, combatants carried small pieces of paper with their names on them, so that they should receive a named grave if killed. Later, they bought engraved badges that could be attached to their uniforms. In the British Army, identity was similarly provided by paper; the Soldier's Pay Book (Army Form AB64), which was carried in the right breast pocket of the Service Dress.

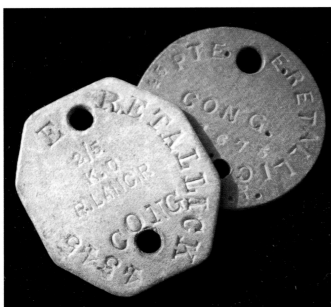

Clearly inadequate, this form of identification was supplemented by the addition of a single stamped aluminium disc, which carried the name, rank, serial number, unit details and religion (where appropriate), and which was issued on mobilization in 1914; later issues involved a single red fibre disc (top). This was hardier than the pay book, but it did none the less cause problems; once this single disc was removed from the body, as stipulated in Field Service Regulations, *the chances of identification were much reduced. In August 1916, a two-disc system evolved, the discs carrying the same information as before, in duplicate, but this time stamped on compressed fibreboard discs (left). The green octagonal disc was intended to stay with the body, while the red disc was to be taken as part of the accounting procedure. Both were worn on a string around the neck, but, as this often became dirty and clammy, soldiers were wont to carry the discs separately in the haversack or pack, or to rely on the commercially available metal versions that were produced at home and abroad. All were to be given the brutally frank nickname 'cold meat tickets' (since they resembled the tags used in butchers' shops), as the war dragged on. Typically, local entrepreneurs soon adapted their trade to produce engraved or stamped versions for the troops in rear areas and base camps. Examples (several of which are illustrated below) include functional aluminium or finer silver versions of identity bracelets, foreign coins modified for use, or trench art bracelets made from scrap materials.*

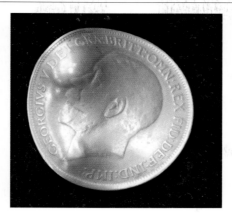

Good Luck Charms

In waving goodbye to their men, relatives and sweethearts put their trust in luck; and bought a variety of charms that might carry that luck with the soldier to the front. The men themselves would have their own versions, from lucky pennies to pieces of shrapnel from near-misses, spent bullets and so on. The penny illustrated, struck by a bullet, undoubtedly saved the life of its anonymous owner. In the early stages of the war, there were several commercially available charms, including 'Tommy Touchwud', which provided a piece of wood that could be touched in the pocket, and 'Fums-up', a silver charm with rotating arms and erect thumbs, which also had a wooden head. Crucifixes were also carried, and commonly worn with the identity discs, or stowed in a convenient pocket.

Pay Books

As part of their official record of service, soldiers were issued with a document that served as a log-book, incorporating personal and family details (including next of kin), regimental number, dates of enlistment, ranks and awards attained, skill at arms, charges, a sick record and a record of pay issued. Pre-war, the soldier was issued with a linen-covered 'Small Book' (right); this was replaced by the issue of AB64, the 'Soldier's Service and Pay Book', to every soldier on enlistment (below). This 'passport' was to be carried at all times and to be produced on request for examination by officers or regimental/military police. The AB64 was a valuable document – proof of identification both as a battlefield casualty and when receiving pay. Covers, like that illustrated, were produced as gifts (this one from a NZ army hospital), or made when there was a quiet moment by the soldier himself. Page thirteen of the AB64 was a will; soldiers moving up the line for the first time were required to complete this in an act that was seen by many to be tempting fate.

Field Service Pocket Book

The officer's 'bible' was the Field Service Pocket Book, *a handy reference guide that provided advice on everything from the construction of trenches and latrines to the maintenance of discipline. Other texts were equally valuable to the keen officer, including the official text on field engineering and the* Manual of Elementary Military Hygiene. *These would guide the raw officer through his initiation into military leadership; in this case, it was 2nd Lieutenant Herbert Smith of the Bedfordshire Regiment who charted his progress in 1915–16 within the covers.*

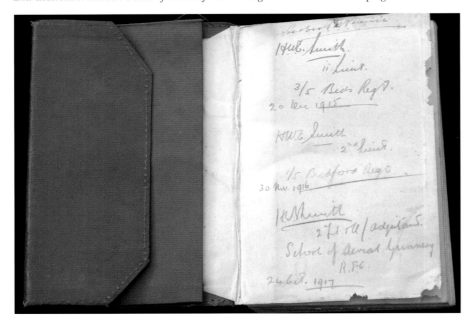

Testaments

Many soldiers found comfort in the New Testament, and the army obliged by the issue of small-volume service testaments; other organizations, such as the Church Army and the YMCA, also produced similar pocket versions. A selection is illustrated.

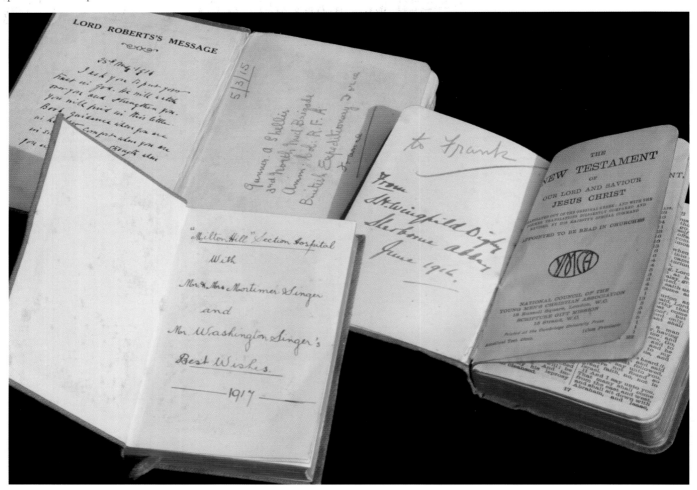

'Trench' Watches

The wristwatch – or 'wristlet' as it was then called – was not a new invention, having been used by the forces during the Boer War, and having been fashionable as an accessory for ladies at the turn of the twentieth century. It was the very femininity of these early watches that had meant that, prior to war, men had spurned them in favour of the traditional pocket watch, the perfect adornment to the Sunday-best suit. But in wartime, the need for an accurate and easily observable timepiece was of paramount importance, and the wristwatch was re-branded for a short time as the 'trench watch'. Trench watches were worn by men and officers alike, and were manufactured by a wide variety of companies, usually Swiss, with import marks indicating their date. Trench watches have fixed wire attachments for the straps, and are found in a variety of cases, from gold and silver to steel, and with a variety of enamel faces. Typical examples are illustrated. One notable fashion denoted the twelve numeral with a red colour, usually on a white enamel face (presumably to draw attention to the 'o'clock' position and, thereby, to zero hour). Another fashion involved the use of luminous material for the numerals, again essential in the darkness of the trenches. Watch crystals being fragile, watch guards of many types were developed to protect them, varying from integrated components of the watch through to additional accessories. In all cases, the image of the officer staring at his watch, whistle poised, at zero hour is a potent one.

SERVICE DRESS INSIGNIA

Clad in drab khaki uniformity, the British soldier of the Great War often appears to blend with the landscape, particularly since the modern-day view of the war is so heavily influenced by monotone photographic images, which trick the senses into thinking that the war was fought in black and white, and that the sun never shone. Recent rediscoveries of original colour images of French troops of the Great War give the lie to this. Nevertheless, when Tommy went to war in 1914, he was largely unadorned, other than by his cap badge, buttons and shoulder titles. By 1918, however, a bewildering array of colourful 'battle patches' and formation signs were available, which transformed the arms of the average soldier into a riot of colour and design in a code that could be deciphered only with specialist knowledge.

General Service (GS) Buttons

Most other ranks' Service Dress was issued with the General Service (GS) button, a brass button of approximately one-inch in diameter, with a 'floating' loop shank, which bore the royal arms. This had been introduced for wear with the traditional red coat of the infantryman in 1871, and survived unmodified (with the exception of a change in crown, with the accession of King Edward VII to the throne) until the Second World War. The Service Dress tunic had five such buttons, with smaller pattern versions being used on pocket flaps and shoulder straps. For Empire troops, GS buttons carried appropriate national devices. Economy issue Service Dress had unadorned buttons, and in certain regiments regimental patterns were obtained and used in replacement. Particularly favoured were the use of black composition or hard rubber buttons by rifle regiments, which carried a significant cachet among officers and men alike, as in the studio portrait of a proud rifleman illustrated. In some cases, regimental-type buttons were replaced by the soldiers themselves, who obtained them from the regimental canteen at their own expense. In others, they were replaced by the battalion tailors. The HAC Service Dress illustrated on page 54 is typical, with regimental buttons, identical to those of the Grenadier Guards, replacing GS buttons. GS buttons found on the battlefields today are a most poignant reminder of Tommy's service in the Great War (right).

Shoulder Titles

Shoulder titles were adopted as a regimental identifier with the Service Dress tunic. Most commonly these were brass, attached with lugs to the shoulder straps at their widest, closest to the upper arm. Early, pre-war tunics had detachable straps and, as such, titles were in cloth, produced in red (for infantry) and green (for rifles) with white lettering, sewn to the upper arm; they resembled those adopted later, at first unofficially, for wear with battledress in the Second World War. Early examples are noticeably more heavily embroidered than WW2 versions, however. Some regiments, including certain territorial battalions and the Guards, continued the practice throughout the war. Examples from the First Surrey Rifles, 3rd London Regiment (both Territorials) and Household Battalion are illustrated. Metal titles are more common, with a bewildering array being produced. Typically, fusilier regiments would be distinguished by a flaming grenade as part of the design, as in the Northum-

berland Fusiliers version illustrated above; light infantry were represented by a bugle. Territorial battalions would be distinguished by two or three tier titles, usually with T for territorial, the name or number of the battalion or arm, the regional distinction, as with the artillery version shown (left). A huge array of different types was issued for service battalions. Several are illustrated. Finally, as brass was a valuable war commodity, cloth slip-on titles were to appear later in the war, both embroidered and printed versions (as illustrated) – these are sometimes seen cut-down and sewn on to the strap or upper arm. An array of other unofficial types was also produced, such as the red-on-black HAC titles shown on the SD tunic illustrated on page 54.

221	222	223	224
INFANTRY PIONEER †	ROUGHRIDER	SCOUT-CORPORAL † (HOUSEHOLD CAV.)	TRAINED SQUADRON-SCOUT
225	226	227	228
BUGLER	BUGLER (RIFLE REGIMENTS)	SERGT.-TRUMPETER (R.E. & R.A.)	TRUMPETER
229	230	231	232 †
DRUMMER OR FIFER (EXCEPT IN FOOT GDS)	BANDSMAN (EXCEPT IN CAVALRY)	GOOD CONDUCT BADGE	R.A.M.C. 2ND CLASS ORDERLY
233	234	235	236
ARMOURER-SERGT. † MACHINY.-GUNNER	FARRIER & SHOEING SMITH	SADDLER (EXCEPT IN CAVALRY)	WHEELER & CARPENTER

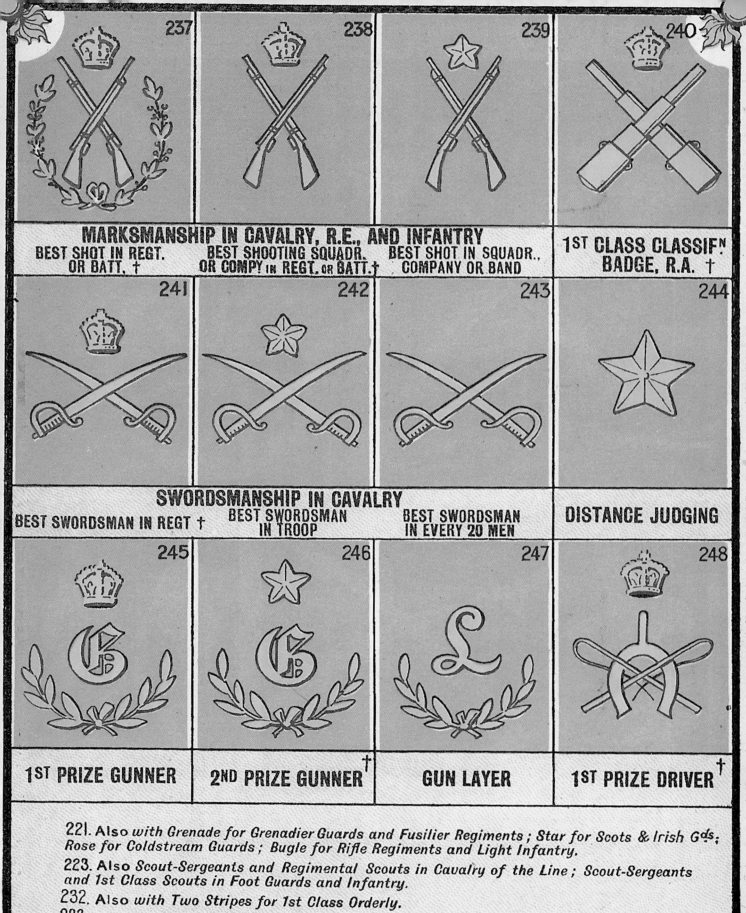

MARKSMANSHIP IN CAVALRY, R.E., AND INFANTRY

237 BEST SHOT IN REGT. OR BATT. †

238 BEST SHOOTING SQUADR. OR COMPY. IN REGT. OR BATT. †

239 BEST SHOT IN SQUADR., COMPANY OR BAND

240 1ST CLASS CLASSIF'N BADGE, R.A. †

SWORDSMANSHIP IN CAVALRY

241 BEST SWORDSMAN IN REGT †

242 BEST SWORDSMAN IN TROOP

243 BEST SWORDSMAN IN EVERY 20 MEN

244 DISTANCE JUDGING

245 1ST PRIZE GUNNER

246 2ND PRIZE GUNNER †

247 GUN LAYER

248 1ST PRIZE DRIVER †

221. Also *with Grenade for Grenadier Guards and Fusilier Regiments; Star for Scots & Irish G*ds*; Rose for Coldstream Guards; Bugle for Rifle Regiments and Light Infantry.*

223. Also *Scout-Sergeants and Regimental Scouts in Cavalry of the Line; Scout-Sergeants and 1st Class Scouts in Foot Guards and Infantry.*

232. Also *with Two Stripes for 1st Class Orderly.*

233. Also *Machinery Artificer and Smith.*

237. *For Sergeants and Lance-Sergeants.*

238. *For Section-Commanders.*

240. *For Batteries and Companies.*

241. *Also in each Squadron.*

246. *Also without Star for 3rd Prize Gunner.*

248. *Also without Crown for 2nd, 3rd and 4th Prize Drivers.*

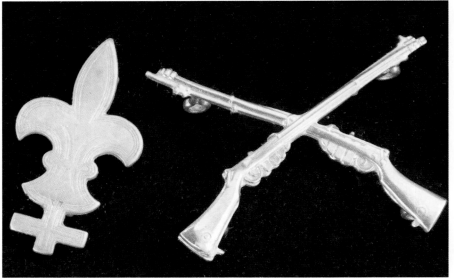

Specialist Insignia

Trades were identified by a number of badges that are attached to the lower right sleeve of the Service Dress. Some, such as that of Farrier, date back centuries, while others, including Machine Gunner and Gun Layer are much more in tune with the period. In the early part of the First World War these were invariably in brass, attached through the sleeve by the addition of a back plate and split pin. However, as the need for brass in the munitions industry grew, so did the demand for trade badges to be produced in cloth, which was easily sewn directly to the sleeve. All such badges were worn with pride (reproduced in the preceding pages), and publications such as Rank at a Glance *were produced to help both passers-by and new soldiers, the brass examples illustrated are typical of the early war period, and include Marksman (crossed guns), Scout (fleur de lys) and Signaller (crossed flags), none of which would be awarded easily. Rifleman Dennis of the 21st KRRC was so proud to have passed his Brigade Signalling Course that he bought his own flags; his example is by no means unusual. Also illustrated are Pioneer, Armourer and Wheelwright badges (top). Most commonly seen were Machine Gunner, Bomber and Trench Mortar badges; examples of these are illustrated in Chapter 4.*

Formation Signs

With so many units in the field by 1916–17, there came about a need for an effective system of identifying them as components of a larger formation, to be used widely on the transport, headquarters and men themselves. Their design left largely to the whim of the commanders of these units, a series of identifying badges was developed that could be painted on battalion transports and the like. Sufficiently colourful to be the subject of two inter-war series of cigarette cards, these badges generally referred to the regional origin of the formation – the thistle of the 9th (Scottish) Division, Welsh dragon of the 38th (Welsh) Division or red rose of the 55th (West Lancashire) Division – or used a symbol that indicated the number or origin of the division – such as the bantam cock of the 40th Division, modified with the addition of an acorn to commemorate the capture of Bourlon Wood on the Somme in 1916, or the broken spur of the 74th Division, composed largely of dismounted Yeomanry troops. Late war, these patches would be sewn to the upper sleeve of the Service Dress; typical examples are illustrated.

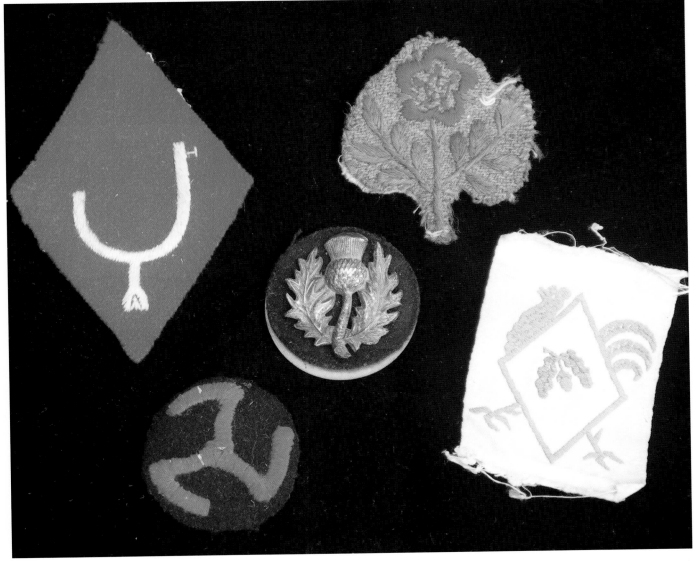

'Battle Patches'

In addition to the formation badges, a series of plain patches were worn on the Service Dress in order to distinguish brigade and battalion; these have become known as 'battle patches' by collectors. That illustrated below is from the 31st Division: the red and white rectangle illustrates the brigade; the three red bars, the third battalion within the brigade. The system as evolved was complex, at least in the bewildering array of badges displayed, and today many cannot easily be identified. Patches were often worn on the rear of the tunic; this would serve to identify the unit to soldiers following in battle. An example from an officer's tunic of the 55th Division, 166th Brigade – a plain black felt square – is illustrated below. Unofficial regimental patches were also worn in some cases; examples from the Hampshire Regiment, Somerset Light Infantry and King's Shropshire Light Infantry are illustrated.

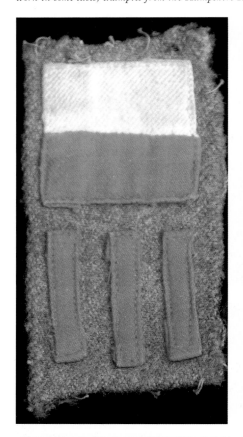

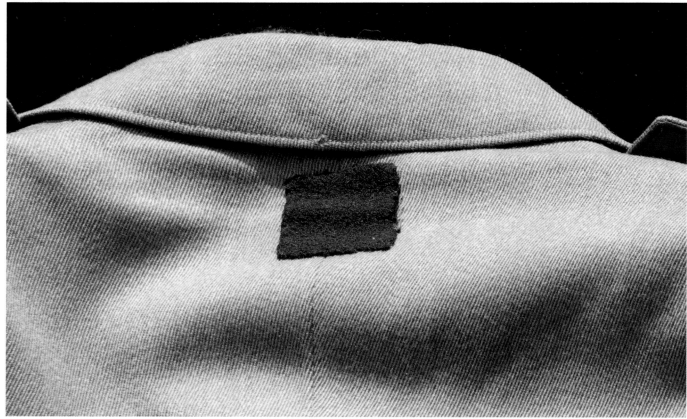

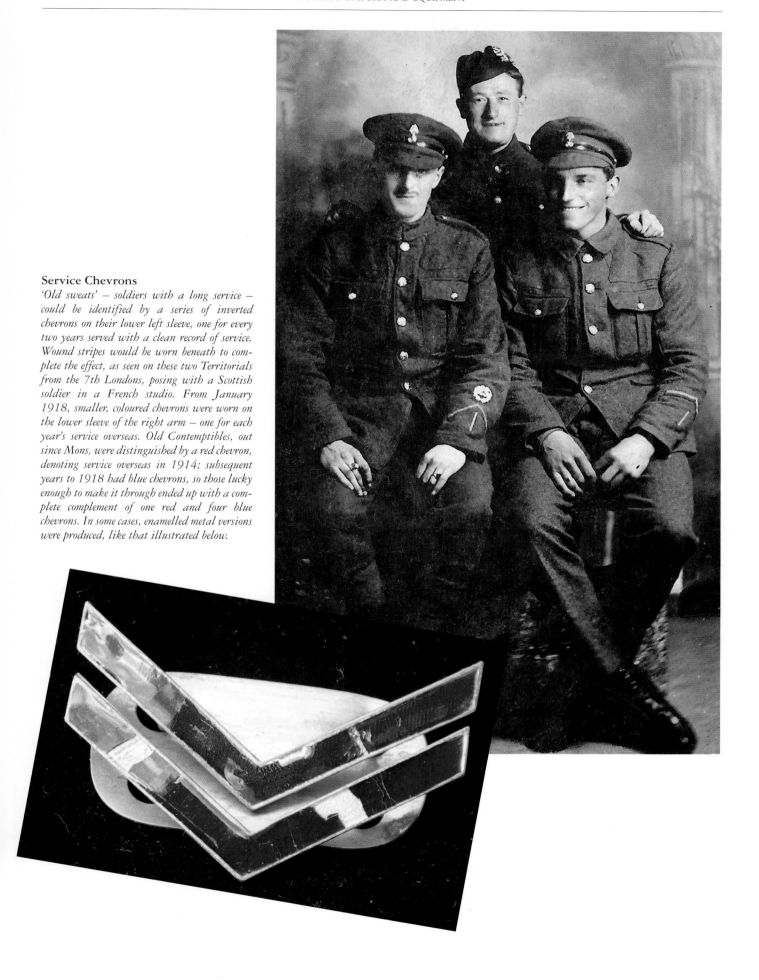

Service Chevrons

'Old sweats' – soldiers with a long service – could be identified by a series of inverted chevrons on their lower left sleeve, one for every two years served with a clean record of service. Wound stripes would be worn beneath to complete the effect, as seen on these two Territorials from the 7th Londons, posing with a Scottish soldier in a French studio. From January 1918, smaller, coloured chevrons were worn on the lower sleeve of the right arm – one for each year's service overseas. Old Contemptibles, out since Mons, were distinguished by a red chevron, denoting service overseas in 1914; subsequent years to 1918 had blue chevrons, so those lucky enough to make it through ended up with a complete complement of one red and four blue chevrons. In some cases, enamelled metal versions were produced, like that illustrated below.

4 Up the Line

The First World War will for ever be viewed as the 'war in the trenches'. Trench warfare was always seen as a 'temporary phase' by the generals, yet in many ways it was inevitable in 1914, given the extent of the development of weapons effective in a defensive role. The use of quick-firing artillery and machine guns against infantry trained to expect open warfare, meant that the gaining of cover and the seizing of vantage was to become paramount. The war became one of artilleryman pitted against engineer in a gigantic siege – with the infantryman in the middle. The largest and greatest siege in history led to the development of new ways of warfare; of new ways of creating fortifications and of breaking them with latter-day siege engines. Tanks, high-trajectory artillery, detailed artillery plotting and mapping, undermining, gas warfare, storm troops – all were developed as a means of grabbing the advantage, puncturing the line, and gaining access, 'through mud and blood, to the green fields beyond' – in the words of the motto of the Tank Corps.

And, while the High Command turned its efforts to combating the problems of the breakthrough, the individual soldier's ingenuity was hastily directed towards new ways of making his lot easier in the front line. Increasingly, the military mind was focused on improving the efficiency of trench warfare, and improving the protocols and structures of its day-to-day efficiency. The pronoun 'trench' was added to everything – trench stores, trench boots, trench cap, trench foot, trench fever, trench boards and so on. Committees were established to examine the efficiency of the trench system of working. Locally, officers set about improving their lot, and creating order from chaos, and the man in the trenches sought ways of developing his own 'comfort zone'. While constantly on the lookout for incoming trench mortars (*minenwerfers* or 'minies') and gas shells (which made a peculiar 'plopping' sound) in his patch of sky, he became adept at making the best of a bad job, improving his lot through comforts sent from home, food, clothing, rudimentary cooking devices such as 'Tommy cookers' (using solid fuel), candles or, rarely, the much-coveted primus stove.

To the unseasoned volunteer and conscript, the phrase 'up the line' signified that, for them at least, the war had definitely arrived. To those new to the front, the first taste of trench duty would be a defining moment in their military career, if not their life. Issued with iron rations and a full complement of 250 rounds of ammunition (150 in pouches, 100 in two cotton bandoliers) it was an ominous sign that soldiers were instructed to destroy any personal papers that could identify them, and to fill in the personal will section of their pay book. At this point, letters would be hurriedly written – 'in the pink' – and the men would move up the line via duckboards and communication trenches (CTs), to replace soldiers only too happy to leave. Trench stores would be handed over from one battalion to another, the officers would set to work ensuring that sentries were deployed, and the nocturnal life of the trenches could begin. For most soldiers, serving 'up the line' had a special cachet; the wound stripe, the authentic wear-and-tear on the uniform, mud on the boots would all mark out the soldier who had done his tour, typically five to seven days in the front-line trenches, before going out in reserve and finally on rest. 'Rest', anathema to the army, meant training by day, and by night, up the line again on fatigue parties.

TRENCH ARCHITECTURE

Trenches and their construction had formed part of the instruction manuals of the Royal Engineers (RE) – that most versatile of corps – and had been developed through experience and the application of the modern theory over centuries. It was the role of the RE to direct the construction of fortifications, and to engage in the active destruction of the enemy's own works. The commonest name for a military engineer in the British Army – a member of the Royal Engineers – was 'sapper', a name derived from the Italian word for spade (*zappa*), signifying someone who dug 'saps', or trenches and short tunnels. It was the sappers who provided the know-how to build the fortifications of the Western Front and its 'sideshows' of Gallipoli, Salonika and a myriad of other places. When the army went to war it was equipped with the basics – picks and spades; by the war's end, vast swathes of forest in Britain and Canada had been felled to provide supports and boards for the trenches and innumerable sandbags had been manufactured and filled. New pieces of equipment had been developed, from the simplest staple, through to the most complex frames, and innovative thinking had been applied by the military mind in action.

Barbed wire was part of trench warfare from its inception on the Western Front. Its earliest successful use was in the late nineteenth century, where it was used in the American West as a means of cattle control; deterring humans instead of cattle was an obvious development, and the military use of wire was advocated from the 1880s onwards. By the early twentieth century, wire had become accepted by the military, and contemporary engineering manuals indicate the ideal: an array of methods to deploy the wire to maximize its effect. In fact, in the early days, this might have amounted to a few strands sufficient to hold up the enemy ('Gott strafe this barbed wire', as depicted by Bruce Bairnsfather); by 1917–18, massed ranks were used in the German defences of the Hindenburg Line.

OPPOSITE: *The impedimenta of trench warfare: British close-combat weapons, tools and construction materials.*

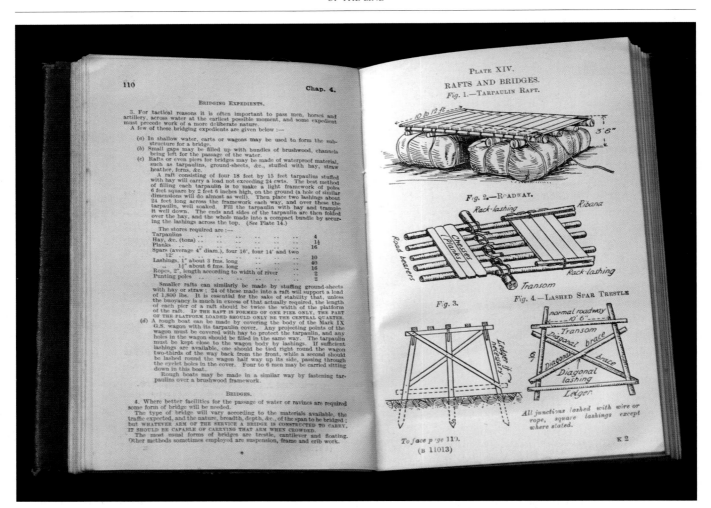

Manual of Field Engineering

This manual dates from 1913, and was the current treatise on the construction of field fortifications when the army went to war in August 1914. Given to new officers such as 2nd Lieutenant Martin, newly commissioned into the North Staffordshire Regiment in 1916, its issue (together with other manuals and an officer's Field Service Pocket Book) was to mark the attainment of responsibility in the army. It was the first theoretical introduction to trench warfare for such officers, containing all the basics; what was not expected was the way in which the war would develop into an extended siege, with the trenches forming the fortifications. For the engineer, one of the main tools in planning these complex fortifications was a field level like the one illustrated opposite; this facilitated the planning out of the bays and traverses required so that the effects of the blast of shells, mortars or grenades would be confined laterally, and to prevent the opportunity of trench-long enfilade fire when captured or otherwise compromised. This level also indicated the all-important one-in-four batter that was to be the standard slope of all trench sides during the war.

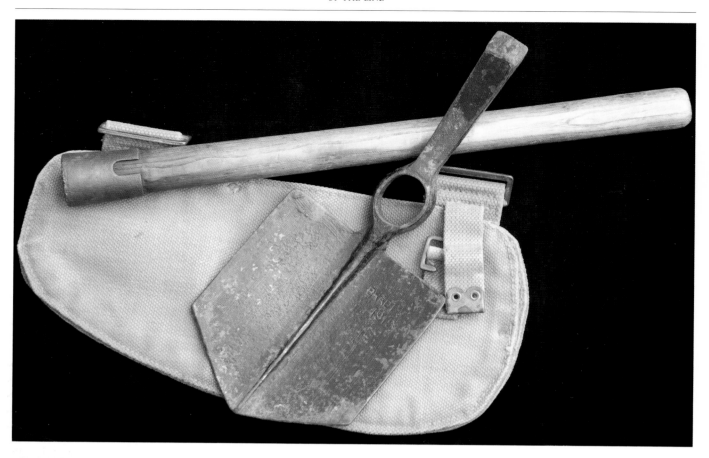

Entrenching Tools

Getting close to the earth was a natural reaction under fire; if he was to improve the cover of his position, the soldier required tools. All British infantrymen were equipped with a clever personal entrenching tool, which comprised a steel head of combined spade and pick, and a separate wooden handle, called a helve (above). Carried in either a webbing or leather (in the 1908 and 1914 pattern equipments, respectively) holder, these tools were supplied to provide a means of digging a shallow scrape in an emergency, or for a multitude of other small jobs in the field, acting as hammer, pick and digging tool. It is doubtful that entrenching tools were used to dig many trenches; for that, the ubiquitous British GS or 'Bulldog' (named after their Lancashire manufacturer) shovels were needed. GS shovels were issued at the rate of 110 per battalion; open-mouthed, with a turned-back top to protect the spade from the heavy boot of the infantryman, these spades were used in earnest in the digging of front-line trenches. The time estimated in 1914 (as prescribed by the officer's Field Service Pocket Book*) for digging a man's length of fire trench – two paces or forty-five cubic feet – was 100 minutes under normal conditions. Heavy picks were also provided where the ground was hard enough to warrant them, at the rate of seventy-six per battalion. Both tools would be used in digging trenches throughout the war, under the orders of sapper officers and NCOs, with the*

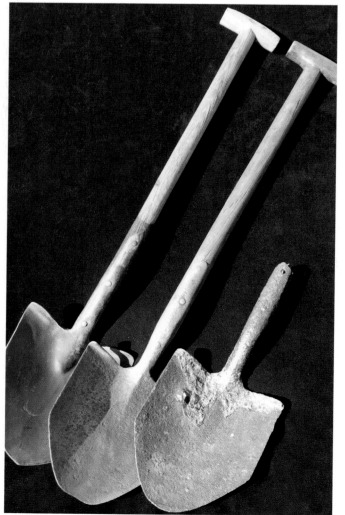

infantry providing the manpower. Infantrymen often carried spades (and picks) into action, most famously in the case of the leading assault troops on the Somme in 1916. This was to allow for the turning of trench lines once they had been captured, with the reversal of the fire step from one side to the other. This would account for the bullet hole in the third spade illustrated (right), a relict of the front-line trenches of Arras in 1917.

Barbed Wire

Barbed wire was to form a significant component of the field defences of the Great War, and it needed constant attention. Wiring parties on both sides would enter no man's land under the cover of darkness. In patrols of two to three men, they would inspect the integrity of the defences or cut paths through their own wire in preparation for a raid; larger fatigue parties (gangs of anywhere between twelve to eighty men) would go out to repair and improve the front-line wire. Wire was brought up the lines by fatigue parties, who, usually under the instruction of a sapper officer or NCO, would carry out the work in darkness. Such parties would be in a constant state of readiness; any noise would trigger off a flurry of star shells and Very lights intended to illuminate the interlopers, picking them out in stark silhouette against the night sky, and making them an easy target for a sweeping machine gun or targeted artillery barrage. Pte Groom of the London Rifle Brigade recalled the activity: 'The fear of noise, the desperate whisperings when the wire wouldn't roll, the ping of the wirecutter, the tin kicked in the dark.' The more complex constructions involved hammering in wooden or angle-iron stakes by a maul, so it was not surprising that soldiers feared the attention of the other side. The invention of the screw picket – which spread like wildfire on both sides of no man's land – meant that complex wire barriers could be constructed relatively noiselessly, soldiers using their entrenching tool helves or other suitable post to wind them into the ground. Examples exist with one, two, three or four loops; standard three-loop versions are illustrated. In fact, the wire used by the British and German armies differed to a great extent. British wire was double-strand with modest barbs, while German wire, tough to work with, was single-strand, 2.5mm square-section wire with murderous barbs. Relics of both are illustrated. The same German wire would be used to great effect by another of the Central Powers, the ailing Ottoman Empire, which wired the fatal shore of Gallipoli to great effect. Elsewhere, wire would be feared; a typically fatalistic soldier's song of the time spoke of 'hanging on the old barbed wire', but is was made light of in Bairnsfather's famous cartoon 'Gott strafe this barbed wire'.

"GOTT STRAFE THIS BARBED WIRE"

Sandbags and Trench Architecture

Sandbags, simple hessian bags filled with sand, clay or earth, became an important part of trench life, filling gaps in the line, creating a parapet or ultimately being built upwards as High Command Breastworks. They would be used to disguise periscopes, and sniper loopholes would be built into them; they would be used as additional leg coverings, to bring up the rations and could, like the original example illustrated below, be packed with explosives. The sandbag has become part of the archaeology of Flanders, fossilized, its hessian material impressed into damp clay (below). It has also entered the vocabulary of the Great War, with soldiers going 'over the bags' in the main assaults. Trenches were much more than simple accumulations of sandbags of course; timbers, corrugated sheeting and expanded metal (xpm) were all used to maintain the trench slopes, while duckboards (like those illustrated accurately in Mackain's postcard) were designed so that one end was narrower than the other, fitting together to create a continuous line of wooden flooring for each trench. Hardware was designed to keep all these things together — steel staples were used to hold timbers together in dugouts (right); the rare, unobtrusive, steel hook was actually a pin to bond sheets of xpm together (bottom). Many other items were designed and manufactured for the simple purpose of keeping trenches under continuous bombardment in a fit state.

I've got a cushy job now!

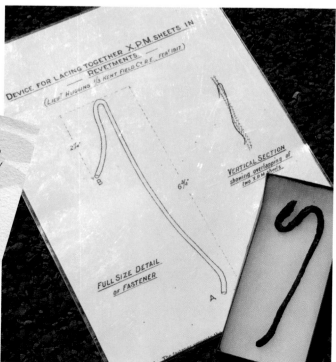

TO FRONT LINE

FIFTH AVENUE

RESERVE LINE

CHEERO TRENCH

Sketches
of Tommy's life
Up the line — N° 10

Sometimes you get so far in the rear, marching in, you are as good as lost
when you come to a spot where different trenches branch off.

F. Mackain

Visé Paris 763

Bystander copyright.

THE COMMUNICATION TRENCH
Problem—Whether to walk along the top and risk it, or do another mile of this.

Bruce Bairnsfather

Signboards

It was vital to direct soldiers through the maze of trenches, for, although they were theoretically constructed in parallel lines — at least in the early stages of trench warfare on the Western Front — the re-entrants, salients and redoubts were interconnected by communication trenches (CTs) and minor trenches intended as latrines, entrances to dugouts, trench mortar batteries and so on. It was quite a challenge for the soldier to find his way around. Most soldiers would travel to the front line from the rear areas at night, along crowded CTs that were bustling, narrow thoroughfares six feet deep with barely enough room for men to pass. Although relieving battalions would be guided to the front by experienced soldiers from the battalion about to be relieved, to direct them, signboards like that illustrated above would still be necessary, picked out by candlelight. Many of the long CTs had picturesque names, chosen at will and whim; these would be painted on rough and crude boards to aid in direction finding — Mackain illustrates the bewilderment of a new sector. Such boards would also exist in the front line, while others imparted a more urgent message, perhaps warning of the dangers from snipers, artillery fire or the physical hazards of loose or low wires, or treacherous duckboards. Once common, signboards are now very much rare survivors of everyday trench life.

TRENCH EQUIPMENT

Living in the trenches meant that, inevitably, there would be a need for specialist equipment that could improve and protect the life of the average infantryman when in the front line. Living in a six-foot-deep ditch meant that the environment of the soldier was peculiarly constrained, with little chance to find out – in safety at least – what was immediately to the front of his particular patch of earth. By day, periscopes were the only means of observing in relative safety, and a great variety were developed through the war.

The vulnerability of the head, exposed albeit briefly where the parapet was damaged, or when the soldier was tempted to peer over the top, meant that, by 1915, soft caps were no longer viable head coverings in the trenches. The steel helmet arrived *en masse* in the British Army in 1916, and was to provide Tommy with a distinctive silhouette for the rest of the war – and beyond. The necessity of trench warfare brought with it its own language, and an inventory of stores never before encountered.

Steel Helmets

Steel helmets were an innovation that was born out of the necessity of modern war. In 1914, all armies were equipped with some form of uniform cap or ceremonial helmet – the German Pickelhaube *being an example of this type – but these were generally gaudy, impractical and affording little protection from either the elements or the ballistic attentions of bullets. Up until 1915, Tommy was to wear the Service Dress cap in all its forms in the front line. In action, this meant that head wounds were common, especially in its static phases when the attention of snipers was concentrated on the movement of soldiers past loopholes and dips in the trench sides. Soldiers were vulnerable to snipers, but they were also subject to the random tragedies of spent bullets, air-burst shrapnel and shell fragments. Clearly there was a need for increased head protection, and this was to be introduced in late 1915, with innovation by the French, Germans and British producing markedly different steel helmets.*

The British helmet was invented by John Brodie, and was pressed from non-magnetic steel, its dish-like form and wide brim intended to supply protection from above – hence the widespread use of the term 'shrapnel helmet'. The real innovation, it was claimed, was the liner, which provided space between the head and the helmet, allowing for dents and dings without impacting with the cranium. The helmet had two prototype designs, varying in the depth of bowl and width of rim. These have been named 'Type A' and 'Type B' helmets, but it appears that they were just variants of the first helmet in production, the War Office pattern, first introduced in 1915. Characteristically, this had a sharp, unprotected rim, and was painted an apple green colour, like the interior helmet shell illustrated. Problems with the sharpness of the rim and the smooth reflective surface of the helmet (and complaints to that effect from General Plumer) led to the introduction of an improved helmet, which was known as the Mark I Brodie, which had a steel protective rim added, and a non-reflective sand finish. The War Office pattern, with simple Mark I liner (top) (and some added sand finish) and the Mark I helmet (bottom) (with the improved Mark II liner) are illustrated. In most cases, the distinctive silhouette of the 'Tommy helmet' was disguised by sacking or sandbags in close-fitting covers. Some battalions painted divisional signs or attached regimental badges to their helmets, or covers.

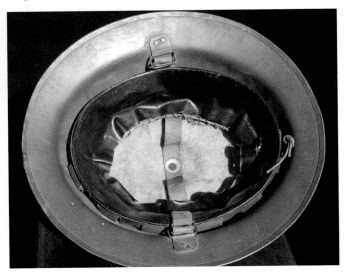

Officers frequently used their own privately purchased helmets, fitted with expensive liners fitted in fashionable outfitters. Prior to the widespread introduction of the Brodie helmet, officers purchased other patterns of helmet, for example, the single-piece tempered steel acier trempé helmet, which resembled the stylish but complex Adrian helmet issued to French troops in 1915. This was notoriously brittle, and was withdrawn from French service. Some officers, like Francophile Winston Churchill, serving as Lt-Colonel in the Royal Scots, appropriated standard Adrian helmets (like that illustrated) for use in the field; his example is preserved at Chartwell, his country house in Kent. Other, fluted helmets were also in relatively wide circulation, sometimes with a rakish leather band around the base of the helmet. This type of helmet was adopted by the Portuguese ('Pork and Beans' to the British) troops on the Western Front (below). Although this design was said to give greater protection, it was actually thought to be inherently weak, its flutes catching shell fragments, and its mild-steel construction was less strong than the manganese steel of the British. A battle-damaged German Stahlhelm – introduced in 1915, and widely believed to be the most effective design – is illustrated (below right) for comparison.

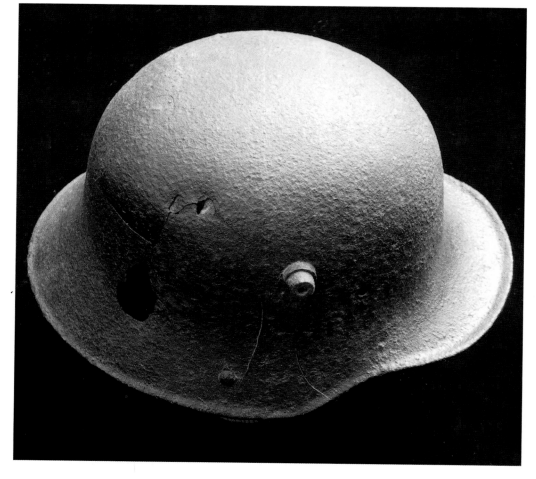

Trench Maps

With the development of trench warfare came the development of trench mapping. Good maps are, of course, a significant issue in any battle, supplying as they do a wealth of information about topographical position for vantage, and the nature of the 'going', the surfaces over which man and materiel would need to travel. When the Allies went to war they relied upon their state surveys, and those of their friends, to provide military maps that might aid in the deployment of troops and the ranging of artillery. While those for the Western Front – France and Belgium – were of good quality generally, information available on fronts in the Middle East was in some cases less reliable, although new evidence shows for Gallipoli that this hand has been overplayed in post-war recriminations over the campaign. In 1915, with the move to static warfare on most fronts, trenches started to be overprinted on existing maps, with the best examples being in France and Flanders. Here, at scales of 1:20,000 and 1:10,000, special trench maps were produced, which plotted the location of trenches, and used a semi-formal nomenclature for ruined structures and trenches that grew up in the front line (perpetuated by the survey companies of the Royal Engineers). Some examples are illustrated overleaf from the Somme and the Ypres Salient, and these were backed up by topographical maps at 1:40,000 and 1:100,000 scales. For Gallipoli, detailed maps like that shown overleaf were available only after the capture of Ottoman examples. The convention for trench maps from 1915–17 was to show the German trenches in red, and the British – in outline only – in blue; in 1918, this convention was reversed. Unsurprisingly, millions of trench maps were produced during the war, at all scales. Regular updates were created in advance of trench raids and offensives, along with secret editions. From these humble documents, great offensives such as the Somme, Passchendaele and the Advance to Victory in 1918 were planned and prosecuted; in developing them, many men of the Royal Flying Corps, flying stable camera platforms vulnerable to enemy 'scouts' (the modern fighter), would lose their life capturing aerial photographs.

Trench maps at 1:10,000 and 1:20,000 scales from France and Belgium. Obtaining adequate maps for Gallipoli required the capture and reprinting of Ottoman versions, like this example.

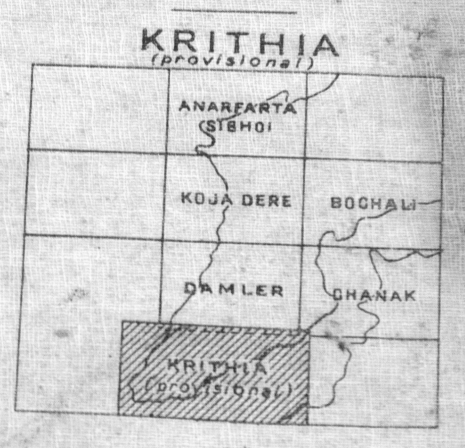

Torches, Lamps, Candles

As the trenches came alive at night, with a host of activity from trench repairs to sorties out into no man's land, it was necessary to provide some form of light, and for the most part, this was obtained through the use of the humble candle. For the average soldier, a candle stub provided both light and a rudimentary means of cooking – or, at very least, in the hands of an old soldier, the boiling of the water for tea. Such stubs have been found beneath trench duckboards on archaeological digs. Light was a comfort, particularly in the underground world of the dugouts, and candles would be requested in parcels sent from home. They could also be obtained from the Expeditionary Force Canteen, the YMCA and other charitable organizations set up to administer to the needs of the troops, and were often exchanged between soldiers coming in and out of the line. Birmingham manufacturers Albion Lamp Co. created a series of mild-steel cases for candles, as well as folding candle lanterns that fitted into a steel carry case (illustrated, dated 1915). Care had to be taken to ensure that such lights did not bring down a hail of artillery, a minenwerfer attack, or sweep of a machine gun. Other examples included clever folding and hand-held candleholders (below), together with sophisticated dry-cell battery-powered torches, used mostly by officers. The Orilux is the best known; Winston Churchill's own example is currently on display in the Churchill Museum in London. This leather-covered torch was sold with a leather case (often monogrammed), or webbing pouch to be carried on an officer's belt. The version below has red, clear and green lenses, the combination intended to complement that used for signal flares. More cumbersome torches, like the one dated 1918, also illustrated below with an Orilux, were also used.

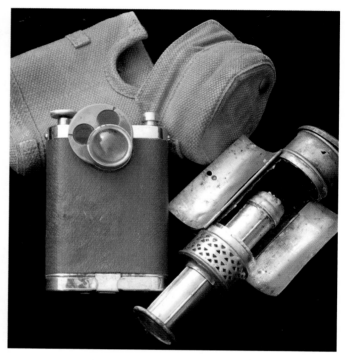

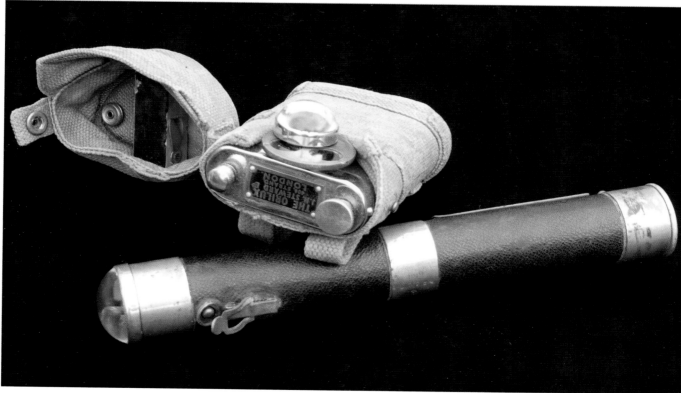

Sketches
of Tommy's life
Up the line — N° 2

The first trench I ever saw was an old communication trench where we were taken one night on fatigue. We did more star shells gazing than trench repairing that night!

Visé Paris 763

Bystander copyright

THAT EVENING STAR-SHELL.
" Oh, star of eve, whose tender beam
Falls on my spirit's troubled dream." — *Tannhäuser*.

Star Shells

Star shells and warning flares were used extensively in the front line. Intended as a means of illuminating suspicious activity in no man's land – working parties and trench raiders would be starkly silhouetted against the night sky – star shells like that depicted in the classic Bairnsfather and Mackain postcards could be fired by the artillery, or from a hand-held Very pistol, which was issued generally at a rate of two per platoon. Rockets were also available, intended, when fired in colourful variations, to bring emergency aid from artillery in the face of a raid or larger-scale attack.

Periscopes

Looking over the parapet in daylight was most unwise; snipers would have weapons fixed in position, targeted at dips in the parapet, at latrines and crossing points, and at loophole plates. There was continual loss of life on the Western Front through the actions of snipers, combined with the random attentions of the artillery shell. From early on, the need to look over the parapet to observe activity in no man's land led to the production of specially designed 'trench periscopes'; these objects, as illustrated on this contemporary postcard, were to enter popular culture of the day.

In an issue of the Transactions of the Optical Society *for 1915, the basic parameters were laid down for a trench periscope, the object of which, it was stated, was 'to give the soldier a view of his front whilst his head and person are sheltered'. Its author W. A. Dixey distilled these parameters into four points: 1, portability; 2, degree of shelter provided; 3, field of view; and 4, camouflage to the enemy. Many patent versions were produced to try and achieve these aims; several of them were adopted officially, others were available for private purchase. Most provided a non-magnified field of view, but magnification could be gained by the use of binoculars in association with the periscope.*

For portability, a simple mirror attached to a stick or bayonet was the most effective. For 2nd Lieutenant Bernard Martin, such contrivances were more effective than larger box periscopes, which were much more susceptible to damage from shellfire. Both official issue (the No. 18 bayonet periscope) and commercial versions (the Vigilant) are known; the one opposite was the property of Corporal John Rogers of the Royal Fusiliers. Mirrors could be used fixed in position for sentries; Private Hodges of the Bedfordshire Regiment recalls his sentry's eye view of long grass and glimpses of barbed wire in 1918. More commonly, day sentries would be at station next to a No. 9 box periscope, which was in the form of a collapsible and reasonably portable (in the bag illustrated) simple wooden box over twenty-five inches long (to provide the shelter required), and with a clear field of view sufficient for most trench duties. The original No. 9 (the Mark I) was manufactured by Adams and Company and R & J Beck in 1915, with the later Mark II, like the example illustrated opposite, manufactured by Trenchscope later in that year. As the top mirror was susceptible to sniping, care was taken to protect the observer from glass splinters with a simple shield in the later version. Although portable, such periscopes were fixed at sentry posts throughout front-line trenches, effectively disguised from sniping by the use of sandbags and sacking.

I wish I had a Periscope made big
enough to view,
Across the Miles of Hills & Dales,
That separate we two.

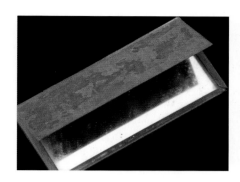

THE OUTPOST

A British "Tommy" watching the enemy through his periscope

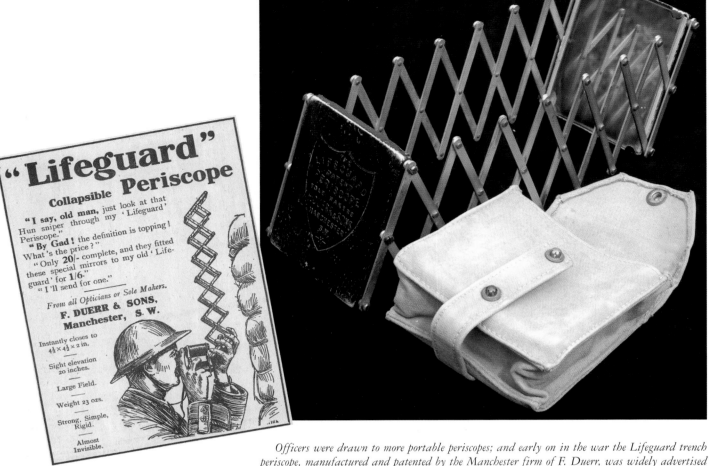

Officers were drawn to more portable periscopes; and early on in the war the Lifeguard trench periscope, manufactured and patented by the Manchester firm of F. Duerr, was widely advertised in the press. This periscope was constructed on the expanding 'lazy tong' principle. When extended, it provided the required two opposed mirrors separated by two feet; when collapsed, it was only two inches deep. The version illustrated is a second pattern with struts intended to make the expanding metal tongs more durable; officers could also buy a canvas cover like that illustrated to protect it. The most commonly encountered periscope used by officers was the Beck's No. 25, issued from 1917, which comprises a simple small-diameter brass tube, with detachable handle and a focusing eye-piece (opposite). This effective piece of equipment was not only light, durable and difficult to spot at a distance, and long enough to provide the observer sufficient protection, it was also a magnifying periscope, and popular with officers. A great many other types are also known.

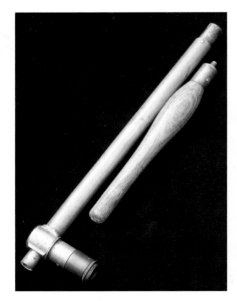

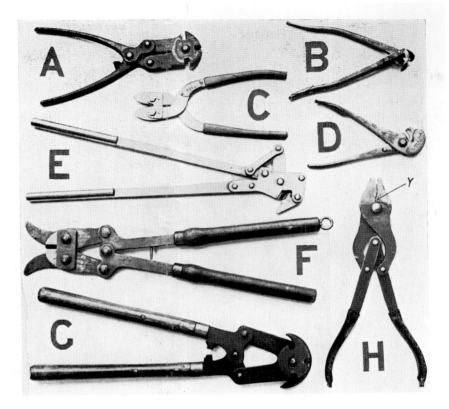

REFERENCE.

A. Cutters, wire, small, Mark V.
B. Beauchamp pattern, with horns.
C. Stokes pattern.
D. Ironside pattern.

E. A long steel cutter
F. A long cutter with wood handles.
G. Cutters, wire, large, Mark I.
H. Holtzappfel & Co. cutter.

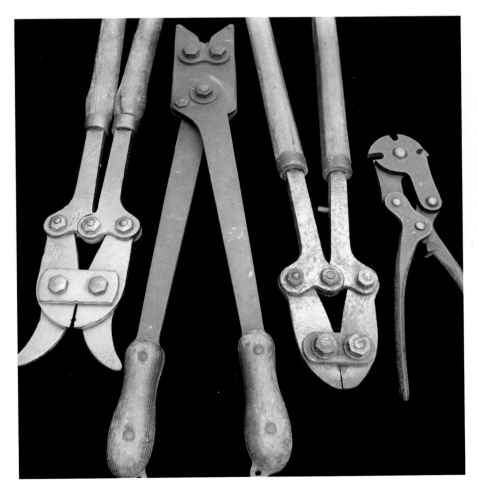

Barbed-Wire Cutters

With the increased complexity of barbed wire came the increased necessity to cut it, to avoid being left 'hanging on the old barbed wire'. Every soldier's own wire was almost as hazardous as that of his enemy, and special paths often had to be cut through a tangled maze, lanes that could be targeted by enterprising machine gunners and snipers. Cutting the enemy's wire was a hazardous job; wire would be attached to such warning signals as empty tin cans that would clatter alarmingly if disturbed. Early cutters were largely inadequate; Captain Siegfried Sassoon of the Royal Welsh Fusiliers would famously go in search of a decent pair from the Army and Navy Stores in London; 2nd Lieutenant Bruce Bairnsfather had to resort to French ironmongers with the same aim in mind. A great variety were tried and patented, and many were tested by the Royal Engineers experimental trench workshops (left). Makers Chatter Lea produced a variety of long-handled versions from 1917 that were more satisfactory, but there were still many difficulties when it came to actual use. Wire-cutter attachments were also made, to be fixed to the muzzle of an infantryman's SMLE rifle (below). At least three versions were put into use during the war; this ungainly piece of equipment fed the wire on to jaws, which then pivoted when withdrawn to provide a cut. In view of the great tangles encountered, these cutters were never really a practical proposition in the field. In many cases, cutting the wire was left to the artillery; it was a skilled business, requiring shrapnel to burst at the correct height to obtain the right effect. History shows that this was not always achieved.

TRENCH LIFE

Life in the trenches was dominated by its routine; the rhythm of daily existence began with the 'morning hate' at stand-to, an hour before dawn, through to its equivalent at dusk, when the soldiers would man the fire step in anticipation of attack, often firing off amunition into no man's land. By day, sentries would be posted at box periscopes or their simple mirror equivalents, one per platoon, looking out for *minenwerfer*, gas and unusual activity. By night, sentries would stand nervously on the fire step, nervous in case of the casual and random play of a machine gun across no man's land. Between times, there would be inspections, trench repair and the issue of rations. In fact, it was the supply and issue of rations that had one of the greatest effects on morale in the front line; the supply of hot food was the most important. All too often, soldiers were required to fall back to the standard rations of corned beef, or 'bully beef', and biscuits, or 'iron rations', as they were known. Welcomed by many – but not by all – would be the issue of the rum ration, under close inspection of an officer; the fiery effect of this viscous liquid was a boon in the cold, damp conditions of the trench.

Rations

Food was a difficult issue for High Command; tinned food was relatively plentiful, but 'bully beef' – ration corned beef – was hardly warming in the cold of Flanders, and could be inedible in the baking heat of the Middle East. Food was a major factor in maintaining morale in the trenches. The rations would be brought up at night by ration parties, usually men 'out at rest' detailed for work up the line, who returned to their rest camps at night. As the military machine became increasingly sophisticated, hot rations in specially designed ration carriers were brought up the line; negotiating long communication trenches in the dark meant that this was often an arduous duty, but the hot food was much appreciated by the front-line troops. All other rations would be brought up in sandbags, often in a hopeless jumble of loose tea, sugar, bread, bacon and tinned rations, intended for a forty-eight-hour period. Bully beef was imported then, as now, from South America, and was variously received. The tin illustrated, kept by an old soldier, is dated 1918.

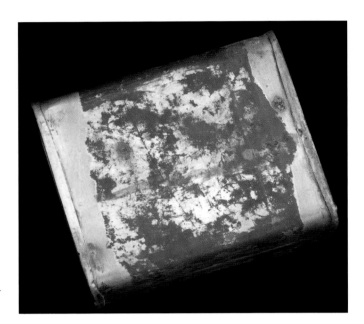

The origin of the term 'bully beef' is obscure – the most likely explanation is that it came from the French bouilli, *meaning 'boiled', but it may have been derived from the use of bull images on the tin. Other tinned food staples included 'pork and beans' – tinned beans with a small cube of pork fat at the bottom of the tin – and the universal Maconochie ration, a tinned vegetable and meat concoction that at least served to break the monotony of bully beef. This issue was to be memorable enough to warrant an epic poem* The Rubáiyát of a Maconochie Ration *(based loosely on the four-line verse format of the ancient Persian* Rubaiyat of Omar Khayam*), which was published just after the war:*

> *'Thou! Oh Thousand Mysteries in a Can*
> *Ingeniously contrived as food for man–*
> *On Moab's Mountains {in Palestine} or in Flanders Mud–*
> *You're welcome unto us as Tickler's Jam!'*

In Suvla Bay, Gallipoli, rusted bully tins and the round tins from Maconochie rations still litter the beaches from which the Allies evacuated in December 1915–January 1916 (opposite). Jam – 'pozzy' in soldier's slang – was another welcome ration, but the frequency of Tickler's Plum and Apple variety raised the eternal question, famously posed by Bairnsfather, 'When the 'ell is it going to be Strawberry?' Fresh rations of meat, bacon and vegetables would also be supplied, brought to the front in the ubiquitous sandbag. Braziers – buckets with holes punched in them – were one way of keeping warm (well illustrated by Pte Mackain), as well as cooking, but their glow could be seen for some distance. Pte Groom of the London Rifle Brigade was impressed by the improvisational skills of one 'old sweat', who used a candle stub, cigarette tin and 'four b' two' flannel to boil, very slowly, enough water for a mug of hot 'char'. Most coveted was the paraffin-fuelled Primus pressure stove, a sophisticated and efficient piece of engineering invented in the late nineteenth century, and a rare luxury in the trenches.

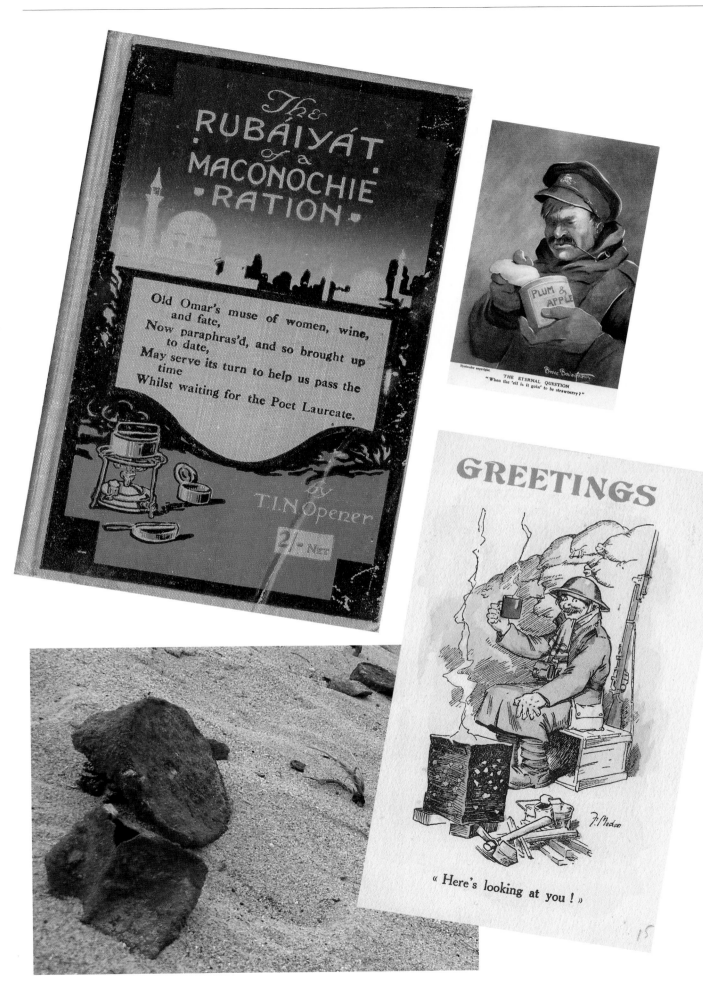

THE ETERNAL QUESTION
"When the 'ell is it goin' to be strawberry?"

GREETINGS

« Here's looking at you ! »

Water

Obtaining sufficient quantities of water was a major issue in the static lines of trench warfare. Both sides employed geologists whose role it was to survey the rear areas for sources of water; this was not an easy job in some places, for example, the water-starved areas of the Middle East. Supplying water to static locations such as camps and field hospitals was also especially difficult. For the soldier in the front line, water was supplied in petrol tins, carried to the front with ration parties. As Shell Oil was the main supplier of fuel to the British Army, Shell petrol tins like those illustrated were undoubtedly seen in the front line as water carriers. Unfortunately, the water never quite lost its petrol taste, and even the strongest tea could not disguise it. As recalled by Harry Patch, the last surviving veteran of the trenches, it was a standing joke that front-line soldiers could tell whether their water had come from a Shell tin or from the BP version. Empty rum jars were also used for water, resulting in, it is presumed, a more palatable undertaste. Mineral waters and sodas sent from home also provided some respite from the petrol-tainted water, and discarded Schweppes bottles are commonly found in the trenches.

Rum Ration

A rum ration in the armed forces was a British institution. Service rum was thick and fiery, and its positive effects after a night on the fire step are recalled in most soldiers' memoirs. It was issued from ceramic jugs labelled 'SRD'. These initials spawned a host of interpretations, from 'Soon Runs Dry' and 'Seldom Reaches Destination' to 'Service Rum Dilute' (although dilute it was not). Despite the enduring mythology, the initials stand for something rather more prosaic: 'Supply Reserve Depot', referring to a large establishment based in Woolwich, the repository of many such stores. Rum was issued at dawn and dusk, following 'stand to'; its fiery warmth was intended to dispel some of the ague brought on by the cold, wet and miserable trench conditions. Famously, it was also issued to those men about to go 'over the bags', either at dawn with a large-scale attack, or at night prior to a raid. The rum ration was issued by a senior NCO, with an officer in attendance, as depicted by Mackain. Drunkenness was a serious offence and the ration could not be accumulated and saved for later; poured into mug or mess tin top, it was to be drunk in the presence of the officer. It was a widely held belief that, as with the issue of strawberry jam, any rum residue left in a jug was taken by the sergeant, and that this was a perk of his position. Soldiers were otherwise not entitled to alcohol in the trenches, although officers' messes did receive such precious liquids from home.

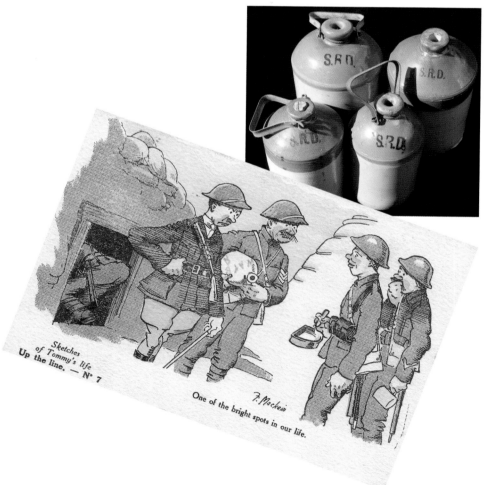

Sketches of Tommy's life Up the line. — N° 7

One of the bright spots in our life.

Mess Kit

In the line, men were to use their mess kit, as issued in the first days of their service in the army, to eat their rations. It was to serve as both container and cooking pot. Officially, the kit comprised the kidney-shaped, two-part mess tin, with a shallow lid with fold-out handle, and a deeper tin with wire handle, contained in a canvas cover. In fact, this was for dismounted troops. Mounted troops were issued with the dish-like circular version illustrated (top). Both mess tins could be used for rudimentary cooking but, as mess kits were routinely inspected by an officer to see if they were clean, this was not a preferred option for the 'old sweat'. In the line, tea would be served in the deeper part of the tin; other cooked items, such as those brought up the line in large 'dixies' – holding twenty pints of food (divided between twenty men) from the company cooks – or in-trench cooked bacon, pork and beans, Maconochie's ration, would be eaten from the lid. Some canny soldiers, fearing the inspection routine, and knowing that there would be little or no hot water for cleaning the tins in the trenches, obtained alternative utensils; enamel plates and mugs (like those illustrated right) were the usual option. The holdall small kit roll that was issued on enlistment contained a knife, a fork and a spoon (see page 79). These came in many different patterns, with the spoon often appearing outsized compared with the others. Stamped with at least the last four digits of a soldier's regimental number (a precaution against the universal practice of 'scrounging' or 'winning'), forks and spoons are commonly encountered – knives less frequently – suggesting that they were discarded in favour of the 'jack knife' worn on a string lanyard around the waist. Mackain's postcard of 'tea in the garden' seems to support this notion.

Your health !

We had our tea out in the garden to day,
as we used to do at home.

Iron Rations

Iron rations comprised a tin of 'bully beef' – the one illustrated below is an original from 1918 – biscuits, and a tin containing tea and sugar (right). It was a 'crime' to dip into these rations unless the order was given to do so from an officer, the intention being that they would be used only in an emergency. Carried in the haversack, or sometimes, in a small cloth bag like those illustrated (intended for the 'unexpired' portion of a day's ration), attached to the belt or equipment, these would be carried into action, along with a full water bottle. Bully beef was so prevalent it was surprising that some soldiers could express a preference for one brand over another, but for Private Hodges of the Bedfordshire Regiment, Fray Bentos was the better brand. The accompanying army biscuits were so hard that men had to have reasonable teeth – a requirement of the medical inspection on enlistment – to bite into them. Alternatively, the biscuits were ground into a powder and mixed with water to make rudimentary desserts or to bulk up food in the front line.

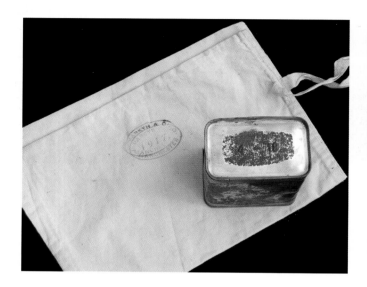

Food from Home

The postal service was surprisingly good to and from the trenches, and parcels could be received relatively quickly – and still intact – from home. Typically, they would contain cakes and tasty morsels in tins, which relieved the unrelenting boredom of front-line food; sardines and meat pastes were typical offerings. Condiments of all kinds would be welcome – Worcestershire, HP and OK sauces (all still with us today) were preferred as they could be mixed with bully to make it more palatable. On the other hand, tins of corned beef were unwelcome, for obvious reasons. Pickles and chutneys such as those produced by Bairds of Glasgow (now defunct) were also popular, and bottles of all these are regularly encountered in front-

line trenches excavated by archaeologists. In many cases these could also be obtained from 'dry canteens' in the rear areas, which supplied their customers with requisites as diverse as cigarettes, Huntley & Palmers biscuits, Nestle's chocolate and basic writing materials. Captain Dunn described the extent of materials available at 'Expeditionary Force Canteens': 'Sauces, meat and fish pastes, and milk in tins, sardines, writing-paper and notebooks, soap and candles, brushes, tooth-powder, button and boot polishes, and laces.' Hearty and warming drinks could be brewed up from meat extracts such as liquid Bovril (in bottles) and solid OXO cubes. Manufacturers of both products were quick to promote the message that the 'man at the front' would be pleased to see these meat extracts in his parcels from home. OXO was particularly clever in identifying a marketing opportunity with its trench heater, a small metal support and solid fuel block that came with a small tin of OXO cubes.

Smoking

Cigarettes came up with the rations, and everyone was issued with a fair share. W. D. & H. O. Wills of Bristol produced many of the favoured brands, including Gold Flake and Woodbine. 'Woodies' were often handed out to wounded men by the chaplain (and poet) G. A. Studdert Kennedy, who quickly acquired the nickname 'Woodbine Willie'. Smoking was a means of killing time, of filling the void between meals and routine. It was also a means of combating both the stench of the war and, in the Middle East at least,

"ARF A 'MO KAISER!"

of deterring the plaques of flies. During the early stages of the war, pipe smoking was common, and a pipe produced by Harrods, together with tobacco, was provided as part of Princess Mary's gift to the troops in December 1914. Pipes were used throughout – stems of the humble clay pipe are commonly encountered at Great War excavation sites – but, as the war progressed, the 'coffin nail' soon supplanted it. With cigarettes being in such plentiful supply, chain-smoking was an inevitable consequence, and this was helped along by organizations such as the Weekly Despatch *newspaper, which organized a tobacco fund intended to provide comforts to the troops: 'Arf a mo Kaiser!', Bert Thomas's famous drawing, much reproduced on postcards and posters, was one item of media that was used to drum up support for the fund. So important were cigarettes to the men that some would risk serious injury to get a 'fag', or would keep their 'emergency fags' and matches in their field dressing pocket, which was sewn into the inside front of the Service Dress jacket. As in the next war, the humble fag was also to be used as a form of currency for exchange or gambling. Rifleman Groom of the LRB recalls that cigarettes cost one franc for a tin of fifty – his usual ration for six days in the line was six tins – and that chain-smoking was the norm in the line, a remedy for frayed nerves.*

Trench Lighters

A means of obtaining a light was obviously important, with matches and lighters being prevalent. The phrase 'three on a match' supposedly relates to a superstition from the First War that lingering too long on sharing a match was a dangerous pastime, the third man being the potential recipient of a sniper's bullet. With matches being prone to dampness, a range of lighters was made commercially available. The lighter belonging to Private J. T. Robinson of the Northumberland Fusiliers was carried by him throughout the war. 'Trench art' lighters are common too, like the pair illustrated below. Many were produced after the war, but some have the ring of wartime authenticity. Three basic types are known: the 'book' type, the 'disc' type and the 'bullet' type. All would have required specialist equipment to construct, and wartime examples were undoubtedly produced in ordnance and engineer workshops of the AOC, RE and ASC.

'The Minor Horrors of War'

Lice were the constant companions of the soldier in the trenches, the inevitable consequence of large groups of men being gathered together without provision for regular changing of their clothes. The adult body louse (Pediculus vestimenti) has a life span of around four weeks, and lives clinging to the undergarments, close enough to the skin in order to feed while still attached to the cloth. Its frequent desire to feed caused great discomfort, sores and, eventually, infections. Yet, the acceptance that lice were part of trench life is illustrated in this remarkable postcard from 1917.

Dr A. E. Shipley, Master of Christ's College, Cambridge, was a zoologist whose essays on lice and other vermin affecting soldiers, originally appearing in the British Medical Journal, *were republished in 1915 as* The Minor Horrors of War. *As one reviewer put it, 'Dr Shipley writes with humour, sharing this part of the Great War task in the same light-hearted spirit in which Tommy holds the trenches. No more cheerful book has ever been written on a more disgusting subject.' Covering a whole plague of vermin, the book gives practical advice: for the louse, removal of clothing from the body leads to starvation of the insect; with the inevitable absence of clothing changes, heat treating seams, or using sulphurous solutions were recommended. Tommy would resort to removal of the 'chats' by hand, running the fingernail through seams or playing a candle flame along them, and hearing the insects 'pop' (but thereby weakening uniforms). Neither method was effective for long, and delousing would be a feature of the bath-houses set up in rear areas, which treated clothing while men were bathing in vats of water, or makeshift showers. That this treatment was not always effective is clear from contemporary accounts of men itching immediately after leaving the baths. Lice were a severe health risk – infections spread with irritated skin, the agent spreading such mysterious 'trench' diseases as 'trench fever', attributed to infection from lice bites. Plagues of flies and rats ('as big as cats' in trench mythology) were other vermin frequently endured, an unavoidable result of the squalid conditions of trench life, and the abundance of unburied bodies in no man's land.*

1ST. TOMMY TO 2ND. (HUNTING IN HIS SHIRT FOR THE ENEMY) "WOT'S THE NEWS BILL?"
2ND. TOMMY: "REINFORCEMENTS COMING UP IN THOUSANDS."

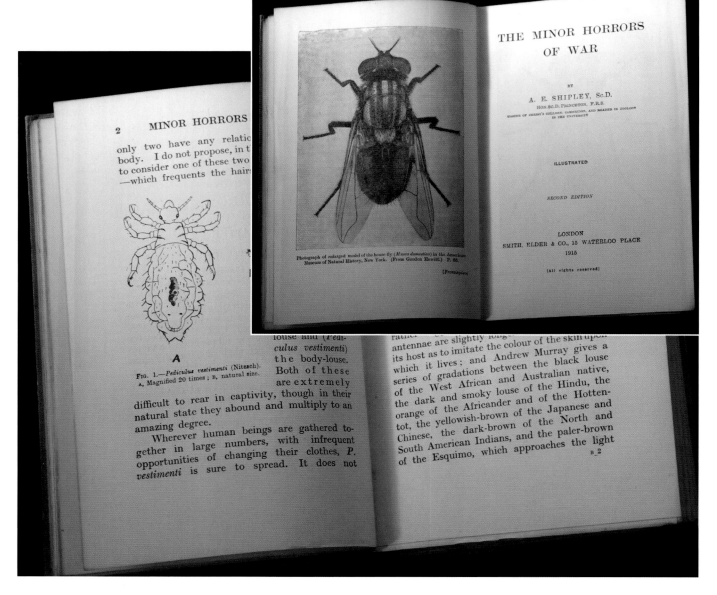

INDUSTRIAL WARFARE

Machine guns are associated by most with the reign of death on the Great War battlefield. They were so effective in scything through the attacking formations that gallantry medals were often awarded for the capture or destruction of machine-gun posts, and the protagonists were at great pains to disguise them. Despite the power of the machine gun, however, it was probably artillery fire that was most feared. Its devastating effects were evident in the destruction of the landscape, and in the often random deaths caused by the explosion of shells of all calibres, when the frailness of the human body became all too apparent. Artillery fire became increasingly sophisticated as the war progressed, with timed barrages designed to 'lift', maintaining a rolling effect in front of an advance, or the isolation of raiding parties in box barrages, deterring the enemy from attacking by walls of shells. Trench maps and other innovations were a function of the need to place shellfire accurately, and a complex system of grid coordinates was evolved for this purpose. The gunners were constant companions in arms to the infantry; providing barrage fire at the opening of offensives, and frequently called upon, through signal flares and fragile telephone lines, to deal with troublesome machine-gun nests, snipers and suspicious activity in no man's land.

Gas warfare was deployed in an active sense in April 1915, when the Germans first used it in a practical manner during the opening phases of the Second Battle of Ypres. Here, cloud gas caused panic and fear among those who faced it, equipped only with wetted handkerchiefs; however, the line held, and the use of gas to achieve the much-anticipated 'breakthrough' was much diminished. From late 1915, with the issue of effective respirators, gas was to become just another weapon to be endured by the man in the trenches. Tanks were the miracle weapon of 1916 – the cause of rejoicing at Cambrai in 1917, and a major element in the new industrial battlefield of 1918.

Machine Guns

The British Army went to war with the machine gun as a specialist weapon, with two heavy Vickers machine guns per infantry battalion. As no one had expected the war to be a static one – with an increased role for the machine gun in both defence (protecting a position) and offence (creating a barrage) – this was hardly surprising. Machine gunners, like those illustrated in the famous Daily Mail War Picture *card below, were to become an elite arm. The power of the British Vickers Mark I machine gun, and of its German MG08 Maxim equivalent, was truly frightening. Fired in short bursts of 200 rounds per minute (although both had a rate of fire of 450 rounds per minute), both guns had a maximum effective range of 2,000 yards, with accuracy and hit rate increasing as the range decreased. Deeper considerations of machine-gun tactics led to the idea that the Vickers guns should be taken away from infantry battalions and given, in larger numbers, to the newly formed Machine Gun Corps (MGC). The role of MGC was guided from the Divisional Commanders, in order that it might provide effective infantry support. In return for their loss, infantry battalions were issued with the lighter Lewis gun, which was more suited to an infantry role. Men deemed proficient in handling both Vickers and Lewis machine guns were awarded badges (illustrated overleaf), to be worn on the right lower sleeve: 'MG' for Machine Gunner, 'LG' for Lewis Gunner. In some cases, unofficial, or Division-specific machine-gun flashes were also worn on the sleeve; some examples are illustrated overleaf. The MGC itself wore a cap badge of crossed Vickers machine guns.*

"Daily Mail" WAR PICTURES

16. BRITISH MACHINE GUNNERS WEARING GAS HELMETS
OFFICIAL PHOTOGRAPH. CROWN COPYRIGHT RESERVED.

The distinctive crossed Vickers cap badge of the Machine Gun Corps is reputed to have changed to match new marks of the gun. Trained gunners wore brass trade badges like those illustrated, MG for machine gunner, LG for Lewis gunner. Some divisions had their own scheme of insignia (above).

Artillery

The photograph shows an experienced field artillery team – members of the Royal Field Artillery (RFA) – with steel helmets and small box respirators in winter. They man one of the 10,000 18-pounder field guns that were produced during the Great War. The British 18-pounder quick-firing field gun had a maximum range of over 6,500 yards, and was capable of firing shrapnel, high explosive and star shells. Heavier guns, such as this 8-inch howitzer depicted on a Daily Mail War Picture *card during the preliminary bombardment on the Somme, were designed to lob shells with a high trajectory, so that they might drop slap-bang into the trench systems of the enemy. This gun was already obsolete in 1916, and was replaced by even heavier siege howitzers, all crewed by gunners of the Royal Garrison Artillery (RGA), farther back from the front line.*

The British shells illustrated are 'duds' – examples that were fired, yet failed to explode. The two deactivated shells are fitted with high-explosive percussion fuses, the larger example being fired from a 4.5-inch field howitzer, the smaller example from the 18-pounder. The paucity of shells in 1915 – and their poor quality, particularly in the manufacture of the complex time fuse – was to be a national scandal that would lead to David Lloyd George being appointed Minister for Munitions. In 1916, the British Army carried out its most extensive barrage of the war in preparation for the Battle of the Somme; thousands of 18-pounder shells were fired in an attempt to destroy the German defences and cut their barbed wire, taking their place alongside heavier high-trajectory howitzer fire with deeper ground penetration and percussion fuses. The precision required in the field gunners in setting the fuses of the shrapnel shells to burst just over the wire, thereby cutting it in a hail of shrapnel balls, was beyond most capabilities, and the adequacy of the fuses to perform the task was once more in question. For farmers working the land today, these shells, often live, are part of the day-to-day iron harvest. The large shell above, still live, was found by farmers on the old German front line on the Somme in La Boisselle. Fired by British siege gunners from a howitzer, it is typical of the type used to try and break the deadlock in 1916. Such shells are regularly encountered, and are left out in full view, for collection by the authorities.

19. FIRING A HEAVY HOWITZER IN FRANCE
OFFICIAL PHOTOGRAPH. CROWN COPYRIGHT RESERVED

Shrapnel Balls and Shell Fragments

It has been estimated that 60 per cent of all casualties were wounded or killed by artillery fire on the Western Front. With increasing precision, artillerymen developed new ways of delivering their goods, with creeping and box barrages intended to provide a protective screen around those attacking, isolating those within from the attentions of the defenders outside the curtain of shellfire. Complex ranging techniques, including the use of aerial spotters, technical apparatus to determine the location of enemy batteries using sound and vision (flash spotting), and increasingly complex artillery maps, meant that the gunners belonged to an extremely professional and scientific Corps by the end of the war. For Tommy, avoiding the attentions of the enemy's artillery fire was paramount. In the 'live and let live' system that developed in some sectors of the Western Front, maintaining the status quo was the soldier's aim, thereby avoiding anything that would bring down a barrage in suspicion of unwanted extra activity or evidence of military preparation. Soldiers soon got used to the sound of incoming fire, distinguishing the 'whizz bang' of the quick-firing field gun from the 'crump' of the heavy howitzer. The explosions of the howitzer would create a forceful blast and plenty of black smoke, and it soon acquired a variety of nicknames, from 'woolly bear' and 'coal box' to 'Jack Johnson' (after the hard-hitting black heavyweight boxer). Heavy shells would kill by the action of the high explosive, which could tear apart fortifications and human flesh alike; wounds from the jagged, cruel shell fragments, like those illustrated below, were particularly feared. Quick-firers could also deliver high explosive, but were often packed with, in the case of the British, 240 lead shrapnel balls that would be propelled with force out of the body of the shell in flight. The wide brim of British 'shrapnel helmets' was designed to protect the wearer from such airbursts. Shrapnel balls like those illustrated are typical of those still found on the battlefields today; these examples are British, larger ones reputedly German.

Trench Mortars

Men of the trench mortars – TMs or 'toc emmas', in the phonetic alphabet of the day – were described as the 'suicide club'. They were a group of soldiers who were very likely to be targeted for retaliatory action by their opposite numbers in the opposing trenches. For this reason (along with many others), TM men were often unpopular in the front line. Trench mortars – simple trench-scale artillery capable of firing high-trajectory shells or bombs – became increasingly sophisticated as the war proceeded. They were used as a means of destroying or reducing enemy trenches, and were capable of killing large numbers of men in any given trenches. The German equivalent – the minenwerfer *– was especially feared. The British experimented with a variety of contraptions – including catapults firing grenades – but the first effective mortars started to appear in 1915. These included the 'toffee apple' mortar, a two-inch diameter tube firing an explosive charge mounted on a long shaft that was liable to destabilize the round in flight. More reliable was the Stokes mortar, a simple three-inch drainpipe affair that was effectively the prototype for mortars in use today in armies across the world. Stokes bombs were dropped into the tube, and a striker would activate the charge and propel the round up to 1,500 yards. Stokes mortar bombs still litter the former battlefields in out of the way places (opposite); they remain volatile, a deadly echo of a past war. Stokes Toc Emma batteries, organized from 1915, were formed from infantrymen. They wore blue flaming grenade sleeve insignia, which distinguished them from battalion bombers, who wore similar, red, grenades (as illustrated opposite). Medium and heavy trench mortars were produced from 1916–17, and were manned by artillerymen.*

Gas Warfare

The use of gas on 22 April 1915 by the Germans, as part of their assault at Ypres, saw the Allies unprepared. The chlorine gas released from cylinders overcame the unprotected French troops manning the front line, with between 800–1,400 men killed and a further 2,000–3,000 men injured. Primitive respirators were extemporized on 23–24 April, with General Headquarters of the BEF issuing a directive that field dressings should be soaked in bicarbonate of soda, an alkaline, to combat the suspected chlorine; urine would also be called upon to do the same job. The 1st Canadian Division, on the right flank of the line, was attacked on 24 April, but their only protection was wetted handkerchiefs and cotton bandoliers. Scientific advice mustered by the British led to the devising of a respirator around a pad of cotton waste soaked with sodium hyposulphite, sodium carbonate and glycerine, held in black mourning gauze, used to tie the mask to the face. The resulting War Office Black Veiling Respirator was to save many lives in May 1915. It was still inadequate, however; under pressure of attack, the veiling could not be tied easily, and it only gave protection for a limited period. Even gas warfare did not escape representation on the humorous postcard – but in truth it was no laughing matter.

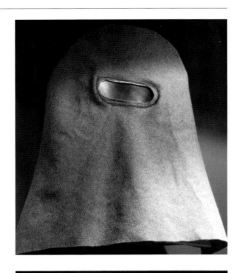

A replacement was desperately needed. The first to arrive, in May 1915, was a flannel hood designed by Captain Cluny MacPherson of the Newfoundland Regiment. The hood covered the whole head and its tail was tucked into the tunic to provide a seal. A simple mica window was provided for vision. The 'Hypo Helmet' (officially, Smoke Helmet) was soaked in sodium hyposulphite and protection was given by the fact that the 'hypo' solution would counteract the gas drawn in through the material by the process of breathing. By the autumn of 1915, this was to be replaced by a more sophisticated version, the 'Phenate (P) Helmet', which used the same basic gas hood design. This was developed in response to the proliferation of gas types, particularly phosgene, which was ten times more toxic than chlorine. This mask was soaked in sodium phenate, and was made from cotton flannelette (wool flannel would be rotted by the phenate), with two circular glass eye-pieces, and a tube valve to expel carbon dioxide held in the teeth, with a rubber outlet. This nightmarish creation, also known as the tube helmet, was famously recorded as the 'goggle-eyed (or googly-eyed) bugger with the tit' by

Captains Robert Graves and J.C. Dunn of the Royal Welsh Fusiliers. It would be used, rolled up in readiness on the head, with the Hypo Helmet in reserve, during the disastrous British gas attacks at Loos in September 1915. Both types are illustrated, together with the simple satchel that contained them. From January 1916 all P Helmets were dipped in hexamine – highly absorbent of phosgene gas – to become the Phenate-Hexamine or PH Helmet. All were clammy, cloying and unpleasant to wear. These nightmarish bags were to become part of the iconography of the Great War, entering popular culture on postcards like that illustrated opposite – the reverse of this card informs its recipient, 'This is what I look like in some of the stunts we have to do.'

'**This puts the tin hat on it !!**'

C'est ça qui vous complète un homme!

Small Box Respirator

The PH helmet could only stop a limited amount of gas, and was likely to fail if pushed to its limit by high concentrations of phosgene. In order to improve this situation, Bertram Lambert, a chemistry lecturer at Oxford, developed the concept of layers of lime and sodium permanganate to deal with a range of gases. His experimentation led to the development in 1915–16 of the Large Box Respirator (LBR), which used a 'box' of stacked granules of lime-permanganate, pumice soaked in sodium sulphate, and charcoal. The box (actually a converted standard-issue water bottle) was carried in a satchel, and was connected to an impregnated face mask with two eye-pieces by a corrugated hose and metal mouthpiece. Large and bulky, it was issued only to Royal Engineer gas companies, and to soldiers in static positions, such as heavy machine gunners and artillerymen.

The Small Box Respirator (SBR), developed from its predecessor, was designed to provide universal protection from a range of gases, while not being an encumbrance to free movement. The first step was to reduce the size of the 'box' by modifying its fill – placing the lime–permanganate granules between two layers of charcoal. Other improvements were an exhalation valve (which also had a device to drain saliva) and a haversack that could be worn slung over the shoulder or, through the use of a lug and leather strap, could be hitched up on to the chest (strap over the head) into the 'alert' position. The face mask was issued in four sizes, its number stamped on the mask and on the haversack; the version illustrated is the number three. When he was wearing the device, the soldier would grip the inner rubber mouthpiece between his teeth, and use the integrated nose clip to ensure that his breathing was through the 'box'. When first issued universally in August–October 1916, the masks were individually fitted, and each soldier acclimatized by exposure (when wearing the mask) in a tear-gas chamber for five minutes. This mask was to prove highly effective.

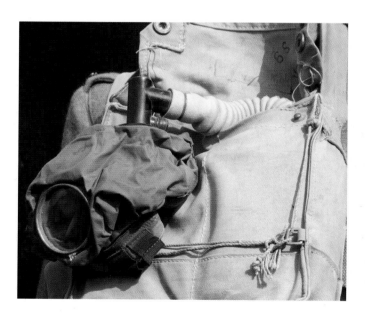

Gas Alarms

With the advent of gas as a weapon of war, some means of alerting the men in the front lines was necessary. From the early days, the army relied upon any number of extemporized warnings, including, typically, shell cases suspended from the trench sides, or from simple tripods near gun sites. Simple gas gongs could be constructed from material that was readily available, and it was simple enough to suspend the gong upside down and provide an appropriate piece of metal or wood with which to beat it. Captain J. C. Dunn, Medical Officer with the Royal Welsh Fusiliers, recalled a typical piece of soldier doggerel:

> *If a whiff of gas you smell,*
> *Bang your gong like bloody hell,*
> *On with your googly, up with your gun—*
> *Ready to meet the bloody Hun.*

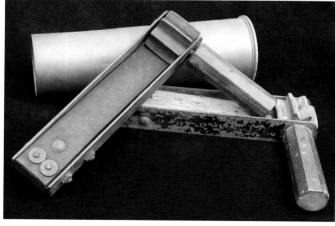

Before they were issued with whistles, the police in Victorian Britain had used rattles, and in 1917 the BEF was to issue these as an efficient means of gas warning; they were to be used again in the Second World War. Rattles had the advantage that, if they were swung with sufficient vigour, they could be heard from some distance. At least two types are known to have been produced in the First World War: the earliest, from 1917, had a wooden frame; the later examples, from 1918, like those illustrated above, had a metal frame, were heavier and could be swung more vigorously. Like their cousins from the Second World War (usually distinguished by their two 'clackers'), these rattles were used, painted in garish colours, in the post-war world by football supporters.

Gas Bottle

When the Germans first deployed gas, at Ypres in April 1915, they did so from cylinders, the resulting gas cloud being driven towards their enemy by the wind. Although it was effective in this first use, the reliance on nature to propel the gas was fraught with difficulty – a fact underlined by the first British use in September 1915 at Loos, where wind changes caused casualties in the British lines. Other means of delivering gas to the enemy were needed. This unassuming small but tough green bottle was designed to hold DA or diphenylchlorarsine – blue cross gas – an agent intended to foil the continued development of effective respirators by the Allies. Blue cross gas was delivered in specially designed 7.7cm shells, the glass bottle held within a charge of TNT. When fired, the shell would explode over

Allied lines, the bottle bursting to release the gas as a fine powder, intended to penetrate gas masks and cause intense pain to the sinuses. The idea was to force the recipients to remove their masks and then succumb to the more deadly effects of phosgene, also delivered in gas shells. In fact, blue cross shells were largely ineffective, and valuable German war effort was wasted on the production of over ten million gas shells in the closing years of the war. This example has been recovered from the fields of Flanders, where gas shells still leak their deadly cargo, and should never be approached.

Livens Projector

The failure of the British cloud gas attacks in 1915 led to the search for more effective ways of delivering the weapon. Like the Germans, the British experimented with gas shells, gas mortar rounds and other approaches. One successful weapon was the Livens Projector, the brainchild of William Livens, a British officer who was spurred on to design weapons by the sinking of the Lusitania by a German submarine in 1915. Comprising thirty-six-inch-long steel tubes dug into the ground at an angle of 45 degrees and resting on a base plate resembling a sombrero, the projector fired 60lb 'drums' filled with liquid gas or flammable oil. Arranged in long batteries, firing was electrical, detonating the propellant charge to send hundreds of projectiles towards the German lines. The tactic was used to great effect in the battles of 1917, at Arras and Messines. Projectors like those illustrated, which were salvaged from the line of the old Western Front, are still encountered today.

Tanks

The tank, a British invention of 1915, was designed to cross trenches, thereby puncturing the German lines, and was to participate in the latter stages of the Battle of the Somme. Its characteristic rhombic shape – an image destined to become an icon used by souvenir manufacturers, trench artists and savings schemes – was intended to give as great a surface area as possible to the tracks in order that they might both cross open trenches and climb gradients. The Mark I was deployed for the first time in the latter stages of the Somme; these Daily Mirror *war cards depicting the tanks were extremely popular in their day, the* Mirror *having already carried the first pictures of the tank in action to be released. The tank evolved during the war, with increasing reliability, the Mark IV being the main battle tank of the later war period. It was to be deployed in two basic forms, with six-inch guns (male) and with Lewis or Hotchkiss machine guns (female) arming their side-mounted sponsons. Both, travelling at an average speed of four miles per hour, were vulnerable to shellfire. At first, they were operated by men of the Machine Gun Corps (Heavy Section) but, by July 1917, a new Tank Corps had evolved, with its own distinctive insignia; a soldier's cap badge and paired officer's collar badges are shown here. The use of tanks was to be decisive in the final battles of the Great War.*

A BROADSIDE FROM OUR LAND-SHIP.

Canadian Official

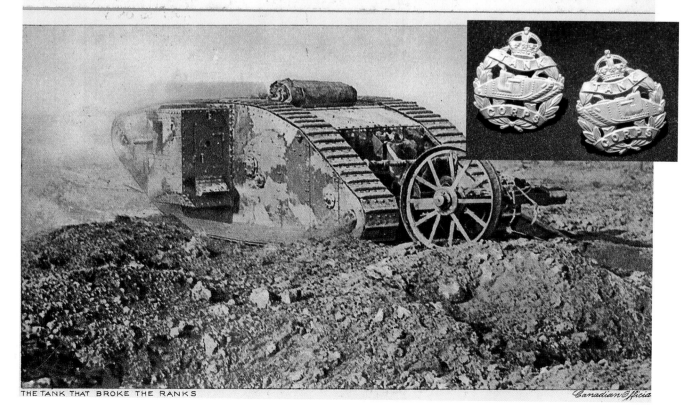

THE TANK THAT BROKE THE RANKS

Canadian Official

'OVER THE TOP'

For the infantryman, going 'over the top' or 'over the bags' was, relatively speaking, a rare event. The large set-piece battles so commonly associated with the Great War took a considerable amount of planning, with extended periods of artillery preparation and the gathering of reinforcements in the rear areas, clogging transport arteries and communication trenches. Nevertheless, most infantry soldiers would experience at some point the terror of rising out of the trenches in broad daylight to face an enemy that they had previously only glimpsed through trench periscopes, and the resulting battles have become the subject of heated discussion over the decades since the end of the war. More common were trench raids, which involved many activities, from single officers exploring no man's land to organized miniature offensives protected by complex box barrages. Trench raids were deemed by the High Command to be an operational necessity, required for at least two reasons: to provide information on the enemy in the trenches ahead, and to maintain the offensive spirit.

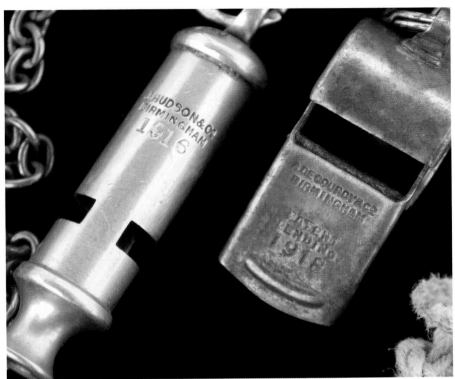

Whistles

The whistle has entered into the mythology of the war, the image of the junior subaltern blowing whistles at zero hour to signify the attack 'over the bags' being a favourite of film directors. Most were made by the famous firm of Hudson's, in Birmingham, which had manufactured the 'Metropolitan' police whistle and its military versions since the middle of the nineteenth century. Great War whistles are usually stamped simply with the date, like the example illustrated from 1916. Acme referee's whistles, with a completely different timbre, were also used; this example is from 1918. Whistles were employed on other tasks, warning of gas attacks, for instance, or, more usually, by day sentries keeping watch through periscopes for incoming 'minies'. The minenwerfer trench mortars were easily spotted in flight, and sentries would blow their whistles and shout 'minies to the left or right', as appropriate; this activity was illustrated in one of Mackain's 'Up the line' postcards, below.

Sketches of Tommy's life
Up the line — No 5

The main duties in the Front Line in the daytime are watching the periscope, and looking up in the air for "trench mortars", with a whistle ready to blow for a warning.

Trench Clubs

Of all the items associated with trench warfare, the rediscovery of clubs and knives as weapons most clearly indicates the descent of warfare from the ideal of open battle to the extended and stalemated nightmare of the trenches. The club as a weapon has a history that extends back millennia. Rifles with fixed bayonets could not be wielded effectively in the strict confines of the trench, and the club, knife, revolver and grenade found favour in night-time trench raids where a modicum of surprise was needed. In most cases, clubs and knives were fashioned from whatever material was to hand. There was no official issue of such weapons in the British Army (although they were relatively common in the US Army, at least at the end of the war). There is much debate among collectors as to the whether clubs and knives were made by soldiers themselves or in the workshops of the Royal Engineers, Army Service Corps and the like, but the fact is that they follow a familiar pattern. A number of typical clubs are illustrated. The first is an example of a semi-official type, a club with a long turned-wood handle studded with boot cleats. It is missing its lead top, which would have given it weight on the swing. Other examples have nails instead of cleats, with at least one known from the archaeological excavation of front-line trenches in the Ypres Salient. These types may well have been manufactured in army workshops and many have been reproduced in recent years. Other versions were probably extemporized in the trenches, or even prepared at home and then sent to the front. The second example illustrated is constructed from a cut-down walking stick and sheet lead, while the third is typical of the 'folk art' that was to be practised in the trenches, with the soldiers carving and shaping sticks and clubs from any wood that was available. This particular example, fashioned out of wood from a stunted oak found on the Gallipoli Peninsula by an Irish soldier, depicts a Turk's head. Whether it was simply an occupation piece to pass the time, or an actual weapon of trench warfare, is difficult to determine.

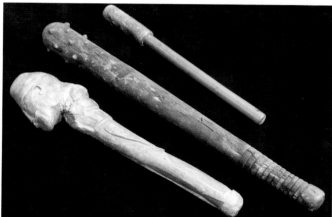

Trench Knives

In most cases, the 1907 pattern bayonet was too long to be of any effective use in trench raids. As no official trench knives were issued to British troops, home-made examples were actively employed. According to expert Anthony Saunders, the knife was not a preferred weapon on British trench raids; using a bayonet on the end of rifle as trained was one thing, but getting close enough to stab a man with a knife was another. The trench club was a more commonly used weapon. While the Americans, the Germans and even the French were to be issued with short knives for battle use, the British would resort to privately purchased examples from such stores as The Army and Navy in London, or to manufacturing their own, close to the front line. Typically, soldiers would use a bayonet, like this 1907 pattern Lee Enfield, cut down and shaped to a more manageable blade. The Canadian Ross bayonet (for the ill-fated Ross Rifle, which was withdrawn as being unfit for front-line service in late 1916), already relatively short, was another popular choice for modification. Any other suitable piece of metal that would carry a blade was also pressed into service; Saunders records the use of ground-down metal files, and the example illustrated, based on a file undoubtedly made in Sheffield, England, is typical of this type. Together with trench clubs, these crudely fashioned knives are gruesome reminders of a terrible war.

Grenades

The hand grenade was to replace the rifle as the primary offensive weapon of trench warfare. Its use required little training (although fatal accidents were common) and, placed correctly, it had a wide kill radius that was more efficient than the well-placed shot of even the most skilled marksman. The British Army went to war with an extremely cumbersome grenade – the Mark I – a sixteen-inch stick grenade with a cast-iron explosive chamber and streamers to make it stable in flight. It had a fatal flaw – it was detonated by a percussion striker, which meant that the bomber had to be extremely careful not to hit the side of the trench when preparing to throw it, and this was a difficult proposition, given the length of the handle. This, together with difficulties of supply, meant that by 1915 soldiers were making their own version, which was ignited by a slow-burning fuse, usually at the rate of 1 inch of fuse per 1.25 seconds of delay. Typical is the 'jam-tin' bomb – literally a tin filled with explosive gun cotton and shrapnel balls – that is particularly associated with the Gallipoli Campaign of 1915. In France, the Battye Bomb (top right), named after its inventor Major Basil Battye RE, was manufactured at Béthune. It consisted of a cast-iron cylinder containing 40 grams of explosive, sealed with a wooden stopper and ignited by a Nobel fuse, and was activated by banging down a friction cap.

The Type 15 (right) was the first grenade to be mass-produced, again in 1915. Resembling a cricket ball, it could be thrown a reasonable distance, but, with its simple cast-iron body and cord fuse, it resembled a traditional 'anarchist's bomb' of the nineteenth century. Also ignited by friction, the Type 15 was badly affected in wet weather, with the special friction brassards issued to bombers becoming useless, and this factor was to present a major problem in the Loos Campaign of September 1915. Although half a million grenades of this type were eventually produced, they were unreliable, and were to decline in popularity with the introduction of the Mills grenade in May 1915. Named after its inventor William Mills, and officially designated the Number 5 grenade, the secret of its success lay with its ignition system, which used a striker that was activated when a pin was removed and a lever released; the lever was then ejected and a four-second fuse activated, during which time the bomber had to throw the grenade. The body of the grenade was formed of cast iron, and weighed one and a quarter pounds; its surface was divided into sections to promote fragmentation, although the value of this has been disputed. An example made by Davis and Mawson in March 1916 is illustrated. A revised model, the Number 36, followed in 1917 (bottom right). The No. 36 was first filled with explosive and then dipped in shellac, a process that sealed the grenade and thus prevented rapid deterioration. Its base plug was also strengthened, for use with a screw-in rod for rifle discharge. Mills grenades were carried in boxes of twelve, with the detonators being carried separately, to avoid unnecessary accidents. Battalion bombers would be equipped with simple tools like that illustrated to enable them to remove the base plate and prime the grenade; hooks were also provided to bombing specialists to enable them to remove the pins quickly and efficiently, thereby increasing the rate of throw. It has been estimated that approximately 70 million Mills bombs were thrown by the Allies during the war, alongside at least 35 million other types, including many rifle grenades, a testimony to the importance of this weapon in trench warfare. A German response to the Mills, the eirehandgrenate *of 1917, is also illustrated (bottom right).*

German Epaulettes

In many cases, the stated purpose of trench raids was to provide intelligence on the disposition and activities of the troops in the opposing trenches. In some cases, this kind of information could be obtained by the 'lone-wolf' activities of officers anxious to see what was immediately in front of the stretch of line for which they were directly responsible. Officers were known to move out into no man's land under the cover of darkness, grabbing unwary sentries, or removing identifying insignia from dead bodies. Such activities were encouraged by High Command, as consistent with the principle of maintaining the offensive spirit; this was anathema to the 'live and let live' system adopted in some parts of the front line farther south. Apart from gaining prisoners, the main target for British raiders was German unit insignia, traditionally the shoulder straps of the otherwise plain tunic. Piped in various colours for branch of service (white for infantry), the regiment would be identified by an embroidered number; the straps illustrated represent the 77th and 58th infantry regiments. These would be cut from the tunics of dead soldiers or prisoners, and sent to the rear, often to be mounted on boards showing the disposition of enemy forces at any given time; one such board is currently on display in the Imperial War Museum in London.

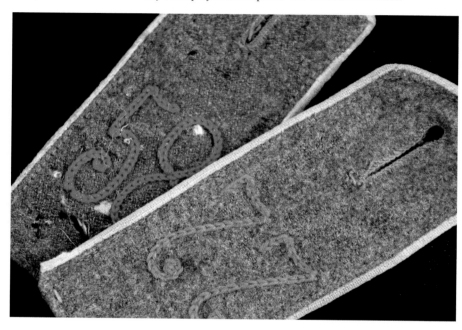

CASUALTIES

Casualties are an inevitable consequence of war, even in today's high-tech and sanitized conflicts. In the Great War, the rate and scale of casualties is breathtaking: infamously, the opening hour of the Battle of the Somme on 1 July 1916 saw at least 50,000 men killed, wounded or reported missing. In fact, the term 'casualty' as used officially is misleading, as it refers to anyone effectively taken out of action, with deaths forming a smaller proportion of the whole. It was relatively rare for a soldier to survive the war completely unscathed, and wounding was a common experience.

Ensuring that men survived their wounds was the responsibility of the Army medical services, and particularly the Royal Army Medical Corps (RAMC), whose role it was to care for the wounded and to evacuate them efficiently from the front line. Most soldiers hoped that their destination would be 'Blighty'. The chain was a long one: first to the Regimental Aid Post (RAP), run by a RAMC doctor and small number of orderlies, which was set up close to the front line and adjacent to battalion Headquarters (usually in dugouts or ruined buildings). Next in the chain was the Advanced Dressing Station (ADS), set up at the farthest front-wards limit of wheeled transport, and run by the RAMC Field Ambulance, with three such units of men attached to an infantry division. The wounded would be transported from RAP to ADS through a variety of means: on foot, by cart, on a stretcher (via a series of relay posts if there was a considerable distance between the two). Men could then expect to be transported down the line to Main

Dressing Stations (MDS), beyond the range of medium artillery fire; then to Casualty Clearing Stations (CCS), set up beyond the artillery zone, and, finally, still within the theatre of operations, to General and Stationary hospitals. From here, Tommy would hope to receive his 'ticket' – a label that marked him for transportation on hospital ships bound for home, or 'Blighty'.

Field Dressing

A First Field Dressing was carried by all soldiers, sewn into a small pouch on the lower right skirt of the Service Dress tunic. This contained a dressing that could be tied on to a small wound with a gauze strip, and a small glass ampoule of iodine, the contents of which were to be poured into the wound before application of the dressing. An example from 1917 is illustrated. It was intended that soldiers would use their own dressing on themselves, and that others finding wounded comrades would use that soldier's own dressing. For more serious wounds, larger 'shell dressings' were carried by stretcher-bearers combing the battlefield.

RAMC Insignia

The RAMC cap badge incorporates the rod of Asclepius, an ancient Greek symbol of a serpent entwined around a staff that is associated with healing. (In Greek mythology, Asclepius, a son of Apollo, was a physician.) The badge was, and still is, worn by all ranks, although officers would invariably wear a bronzed version. Other ranks also wore the RAMC shoulder titles, initials that were unfairly re-interpreted by some as 'Rob All My Comrades' (referring to an accusation of the activities of some stretcher-bearers), or 'Run Away Mother's Coming' (referring to their non-combatant status). In fact, over thirty-one members of the RAMC were to win the Victoria Cross in the First World War, including Captain Noel Chavasse, one of only three soldiers to be awarded the medal twice. The RAMC expanded rapidly during the war; on mobilization the corps consisted of approximately 1,000 medical officers and 9,000 other ranks; by 1918 there were 13,000 officers and 154,000 other ranks of the corps serving across the globe.

Stretcher-Bearers

Stretcher-bearers were battalion men who gave up their arms to carry their stretcher, the bearing of arms by medics being expressly forbidden in war. Ideally, at least six men would be needed per stretcher, but this was not always achievable, and German prisoners were often drafted in to carry wounded soldiers back. It was an offence under King's Regulations to escort wounded soldiers back without the express permission of an officer. Regimental stretcher-bearers would wear a brassard or armband, like that illustrated, bearing the initials 'SB'. Many were bandsmen, others were infantrymen detailed for the job. It was a dangerous task, requiring service under fire, usually in no man's land. Regimental stretcher-bearers' responsibilities ended at the Regimental Aid Post; from here men would be dispatched to the rear areas and would be in the care of the Royal Army Medical Corps or RAMC, men who wore the red Geneva Cross armbands, and the trade badge of the medical orderly, again a red Geneva Cross.

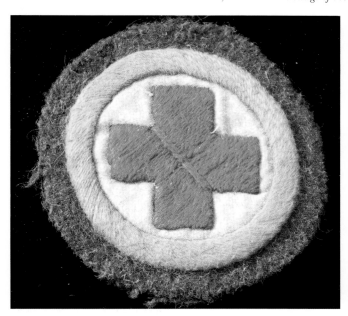

Medical Orderly

Medical orderlies – other ranks within the RAMC – were drawn from all walks of life, and comprised fit men who had specifically volunteered for Field Ambulance service, conscientious objectors who were willing to wear the King's uniform, but unwilling to act as combatants, and, more often deployed in static settings, medically unfit B and C class men. The man illustrated is just one of the 154,000 men who served in the corps with distinction in the Great War, many of whom were themselves to be killed.

Casualty Letters

The delivery of a telegram from the War Office was dreaded by all at home during the war; more often than not it would signify that a loved one had been killed, wounded or taken prisoner. In other households, there might be no news at all of a tragedy until a letter was returned home with the brutal and stark message 'Killed in Action' written or stamped as a cachet on its unopened cover; in other cases, letters would be written from the adjutant or chaplain to soften the blow. More often than not these letters would profess that the soldier in question had not suffered, and had died instantly; the truth might be harder to bear. In the case of Private Charles Chard of Somerset, serving with the Yorkshire Regiment, the colonel of his battalion wrote to the family; according to the letter, Pte Chard was killed 'instantaneously' in the Arras Sector in August 1917 while out on a daylight patrol, and was buried in the Sunken Road Cemetery in Fampoux. 2nd Lieutenant Alexander Joyce MM of the 12th Norfolks, severely wounded across the back and arms in August 1918, was to die of his wounds at the 2nd Australian Casualty Clearing Station, and was buried by Chaplain Williams MC at Longuenesse (St Omer) Cemetery, who would have the duty of writing to his relatives.

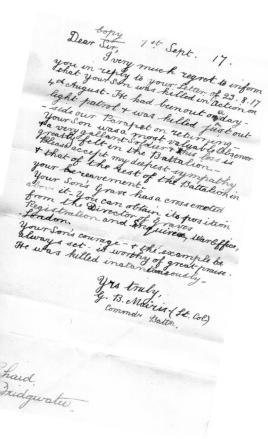

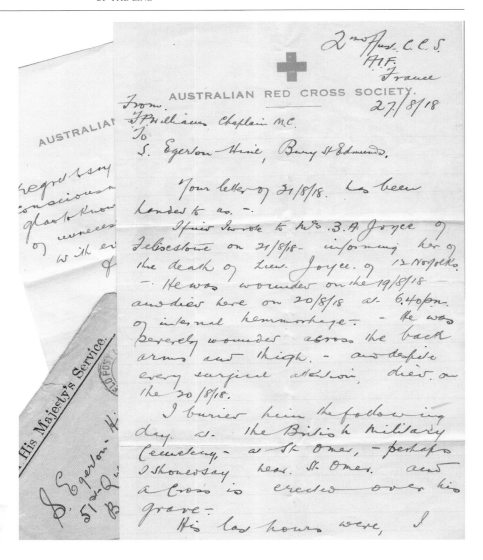

'In Memoriam' Cards

As men were killed, so long lists of casualties were published in local newspapers, often with photographs, and 'Rolls of Honour' issued. For those able to do so, a common way of extending the mourning process and alerting local communities to the loss of a loved one was to have 'In Memoriam' cards printed, in varying styles. These often incorporated a regimental badge or other military device, and usually an image of the soldier himself. Many thousands must have been printed as the war took its course; several are illustrated (below, opposite).

Sergt. Austin H. Holmes
KILLED IN ACTION

Pte. Samuel Walter Johnson,
Killed September 11th, 1915,
at Suvla Bay.

Honour to those in battle slain,
Who died that we might freedom gain;
To their brave memory homage give,
On history's page their deeds shall live.

the three corners of the world in arms, and we shall shock them :
shall make us rue, if Britain to itself do rest but true."

REMEMBRANCE.

Roll of Honour

(To 30th June, 1915).

Names of those who have given their lives for their King and Country.

Trooper FRED LE MAR, D.C.M.,
1st Dragoon Guards, killed in action at Mons, cousin of Elsie Jeffcoat.

Trooper ALBERT LE MAR,
1st Dragoon Guards, killed in action at Mons, cousin of Elsie Jeffcoat.

First-class Stoker GEORGE A. B. ALLUM, R.N.,
Lost in H.M.S. " Hawke," father of Catherine Allum.

Private GRÆME JORDAN,
14th London T. F. (London Scottish), died in Germany of wounds received in action at Messines, brother of Violet, Effie and Stephanie Jordan.

Private ALFRED DANIEL,
London Rifle Brigade, killed in action in Flanders, brother of Dorothy, Kathleen and Irene Daniel.

Private NORMAN PETT,
1st Wiltshire Regiment, killed in action in Flanders, brother of Florence Pett.

Private HAROLD CROXFORD,
13th County of London Regiment, killed in action in Flanders, brother of Irene Croxford.

Lieutenant ERIC W. TALBOT-SMITH,
10th Infantry Battalion, Australian Imperial Force, died in Egypt of wounds received at the Dardanelles, nephew of Miss Chettle.

Quarter-Master Sergeant FRANCIS R. D. ADAMSON,
20th County of London Regiment, died of wounds in France, father of Ruby Adamson.

" Into Thy hands O Lord, I come."

Duty Nobly Done.

IN LOVING MEMORY
OF
JOSEPH HEAFORD
(1st York & Lancs. Regt.),
Beloved husband of Minnie Heaford, of
73, Union Street, Hanley,
Who was killed in action in France, Sept. 29th, 1915,
Aged 35 Years.

Memorial Service in Tabernacle Mission, Union Street, Hanley,
Sunday, October 15th, 1916.

In Loving Memory
of
Private Fred Jenkins
(of the 7th North Staffs. Regiment)
BELOVED HUSBAND OF LOUISA M. JENKINS,
Aged 25 Years.
Killed in Action at Gallipoli Peninsula,
August 11th, 1915.

5 On Rest and at Home

If 'up the line' meant a spell in the front-line trenches, 'out on rest' could mean many different things, depending on the sector, the Army or Divisional commander, or the exigencies of battle. For most soldiers, a period in the front line meant time spent in every present and imminent danger: shellfire, spent bullets, gas, the morning 'hate' – all could spell immediate and random death. Away from the trenches, in contrast, Tommy could resume some connection with normality, and achieve a release of tension.

After a tour of duty in the front line – on average seven days – a battalion would be relieved. Its destination was the reserve trenches, where they were less prone to sniping and trench mortars, but still subject to the random vagaries of artillery fire. Men in reserve could be called upon to reinforce the front when under pressure, and would be the main stock for reinforcements when the front was under severe pressure. The complete withdrawal of a battalion out of the line was more welcome, offering as it did a means of gaining some rest, a chance for officers and NCOs to reassert military fastidiousness, and an opportunity for the average soldier to gain some mental freedom – washing, speaking to locals, buying trinkets. Rest camps were set up in rear areas, which were often still within range of the largest guns. Depending on the theatre of war, they could be based in villages, set up in hutted or tented camps, or simply organized in the least dangerous (a relative term) part of the battle zone, such as that organized at Cape Helles, Gallipoli in 1915 where shallow scrapes in the soil served as billets.

On rest, soldiers could once more feel human. In many cases, they could mix with civilians – those brave or foolish enough to be close to the battle zone would communicate in strange, anglicized versions of the prevailing language with their French, Belgian and Middle Eastern hosts. They could also engage women in hopeful conversations, although most who remained close to the front line were long past an age at which this hope might be fulfilled. The soldiers were paid in the local currency, and their buying power could be put to work in the purchase of alcohol – often of lamentable quality – and to indulge in other vices normally frowned upon at home: gambling, fraternization with women of 'ill repute', visits to brothels. Tommy would also have some freedom to make simple purchases of souvenirs, postcards and the ubiquitous *oeuf-frites* from those civilians brave enough to remain. Huts provided by the YMCA, Church Army or similar continued the good works of the organizations abroad; these 'dry' canteens, funded using money raised through 'flag days' and the like, offered a place for men to gather, drink tea, eat sandwiches, and write letters home on the paper provided. There, they could kill time in between the military duties that persisted 'out on rest', and before their return to the trenches. Expeditionary Force Canteens (EFC), mostly organized and run by the Army Service Corps, also allowed the men to buy necessaries: paper, pencils, food and sauces that would make the ubiquitous bully beef of the trenches more palatable. Finally, 'Toc H' – from signallers' phonetic spelling of T.H., or Talbot House, in Poperinge – still surviving today, provides an example of the various soldiers' respites that were set up by industrious individuals. At Talbot House, Reverend 'Tubby' Clayton welcomed all-comers, inviting them to 'abandon rank all ye who enter here'. Out on rest, military duties – training, lectures, fatigues – still prevailed, but contemporary diarists none the less all record their sense of relief at being set free from the random slaughter of the front line, if only for a short interval of time.

On average, and if they were lucky, soldiers returned home on leave once a year. Officers fared better, with a leave granted at around four months, but it was still a rare commodity. Detailed direct from the front line, the men would have to find their way back on the long, laborious trail home – and if home was in the more remote corners of the British Isles, this could be a trek indeed. Issued with a warrant to travel, those in France and Flanders were at least able to get to 'Blighty' in relatively short order; leave from more remote fronts was more difficult. Once home, soldiers would be surrounded by reminders of the world war still raging. Popular culture bulged with references to trenches, the front line and military materiel – postcards, crested china modelled on military equipment, songs and humorous material – and patriotic manufacturers created a vast array of 'souvenirs of the Great War' that would be avidly collected.

IN BILLETS

Soldiers out on rest were based in a variety of billets. In France and Flanders, this could be a battered village, showing the scars of long-range shelling or the movement of armies in the early days of the war. Billetted upon people grimly holding on to their existence, the men were often accommodated in barns, hay-lofts and outbuildings stuffed with bunks; in other cases, they took up residence in farmhouses, sometimes sharing the kitchen with the family that had remained in residence. Hutted camps were another option – these at least provided reasonably dry and secure accommodation, and were preferred to tented camps. For the men, being in billets and out on rest meant an escape from the tension of front-line life. It was an opportunity to try out the local language – to mangle it hopelessly and mix it with words from the Indian Empire – and to receive and spend the local currency that would be issued while on rest.

OPPOSITE: *Trench art: the reuse of discarded war material, popular with wartime soldiers and post-war visitors alike.*

In and Out

Contemporary postcards by Bairnsfather and Mackain capture the essence of going out on rest. In his celebrated duo of cards, Bairnsfather captures carefully the feeling of troops 'out on rest', the ability of the soldier to escape from the constant tension of the trenches, where random deaths were all too common; the second of the two examines the reverse feeling of depression. Mackain illustrates the freedoms: the ability to walk unhindered down village streets; the freedom to sleep stretched out and warm; the opportunity to read, relax and bathe. Yet, despite this, there was the ever-present reality that, despite being on rest, there were still duties to be carried out that would take soldiers up to the front line on fatigue duties.

Bystander copyright.
IN AND OUT (I)
That last half-hour before "going in" to the trenches for the 200th time.

Bystander copyright.
IN AND OUT (II)
That first half-hour after "coming out" of the trenches.

Sketches of Tommy's life
Out on rest — N° 4
« Ain't it nice to get into a town once more ! »

Sketches of Tommy's life
Out on rest — N° 5
A regular carouse of coffee and fried eggs is one of the things we always have when we get to one of these villages.
F. Mackain
Visé Paris 800

Sketches of Tommy's life
Out on rest — N° 3
Sometimes when you are « out on rest », you think you'd almost rather stop in the trenches.
F. Mackain
Visé Paris 800

Sketches
of Tommy's life

In Training. — N° 7

It was quite a trial the first pay parade; what with the smallness of the sum
laid out for me, and the bigness of the job of stepping up to collect it !

F. Mackain

Payday

A shilling a day, minus stoppages, and plus allowances for proficiency of up to six pence, was all the average British soldier could expect in his pay packet – at least until pay was revised, in 1917. The officer-only Army Pay Department, and its corps of clerks, the Army Pay Corps, handled accountancy in the army. It was a rather unglamorous but nevertheless essential job, handled by a body of men who kept records of the issue of money to the troops, at home and abroad. In theatre, pay was issued to the soldiery by their own officers, drawn from divisional field cashiers, and duly noted in the individual soldier's pay book (AB64). In France, the prevailing exchange rate was around twenty-five francs to the pound; the pound being worth twenty shillings, the average rate of pay per week was ten francs, minus any stoppages. Again, Mackain illustrates the experience. The note most frequently encountered, therefore, was the convenient five-franc. A 1916 version is illustrated, together with the usual two-franc and one-franc silver coins, and numerous centimes, which must have cluttered Tommy's pockets after a night spent in an estaminet *drinking* vin blanc *and weak beer, and eating egg and chips.*

Tommy's French

Thrown into a new country, Tommy quickly picked up enough French to get by, just as he had in India as a pre-war regular. A variety of pidgin French was soon developed, despite the efforts of the authorities to encourage proficiency. 'Napoo' was a particular favourite; meaning 'no more', 'finished', 'broken', 'worn out' or 'useless', it was derived from il n'y en a plus ('there is no more'). 'No compree' – derived from compris, *or 'understood' – meant that there was no understanding on either side, and was also common. For centuries, British soldiers serving abroad had appropriated words from the local language to fill in or supplement their own vocabulary (which, not surprisingly, was also liberally sprinkled with strong, Anglo-Saxon-derived swear words). The languages of the Indian subcontinent had provided many common examples, such as 'khaki' and 'puttee'. Soldier speak used 'Blighty' for home and 'bundook' for rifle. Assimilation of pidgin French was therefore inevitable (as in the cards illustrated, showing Tommy's French dialect); there is evidence to suggest that some of the locals adopted this way of speaking in order to extract the most from their visitors – this Mackain card shows children asking for souvenirs. Numerous French language handbooks and pamphlets – even packet inserts like that provided with Black Cat cigarettes – were issued to tempt the soldiery away from their army slang, albeit with limited success.*

Sketches
of Tommy's life
At the Base. — N° 8

We left the Base in great style and in cattle trucks. We must have averaged a good mile an hour. The juvenile population along the way make earnest enquiries concerning our « iron rations ».

Photographic Cards

Photographers in the rear areas of all battle zones did a roaring trade in providing soldiers with photographic images of themselves as a souvenir of their service. These differ from the photos taken at home in a couple of ways: the soldiers generally carry respirators, and they usually bear the marks of war – dirty uniforms, muddy boots, and miscellaneous equipment slung about their person. Often, the photographs were posed in studios (like those pictured below), but the ruins of Belgium, France and other places were also popular – as used in the photograph of the three signallers of the Royal Engineers serving with the 21st Division. The man on the left, Sapper John Ablitt, was to win the Military Medal and bar, and be awarded the Distinguished Conduct Medal for his actions in November 1918. Sapper Ablitt, and his friend Sapper Archibald Smith (right), survived the war. Sad to say, in many other cases, photographs taken in the rear areas were never collected, their subjects having been claimed as casualties of war.

ENTERTAINMENT

Out on rest gave the army the opportunity to re-impose military standards of cleanliness and bull – the polishing and cleaning of uniforms, and the visiting of bathhouses and showers. Work in the front line was also typical, with soldiers detailed to deliver food and essential supplies, and to take part in reconstruction of the trench line and the development of barbed-wire fences. Despite these military intrusions, there was also the possibility of engaging in harmless pursuits, of escaping with some form of entertainment; the value of such activities to morale was not lost on the High Command. Concert parties, cinemas and canteens were all seen as a means of keeping up the spirits, and helping the men to steer reasonably clear of temptation.

YMCA and Other Huts

The YMCA provided an excellent service for the newly joined men of His Majesty's army, providing home comforts and the opportunity for a get-together in their huts. Under the sign of 'Tommy's triangle', the YMCA operated in quite advanced areas, providing some comforts to the troops, with the provision of basic supplies such as the means to make the unpalatable food palatable, and, most importantly, writing materials. Away from the immediate front, the YMCA and other charitable organizations, such as the Church Army, provided huts that allowed soldiers to gather as they had done at the training camps in 1914. These huts provided a place to gather and kill time, drinking tea, eating sandwiches and writing letters home, before going back to the trenches. Provision of writing paper, envelopes and cards, like the selection illustrated, was particularly important, and would continue overseas, funded by the public's enthusiasm for flag days and street collections at home. These welcome havens were funded mostly from donations made in tins, in return for a paper flag like those illustrated opposite. However, these alcohol-free huts were not always as welcome as they could be, and one soldier, Pte Groom of the London Rifle Brigade, was to remember Arras as 'a deserted town, no egg and chips, no wine, just army canteens, YMCA and Church Army huts in which to spend our pay; how we missed the French estaminets of Flanders'.

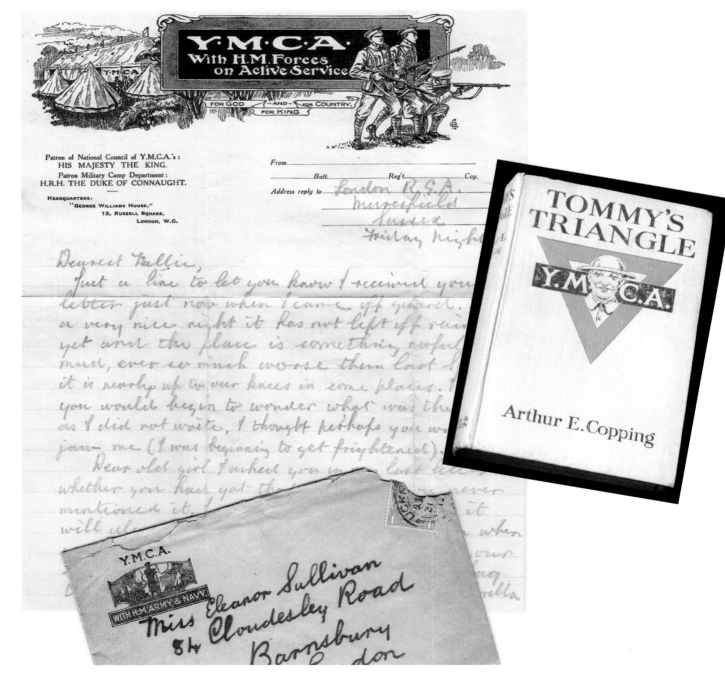

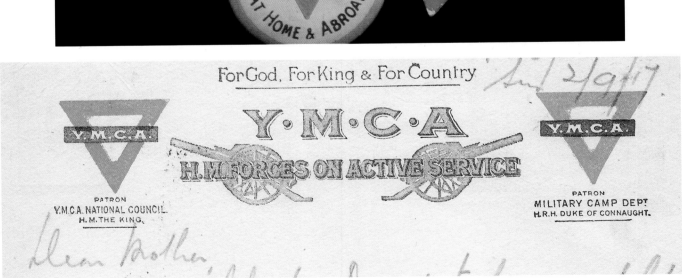

Divisional 'Follies'

In order to keep Tommy's mind off gambling, drinking and other vices, and to maintain morale in general, it was understood at a very early stage that the provision of suitable entertainments would be a benefit. There is no doubt that for men starved of entertainment, and particularly entertainment that might involve women, this form of release was valuable. As early as 1914, concert parties were being created among those servicemen who had a theatrical bent, and the concept soon spread so that every theatre of war, and almost every major unit of the British Army, had its own brand of concert party. Others were laid on by charitable organizations, including the ubiquitous YMCA. Often, these were associated with divisions; in the case illustrated (right), the Pierrot troupe of the 40th Division (whose distinctive insignia was a bantam cock and acorn), 'The Acorns', entertained the soldiers of the division at rest. The Pierrot format has a long tradition in comic theatre and, although strange to today's eyes, with the dress of ruff, white outfit and black

buttons, this would have signified a good turn on the stage. Londoner Frederick Walker (centre), enlisted under the Derby Scheme in 1916, and destined to be gassed before the end of the war, was a keen amateur music hall artiste – singing comic songs alongside his fellow 'Acorns', he would provide welcome entertainment that was very typical of the day. Female roles would be convincingly played by young, slim men, and soldiers could forget they were fellow combatants; in some rare cases, French girls were drafted in to provide a feminine flavour. The celebrated pair from Armentières, 'Glycerine and Vaseline', saw 'action' in many a concert party in the area.

The Cinema

At the time of the Great War, cinema was the new popular medium of entertainment, and the army soon cottoned on to the value of cinema in maintaining morale. The hardworking and ubiquitous Army Service Corps was detailed to provide and run the machinery. The showing of comedy shorts – particularly those of Charlie Chaplin – was well received. Mr Chaplin was to figure widely in many songs of the day, and his name often featured in related puns, as on this postcard from 1916. He was also to figure in at least one song, dating from 1915:

> 'When the moon shines bright on Charlie Chaplin,
>   He's going balmy
>   To join the Army;
> And his old baggy trousers want a-mending
>   Before they send him
>   To the Dardanelles.'

At home, some aspects of the realities of the war had been brought home by films made by the Topical Committee of the Film Manufacturer's Association. Like no film before it, Geoffrey Malins' Battle of the Somme, *which played to packed houses when it was first screened in August 1916, revealed some of the war's realities to a paying public.*

'Tommy's Tunes'

Singing has always been associated with the maintenance of morale among front-line troops, and the First World War is particularly remembered for the extent and diversity of its marching songs – 'It's a Long Way to Tipperary' being the most famous of them all. Written by Jack Judge and Harry Williams and published in 1912, the first recorded use of Tipperary *in the war is credited to an Irish regiment, the Connaught Rangers, as they arrived in Boulogne in August 1914. A number of songs were reproduced on all sorts of media, from headscarves to postcards.* Tipperary *was undoubtedly popular at home and overseas, but it and the other popular songs were parodied mercilessly by Tommy. The revised versions were thankfully preserved for posterity by 2nd Lieutenant Nettlingham of the Royal Flying Corps in his 1917 book,* Tommy's Tunes. *One reworking of* Tipperary *went as follows:*

> 'That's the wrong way to tickle Marie,
> That's the wrong way to kiss:
> Don't you know that over here, lad,
> They like it better like this.
> Hooray pour la France!
> Farewell Angleterre!
> We didn't know the way to tickle Marie,
> But now we've learnt how.'

Such lyrics were sung with gusto while there was some cheer out on rest, the return to the trenches guaranteed to alter the mood:

> 'I want to go home, I want to go home
> I don't want to see the trenches no more
> Where there are whizz bangs and shrapnel galore
> Take me over the sea where the Allemande can't get at me
> Oh my, I don't want to die
> I want to go home.'

More gentle were the lyrics to Take me Back to Dear Old Blighty, *here illustrated as the subject of a series of Bamforth cards, but the sentiment was the same – the desire for a quick escape from the front line.*

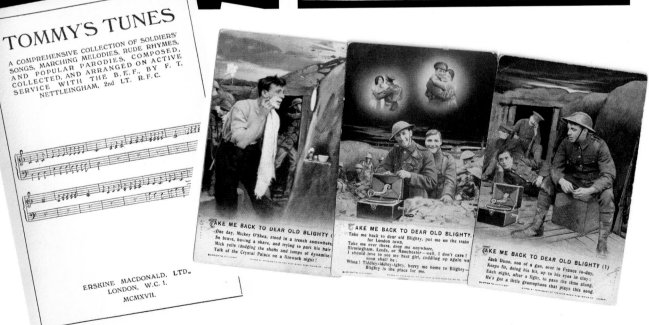

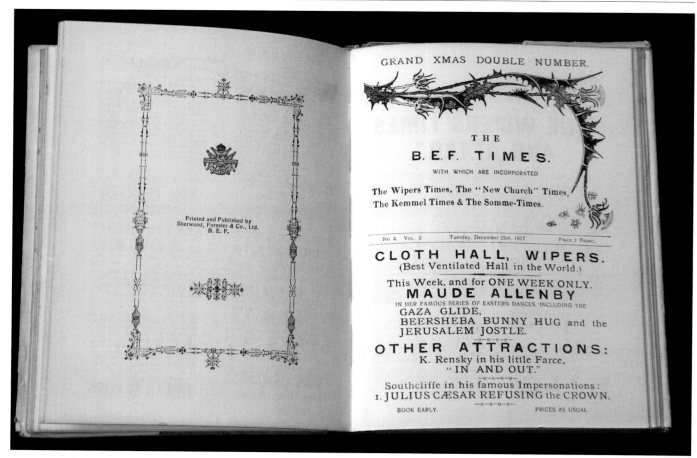

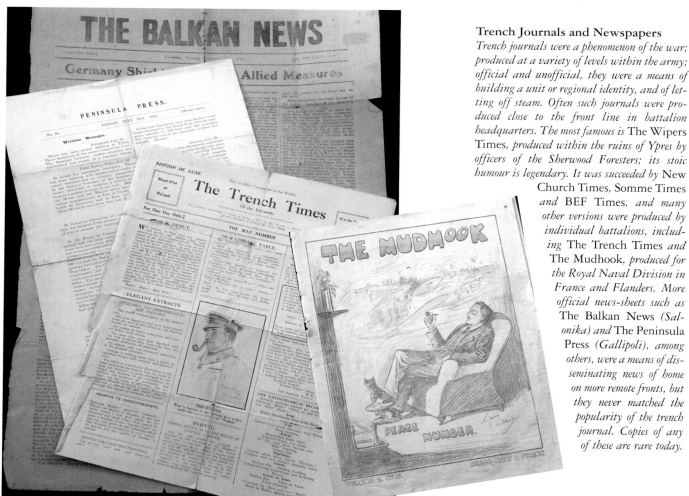

Trench Journals and Newspapers

Trench journals were a phenomenon of the war; produced at a variety of levels within the army; official and unofficial, they were a means of building a unit or regional identity, and of letting off steam. Often such journals were produced close to the front line in battalion headquarters. The most famous is The Wipers Times, *produced within the ruins of Ypres by officers of the Sherwood Foresters; its stoic humour is legendary. It was succeeded by* New Church Times, Somme Times *and* BEF Times, *and many other versions were produced by individual battalions, including* The Trench Times *and* The Mudhook, *produced for the Royal Naval Division in France and Flanders. More official news-sheets such as* The Balkan News *(Salonika) and* The Peninsula Press *(Gallipoli), among others, were a means of disseminating news of home on more remote fronts, but they never matched the popularity of the trench journal. Copies of any of these are rare today.*

LETTERS HOME

The Royal Engineers, that most versatile of Corps of the British Army, was to play a pivotal role in keeping the soldiers in touch with their home life, through its postal service. This had been set up in 1913, with an initial establishment of ten officers and 290 other ranks, intended to support an Expeditionary Force of six divisions. In August 1914, the postal service moved to France with the army.

Mail for the BEF from the United Kingdom was collected by the Post Office and sent to France, gathering at Le Havre, where the RE took over. The main unit was the Field Post Office (FPO), each FPO having its own number and special cachet mark – of which there is a bewildering array. Although each FPO was little more than an iron box and flag of office, it was to provide an essential service for the men of the BEF, MEF and other overseas forces throughout the war.

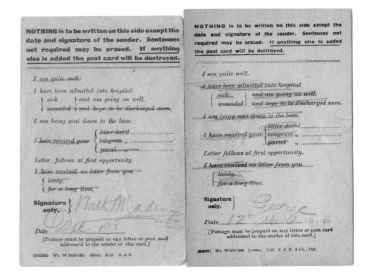

Field Service Postcards

The humble field service postcard, supplied by the military authorities, was a means of getting a simple message home without having to go to the trouble of writing a long letter. The sender simply had to cross out a few lines in order to get his message across, usually expressing the view that all was fine, and that 'letter follows at earliest opportunity'. Some would have caused concern, indicating that the sender was in hospital, sick or wounded. An example, sent home form Gallipoli, is illustrated. Foreign-language versions were made available for soldiers of the Indian Army, too, who first arrived in France in 1914. Millions of active service cards and field service postcards were sent, but some soldiers were reluctant to send them, fearing that their buff colour and official format could be off-putting to the folks back home. These men favoured locally bought cards; with the use of the phrase 'On Active Service', or simply 'O.A.S', on the top of the card, they were sent free by the army postal service. The messages on these cards often relate to the contents of parcels received, or reflect on the soldier's state of mind – 'In the pink' was usual. There is an interesting contrast between the tone of officers' and other ranks' cards illustrated overleaf. As usual, Pte Fergus Mackain captures the spirit perfectly.

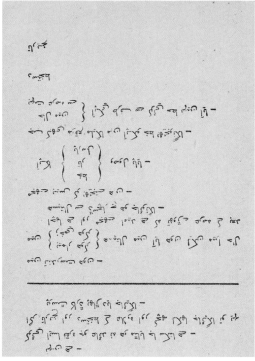

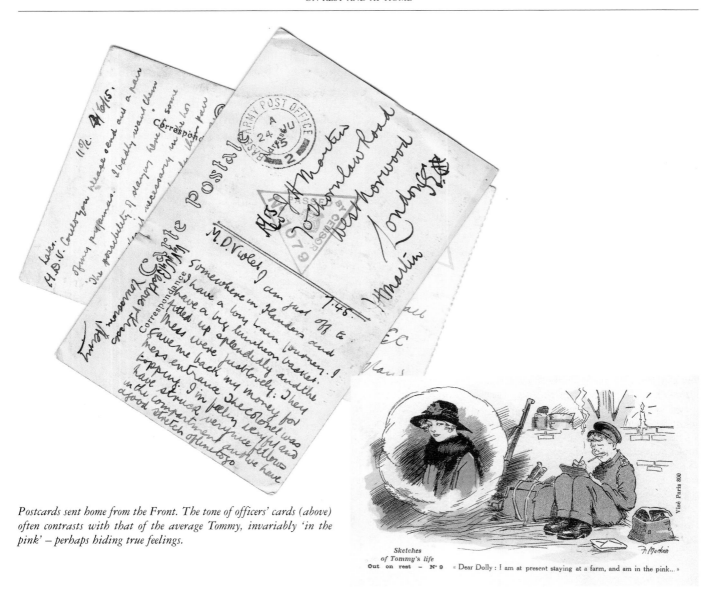

Postcards sent home from the Front. The tone of officers' cards (above) often contrasts with that of the average Tommy, invariably 'in the pink' – perhaps hiding true feelings.

Letters from the Front

Letters to and from the front were of great importance in maintaining the morale of the troops. The soldiers simply had to write 'On Active Service' on a card or envelope, and the letter would be posted for free, carrying the postmark or cachet of the Field Post Office. Each letter would be checked by the relevant officer, who would append his signature to say that he had read its contents, and would strike through offending passages with a blue pencil. Typical 'offences' would be reference to current location, defences, offensives or casualties. A further random check could be made once the letter was in transit – the envelope was then marked 'Opened by Censor'. In response, letter writers would go to great lengths to set up a code system, perhaps using capital letters of consecutive sentences to spell out a place. More innocently, letters from home might have stamps placed in odd positions to indicate love or other personal messages – the card below, with no message, indicates simply 'write soon' with its stamp. Stationery used by the troops was obtained from many sources – bought locally in shops in the base or rear areas, sent from home, obtained from the many YMCA and Church Army huts, or gathered from 'comforts funds' set up at home. Manufacturers were not slow to catch on, and provided special sets of envelopes and paper. For most soldiers, the preferred means of writing their letters was the ubiquitous copy ink pencil; although it was much promoted by companies such as Swan, the fountain pen was just too impractical under service conditions.

The Army Postal Section of the Royal Engineers was in charge of ensuring that letters reached home safely, as well as making sure that letters and parcels arriving for the troops were delivered safely – this was often a difficult task, given the movement of troops to and from the trenches, in many different action fronts. Often, poignantly, a parcel would arrive for a soldier who had been recently killed. In this case, the protocol was to share the consumables among his colleagues, and to ensure that personal items were returned. Letters returned to their sender with the cachet 'Killed in Action' or 'Deceased' were to provide a stark reminder of the fortunes of war.

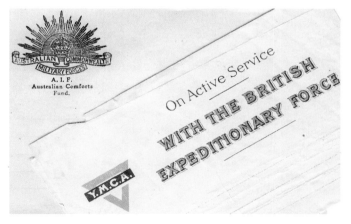

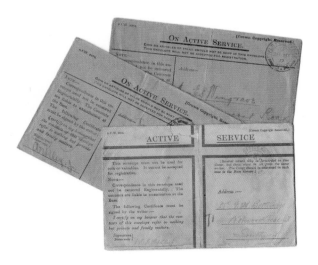

Green Envelopes

Green envelopes were provided as a special concession to the troops, as their contents would not be routinely read and censored by officers. They were an opportunity for the soldier to share his intimate feelings with his loved ones, or to deal with family matters. They replaced the 'red envelope' (which was intended to be used for urgent matters only) in 1915, and were issued to troops at the rate of one or two a week. Single man Rifleman Dennis of the 21st KRRC was more than happy to give his green envelopes to men with families and wives; he contented himself with postcards home. Once the letter had been sealed, the sender had to sign a declaration to say that it contained nothing of military importance. Letters could and would be opened if it was suspected that their contents might give away the location of a given unit at the front, for example, or the impending arrival of other troops, and it is inevitable that some were randomly tested at the base. Nevertheless, the fact that the green envelope was a relatively scarce commodity meant that troops rarely abused the privilege.

Soldier's Diaries

Diaries were expressly forbidden in the field; if found by the enemy, there was the possibility that they might inadvertently provide detailed information about the movement and nature of troops – as such, papers were routinely removed from bodies and prisoners. Despite this proscription, diaries were kept anyway – some companies, such as well-known manufacturers Letts, produced special 'Soldier's Diaries' (like those illustrated below), which contained 'useful information'. Often, diaries were filled while out on rest, usually surreptitiously. Such secretive accounts were usually made using small slips of paper or in tiny diaries, like the examples belonging to Pte J. T. Robinson of the Northumberland Fusiliers (below right), or Pte Frederick Walker of the Kings' Own Yorkshire Light Infantry (below left). Both men, clerks in civilian life, kept meticulous unemotional records of their trench duties.

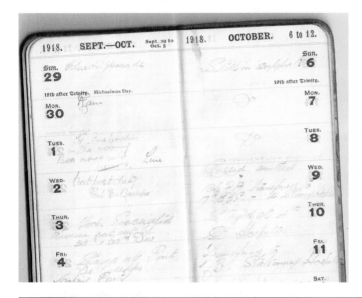

FORGET-ME-NOTS

Tommy was known to be a sentimental soldier, and separation from his loved ones was difficult to endure. Being out on rest meant that he was able to purchase little items that connected him with home – particularly the needlework that was associated with the towns of northern France and Belgium. Silk postcards were avidly purchased, and carefully sent home in separate packages; other objects produced locally used the slips of silk printed with regimental badges that were issued in cigarette packets by the tobacco industry.

Bamforth Song Cards

The Bamforth publishing company specialized in the production of so-called 'song cards', postcards with a saccharine-sweet message of love depicting doe-eyed girls and dreamy Tommies juxtaposed against the words of popular songs. That these were popular with sweethearts is clear from the number and diversity of examples that are found today. For the most part, however, they were sent between sweethearts at home; Tommy, though often accused of being sentimental, was also a realist, and the early editions of these cards were certainly far detached from reality.

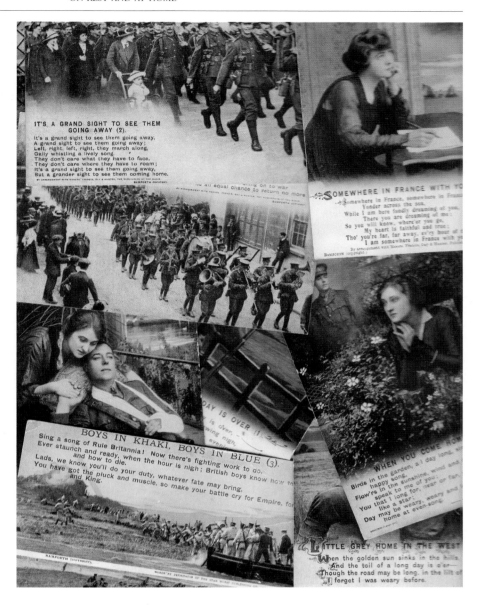

Photographic Tokens

Photographs were essential items of remembrance for loved ones at home and at the front, and most soldiers would carry pictures of their girl, just as most families, wives and sweethearts at home would carry pictures of their men at the front. Often these were just a token of parting; later, when the casualty figures started to bite, they would take on a deeper significance. Manufacturers were not slow to pick up on the manufacture of frames and tokens, even GS buttons, which could hold a picture of a loved one. Some examples are illustrated.

Sweetheart Jewellery

In Britain and abroad, soldiers found further opportunity to pledge their love to wives, sweethearts and family through the purchase – or manufacture – of small pieces of unpretentious jewellery that could be worn as an indication of a loved one 'On Active Service'. Examples from the front-line areas include pieces of 'trench art', such as rings constructed from the aluminium of artillery fuse caps. In Britain, uniform buttons were often made into pin brooches, with the shank removed and a pin added; more elaborate versions include the addition of silver mounts, such as the black bugle horn button, the traditional identifier of the elite rifle regiments. Mass-produced mother of pearl brooches with silver fittings and silver and enamel representations of regimental badges were made for the jeweller's market; more upmarket versions were made from tortoise-shell and silver. Others would bear traditional symbols of luck; horseshoes and wishbones, like those illustrated, are typical. A vast array of these objects was produced, worn proudly by anxious loved ones at home.

Silk Postcards

Silk postcards became a phenomenon of the war, produced early on in 1915 as the locals realized the potential for marketing their skills. Some estimates suggest that as many as ten million hand-made cards were produced during the war, in a huge range of designs. Each card was produced as part of a cottage industry that saw mostly women engaged in hand-embroidering intricate designs on to strips of silk mesh, repeating the design as many as twenty-five times on a strip. The strips were then sent to a factory for cutting and mounting as postcards and greetings cards. Rifleman Dennis and his fellow soldiers of the 21st KRRC were attracted by their sentimental messages – 'Friendship', 'Birthday Greetings', 'Home Sweet Home', and so on, were all popular. The cards gave a small income to civilians trying to scrape a living from supplying the soldiers' needs in the immediate battle zone. For collectors, cards with regimental crests are the most sought after. Other cards had envelopes containing smaller cards for personal messages; most cards were sent back home unadorned in envelopes. For Tommy, it was a chance to send his wishes home 'from the trenches'.

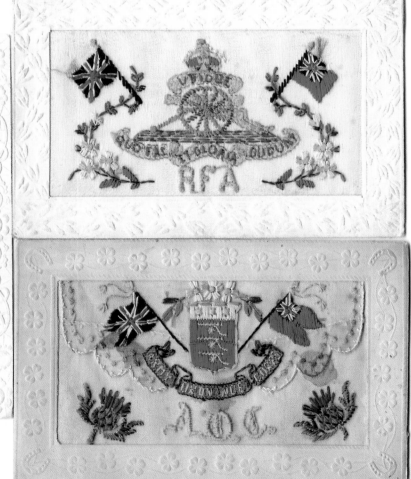

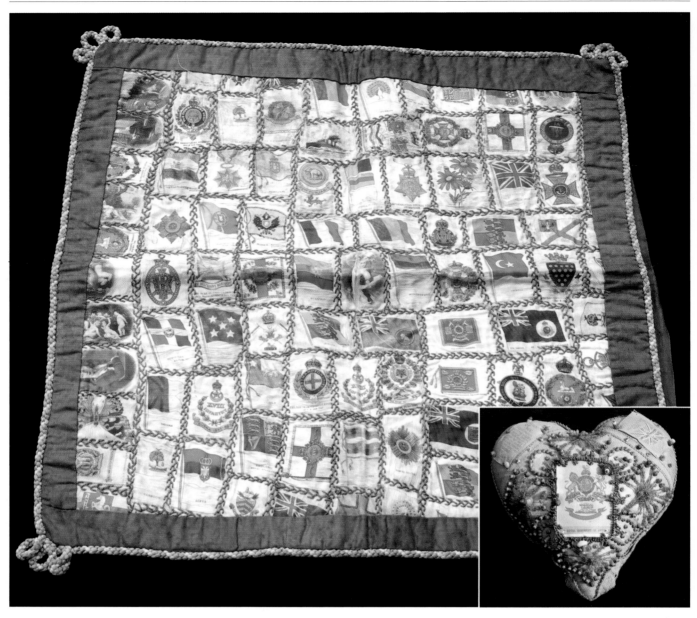

Needlework

Cigarette 'cards' issued during the war by the tobacco companies included small slips of silk with printed designs: flowers, flags and regimental crests were all common, the examples illustrated being typical. The small, delicate slips of silk provided a perfect opportunity for needlework, and were often used on a heart cushion, usually with a regimental crest at the centre, surrounded by elaborate glass beadwork and other cigarette silks with a romantic or sentimental message – 'Forget-me-not' was the most common. The cushions provided a means for Tommy to express his love and longing for home, and to be able to carry home a gift from the war that was not associated with the terrible sights at the front.

Other, less elaborate gifts such as embroidered handkerchiefs were also available; handkerchiefs with flags of the Allies and greetings from France are commonly encountered. The cushion cover above, covered with regimental and flower silks, is another example of the artisan work associated with Tommy in France.

CHRISTMAS WISHES

Spending Christmas in the trenches had an extra poignancy. Separated from their loved ones, soldiers felt a deep sense of longing for home. The festival was commemorated by the purchase and sending of Christmas cards in a two-way traffic that was experienced on all fronts. The cards sent from the trenches still aimed to express the traditional wishes of hopes for Peace on Earth. Famously, in 1914, the sense of goodwill spilled out into the front line, with the Christmas Truce. Christmas gifts were sent from a variety of sources at home, with chocolate, cigarettes and even Christmas puddings being sent from the proceeds of subscription funds. The most famous was the gift issued by Princess Mary's Fund in the first Christmas of the war, 1914, but its delivery clogged the supply lines, and this generosity would never again be repeated.

Princess Mary's Gift

One of the most commonly encountered items relating to the First World War is the brass Princess Mary's gift box. This brass box, well constructed and with designs inspired by the Art Nouveau *movement, was treasured by all who received it in Christmas 1914 – their appreciation is evidenced by the abundance of boxes that exist today. Many still contain the wartime mementoes of the recipient, such as badges, cloth insignia and medals. Princess Mary, aged 17 in 1914, had intended to pay for this personal gift from her allowance, but this was deemed to be an impractical suggestion. Instead it was suggested that a public fund be set up in her name, an idea that took shape at the Ritz Hotel on 14 October 1914. The bulk of the work in administering the fund was carried out by an executive committee, chaired by the Duke of Devonshire. This was established to carry out the wishes of the Princess, that 'every sailor afloat and every soldier at the front' – 145,000 men under the command of Admiral Sir John Jellicoe, and 350,000 men commanded by Field Marshal Sir John French – should receive a gift. It was estimated that up to £60,000 would be needed in public contributions. In fact, over £162,500 was raised, as a result of several high-profile publicity campaigns, with most coming in as small gifts from ordinary people.*

The gift itself was primarily an embossed brass box, designed by Adshead and Ramsay, with four manufacturers initially contracted to produce 498,000. The supply of brass strip to produce the boxes was a major concern, especially when the scheme was expanded to all those 'wearing the King's uniform on Christmas Day 1914' – over 2,620,000 men – in November. A Christmas card and photograph of the Princess also formed part of the gift. The box was to contain one ounce of pipe tobacco, twenty cigarettes, a pipe, and a tinder lighter; non-smokers were to have a packet of acid drops and a khaki writing case (containing pencil, paper and envelopes). Indian troops were to receive boxes with contents varying according to religious beliefs: Gurkhas received the standard gift; for Sikhs, the tin was filled with sugar candies and a tin box of spices; all other Indian troops received the packet of cigarettes, sugar candy and the tin of spices. Nurses at the front were to receive the box with a packet of chocolate. Supply of this complex list of items was a nightmare, especially as there were several manufacturers involved. The order of half a million tinder lighters was to prove too much for Aspreys & Co., and substitute gifts had to be bought in, including the famous bullet pencil with Princess Mary's own monogram.

With the broadening of the recipients to all in uniform, three 'classes' were identified: A, including men at sea and 'at the front', those wounded captured or interned, nurses at the front and the widows or parents of those killed; B, all other troops serving outside the UK; and C, all troops in the UK. The gifts for Class A recipients – 426,724 of them – were ready for distribution by Saturday 12 December, in time for Christmas. The remaining 1,803,147 were to be distributed in January 1915, the wide range of contents simplified to the box, a New Year's card bearing the date 1915, and the bullet pencil. Although common, the boxes are still valued by collectors; unsurprisingly, the rarest items include the Asprey lighter and the non-smokers' stationery set. The box, its contents, the pencil and cards are illustrated.

Other Gifts

The King and Queen also provided a Christmas card, depicting King George V in appropriate naval or army uniform, depending on the service of the recipient. Both are illustrated. Gifts were also distributed on the other side; the pipe illustrated is an example of one given out to the German 4th Army of Crown Prince Wilhelm ('Little Willie'). Other pipes were adorned with Hindenburg, and the Austrian Emperor, Franz Josef. For Tommy, gifts were often sent out to the front sponsored by local authorities, influential people and collection funds for 'soldiers' comforts'. Schools in particular regularly engaged in this activity, the children being rewarded for their efforts by certificates similar to those illustrated. Examples of such 'comforts' included cigarettes and tobacco, Christmas puddings and chocolate. The 'Colonies Chocolate Box' is one example of such a gift, sent from British territories in the Caribbean – today, at least one of these is known to have made it into the front line, found in recent excavations of the former Somme trenches.

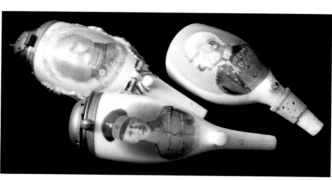

Christmas Cards

Christmas cards sent from the front line were to become one of many postal phenomena associated with the Great War. In 1914, most of the cards that were sent had been obtained from the rear areas, and were based on the commercial versions available, with commercially minded soldier artists such as Mackain also producing cards. Very soon, silk cards were produced for festivals such as Christmas, Easter and anniversaries. Specially drawn and commissioned cards, produced by individual divisions, brigades and battalions, also joined them. Based usually on a piece of art created by a soldier, they were printed locally and sent out in their hundreds. Collectable today, they usually depict a hapless enemy pursued by a plucky Tommy. Some examples, including ones from Salonika, are illustrated.

« I feel like Father Christmas wi'hout the wiskers ! »

GAMBLING AND OTHER VICES

While on rest, Tommy was paid, and used his money to obtain whatever was on offer: food and cigarettes from the expeditionary forces canteens, weak beer and *vin blanc* from the local *estaminets*, egg, chips and coffee from the kitchens of local people, and, where available, the services of women. Gambling was another draw, and the traditional games of peacetime soldiery – such as 'crown and anchor' – would soon relieve the gullible of their money.

'Crown and Anchor'

Gambling has always been a part of army life, and the opportunity to engage in this 'sport', especially when Tommy had money in his pocket, saw the establishment of a large number of illegal gambling schools, particularly engaged in the traditional soldier's games of 'crown and anchor' or 'two-up'. 'Crown and anchor' is a traditional gambling game of the British Navy, using a canvas board and scrimshaw dice. Popular throughout the services, it was usually a mug's game, with the banker, who owned the board, as the likely winner. Private Stephen Graham of the Scots Guards described the game being played in the manner of his forefathers before Waterloo, with huddled masses of soldiery gathered around the 'board', which was traditionally divided into six sections, each marked with a symbol: heart, crown, diamond, spade, anchor and club. Three special dice had the same symbols on their faces and the gamble involved placing money on the board predicting the likely outcome of the dice. The banker – almost always the winner – was usually an old soldier with the gift of the gab. As with other games, the symbols had their own nicknames, recorded by Pte Graham: the crown was the sergeant major; the spade, the shovel; the diamond, the curse; and the anchor the meat-hook. Although it was strictly frowned upon by the army – 'Housey-Housey' (bingo) was the only officially sanctioned gambling game, as depicted by Mackain – there were nevertheless plenty of punters to be found for harder gambling pursuits.

Sketches of Tommy's life At the Base. – N° 3

"House" is the most popular game at the Base. Who hasn't heard those familiar lines: « Eyes down! Legs eleven! Kelly's eye Blind half hundred! And another lucky old dip in the bag! ».

'Two-Up'

'Two-up' involved the tossing of two coins in the air – traditionally two pennies like those illustrated – and gambling on the result: two heads, two tails, or one of each. It is thought to derive from 'pitch and toss', which used one coin, and was particularly prevalent in Australia during the gold rushes of the nineteenth century. This game developed into widespread 'two-up' schools that would follow Australian soldiers into the battlefields of the Middle East and France. It became so closely associated with the Australian soldiery that no post-war Anzac Day would be complete without a game of 'two-up'. These two 1915 Australian pennies may well have seen action.

Women

Women were largely absent from Tommy's life in the battle zone, although he might encounter them at the base, and in the rear areas, where a few hardy civilian souls scratched out a living as best they could. Some soldiers harboured romantic ideals about foreign women, but these were all too soon to be dashed. Rifleman Aubrey Smith of the LRB was not impressed: 'The average Flemish female is an unattractive sight, jabbering hard in a tongue akin to German and frequently showing unmistakeable dislike of the British soldier.'

Farther back in the lines, nurses and, later in the war, members of the Women's Auxiliary Army Corps (WAAC), provided 'decent' women who could be admired with some justification. More often than not, however, men found solace in locally run and officially tolerated brothels (denoted by a red lamp for men, and blue lamp for officers). Risqué postcards such as that illustrated, and racy pin-ups of lingerie-clad ladies published in La Vie Parisienne also provided some mild diversion.

THE IDEAL AND THE REAL
What we should like to see at our billets – and (inset) what we do see.

'BLIGHTY' WOUNDS

Leave was a barely hoped for luxury in the First World War, and it is not surprising that the common soldier secretly wished for a simple wound or debilitating illness that would take him out of the cursed foreign land in which he was serving, back to the green fields of England. Such wounds became known as 'Blighty' or 'cushy' wounds; they were sufficiently serious to be sent home on a hospital ship, but slight enough not to be life-threatening. The casualty figures for the First World War are astounding. The British Empire fielded almost 9.5 million men, of whom almost a million were to lose their lives, while a further 2.1 million were to be wounded.

LUCKY DEVIL!

ARROWE HALL HOSPITAL FOR SOLDIERS.
WOODCHURCH NR BIRKENHEAD.

NAH THEN!! GIT A MOVE ON YER!

HIS MASTER'S VOICE!!

In Hospital

Getting a 'Blighty wound' – a wound that was not life-threatening, but was serious enough to send him home – was dreamed of by most soldiers. The idea passed into popular culture, with songs by Vesta Tilley and postcards like the one illustrated. War hospitals were set up in large private houses and municipal buildings up and down the country, to accommodate soldiers 'from the front'. They were often staffed by 'VADs', volunteer nurses belonging to the Voluntary Aid Detachments. The VAD had been set up under the auspices of the Territorial Associations in 1909, and was run by the British Red Cross Society and the Order of St John of Jerusalem in order to provide a means for women — mostly, at first, from more affluent classes — to give service in hospitals at home. With the requirements of wartime, the VAD would recruit from a much broader cross-section of society. After a short course of instruction, VAD nurses would serve alongside qualified nurses — sometimes with inevitable tension. VADs such as Ethel May, pictured in 1917, would staff all war hospitals, alongside military nurses and RAMC personnel, and some would even use their influence to be sent out overseas, assisting as nurses or orderlies in all the major theatres of war. Londoner Pte George Coppard of the Queen's Regiment found himself transferred to Birkenhead General Hospital at the end of the evacuation trail; others found themselves in large private houses, including Bert Stevens of Enfield, who drew this card while recovering at Arrowe Hall Military Hospital, based in a country pile on the outskirts of Merseyside.

'Hospital Blues'

In both world wars, soldiers sent to hospital, and in convalescence, were ordered out of their familiar khaki and into 'hospital blues', a simple suit of blue clothes worn with a distinctive red tie. In addition, they wore the khaki Service Dress cap, or other head dress appropriate to their regiment or nationality. Cheaply produced, the blue uniform was lined in white, so that lapels would be worn open, contrasting with the bright blue of the jacket. As the trousers were universally long, they were usually worn rolled up. In general, 'hospital blues' provided a poor fit. Depicted in contemporary portraits are contrasting images of Tommy in hospital blues: a typical cheery stoic British soldier of the Royal Fusiliers, complete with 'gor'blimey' cap, pipe and stick; a corporal of the King's Own Yorkshire Light Infantry, an amputee, newly decorated with the Military Medal for bravery; and, at a military hospital somewhere in Britain, a large group of convalescent soldiers from Britain and the Empire. Many would be sent back; others would be downgraded to the Labour Corps; some were discharged. All would be entitled to wound stripes for their uniforms.

'Little Boy Blue'

The blue uniform provided a distinctive sign of a wounded soldier's status, a badge of honour that distinguished him as a man from the front, and this image was used to evoke goodwill in the public. These postcards indicate the generally sympathetic feeling towards wounded heroes in 'hospital blues' that was to persist throughout the war; crowds would often gather to greet the wounded at the main railway termini.

'Our Day'

The image of the wounded soldier in 'hospital blues' was used extensively during fund-raising flag days, which were used to collect money for the Red Cross and other charitable funds committed to providing comforts for the wounded, and to pay for the establishment of VAD hospitals up and down the country. Particularly common, even today, are paper 'flags' bearing the red cross and representations of soldiers in blue, the caption 'Our Day' providing a guarantee that the money would be used for the benefit of wounded soldiers. Other badges and tokens, like this wooden version, are also encountered.

LOOS TRENCHES, BLACKPOOL.

SUPPORT TRENCH RUNNING BEHIND THE FRONT LINE FIRING TRENCHES
THE OVERHEAD COVER AFFORDS PROTECTION FROM HIGH EXPLOSIVES,
AND IS ALSO USED AS A ROADWAY DURING AN ADVANCE.

LOOS TRENCHES, BLACKPOOL.
LOOK OUT POST IN FRONT LINE TRENCHES. THIS USUALLY CONTAINS
A PERISCOPE, FIXED IN THE ROOF, THROUGH WHICH THE OBSERVER
CAN WATCH THE ENEMY'S LINES.

'Loos Trenches'

*The 'Loos Trenches' were a tourist attraction set up in the dunes of Lytham St Annes near Black-
pool. With representations of the front line and CTs, fire bays and traverses, and many other aspects
of current military architecture, these trenches were intended to provide some sense of trench life for
the visitor – rather like the preserved 'trench experiences' do today. They were manned by wounded
soldiers in hospital blues as guides, although these men undoubtedly had more to tell than could easily be shared with the casual day-tripper. These cards were sent by parent and child of the same
family. The message read: 'We have just been to the Loos trenches, it is a very instructive sight and
there are hundreds of wounded soldiers to show visitors around.' Bizarre today, these postcards depict
the result of a 'diverting time at the seaside', completely detached from the reality of the front line.*

Wound Stripe

Soldiers who were wounded were permitted to wear a metal strip on the left forearm of their uniform tunic, to distinguish them from the raw recruit. Wound stripes were an innovation of 1916, and were to be worn extensively by returning soldiers. The stripes themselves were simple in construction. One stripe was worn for each wounding and it is not unusual for contemporary photographs to show soldiers with multiple wound stripes; this family man wears his two stripes proudly.

AT HOME

Leave was much longed for, but it was a rare occurrence, being granted little more than once a year for the average soldier. Getting home was a difficult proposition, even when it was achieved through a 'Blighty wound'. Even when the soldier was at home, he had much to contend with. Air raids were becoming common in 1917–18, and rationing and food shortages were starting to bite. Many men found the experience difficult; one of the images conjured up in the classic novel *All Quiet on the Western Front*, and in Siegfried Sassoon's

famous rebellion against the system, is the alienation of the 'armchair general' from the man at the Front. Certainly, interest in the war was always readily apparent, and took the form of avid readership of newspapers, collection of magazines such as *The War Illustrated*, compilation of scrapbooks, and plotting of advances (or otherwise) on war maps produced by the major newspapers of the day. In addition, everywhere there were reminders of the war for Tommy on leave, from war savings initiatives and crested china to artillery and tanks, the captured materiel of war, in town squares.

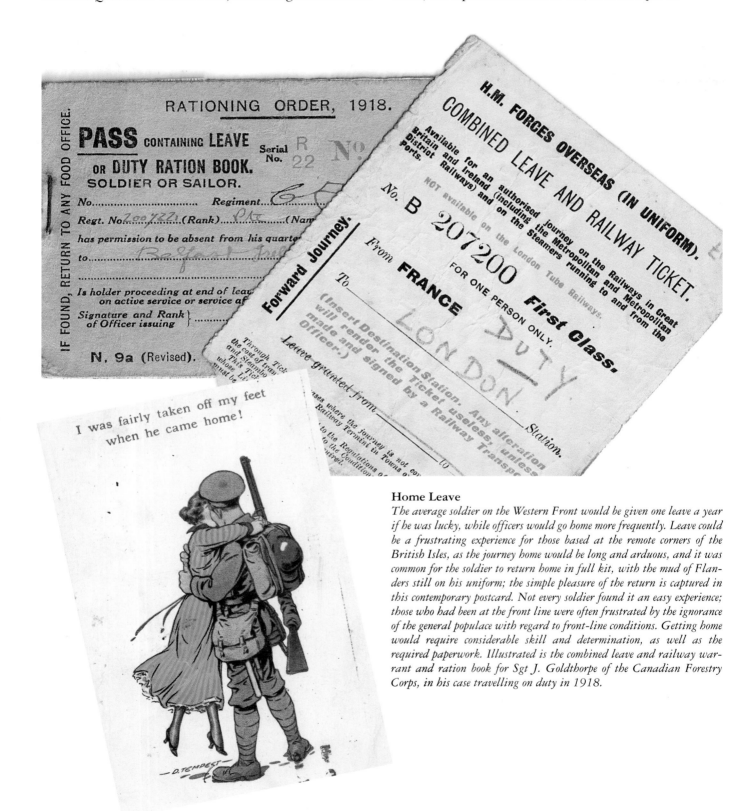

Home Leave

The average soldier on the Western Front would be given one leave a year if he was lucky, while officers would go home more frequently. Leave could be a frustrating experience for those based at the remote corners of the British Isles, as the journey home would be long and arduous, and it was common for the soldier to return home in full kit, with the mud of Flanders still on his uniform; the simple pleasure of the return is captured in this contemporary postcard. Not every soldier found it an easy experience; those who had been at the front line were often frustrated by the ignorance of the general populace with regard to front-line conditions. Getting home would require considerable skill and determination, as well as the required paperwork. Illustrated is the combined leave and railway warrant and ration book for Sgt J. Goldthorpe of the Canadian Forestry Corps, in his case travelling on duty in 1918.

Battle Souvenirs

Tommy was an inveterate souvenir hunter and many battle souvenirs would be parcelled off home or carried back when he went on leave. In his classic Twelve Days on the Somme, Sydney Rogerson describes the lengths that members of his battalion went to gather objects that could be sold on to the 'base-wallahs' and non-front-line troops – enough to fund a desire for extra Woodbines, cheap vin rouge and thin beer when out on rest. The 'flotsam of battle' included shell nose-caps, grenades, German cap rosettes, weapons, gloves and boots, as well as the highly prized hardy perennial, the Pickel-haube (like the Prussian utility version illustrated). Other prized uniform articles were the German belt plate, with its distinctive message Gott mit Uns; the Turkish equivalent was equally highly prized in the Middle Eastern theatre. In Rogerson's experience, by 1916 at least, an Iron Cross was the dream of every souvenir hunter, commanding a good price from those who were away from the firing line. Items could also be removed from prisoners; this 'Hun field postcard' was liberated from a captured German in 1916, and sent home.

Undoubtedly, this passion for collectables put the men at risk. Bairnsfather's classic cartoon, 'Give it a good 'ard 'un Bert', alludes to the dangers of the over-zealous extraction of brass nose-caps from all-too-common 'duds'. Usually, nose-caps were plentiful – shrapnel shell fuses were blown off easily to release the balls within – and not only from enemy shells, but also from 'friendly fire' falling short. In The Great Push, set during the Battle of Loos in September 1915, Patrick MacGill described how local civilians set up shop to sell the 'percussion cap of the death-dealing shell for half a franc'. MacGill, serving in the London Irish Rifles (1/18th Battalion, The London Regiment), was to be wounded in the battle.

THE DUD SHELL—OR THE FUSE-TOP COLLECTOR
"Give it a good 'ard 'un, Bert; you can generally 'ear 'em fizzing a bit first if they are a-goin' to explode."

Trench Art

Trench art represents the folk art of war, reusing bullets, shell cases, copper drive bands, fragments of aircraft, pieces of wood and other detritus of war to create souvenir objects. Trench art was sometimes made by Tommy in the front line, but more often the pieces were manufactured by soldiers in the rear areas where there was better access to tools and equipment. In other cases, prisoners of war would produce such items for sale or as gifts. Typical soldier items include decorated shell cases, letter openers, matchbox folds, lighters, tanks and model service caps. Many pieces available today were actually made by enterprising civilians and garrison (and ancillary) troops in the battle zone, both during and after the war, when a lucrative tourism market began to develop. Some examples are illustrated: tanks made from a variety of materials; service caps made from shell cases; a letter rack; and matchbox covers. There is a bewildering variety, all avidly collected today. Some companies at home also got in on the act, mounting war souvenirs, such as fuse caps, as desk sets (like that illustrated, bottom), or photo frames.

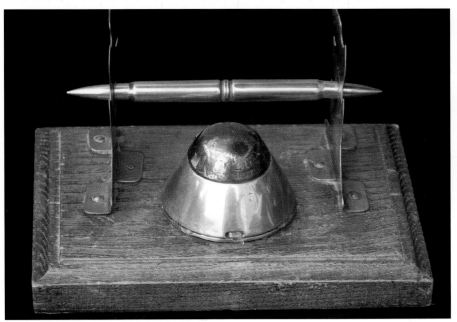

Rationing

Rationing was first introduced in February 1918. Although there had been some concerns over panic buying and stockpiling in 1914, shortages were not felt until late 1916, following periods of unrestricted submarine warfare. Much of Britain's food (around 60 per cent) was imported from Canada and the United States, and the action of the U-boats in sinking merchant ships crossing the Atlantic was a cause of great concern – particularly when wheat started to run dangerously low in April 1916 following the failure of the wheat harvest. Food prices began to rise, and steps were taken to persuade people voluntarily to reduce their intake of bread, with the Royal Family taking the lead. Queues started to grow at high street shops, and not just for the humble loaf of bread, but also for meat, fats and sugar, which were becoming hard to obtain. In response, and following a variety of voluntary schemes, compulsory rationing was finally introduced on the last day of 1917. Sugar was the first commodity to be affected, and meat and fats followed in April 1918 (although this restriction was introduced earlier in the Home Counties). Typical weekly rations included fifteen ounces of meat, five ounces of bacon, four ounces of fats and eight ounces of sugar. Food queues gradually subsided, and ration books like the meat and sugar cards from 1918 illustrated below became commonplace. Postcards (like that illustrated left) and other media from the day reflect this. As illustrated on page 170, soldiers on leave in 1918 also had rationing to contend with.

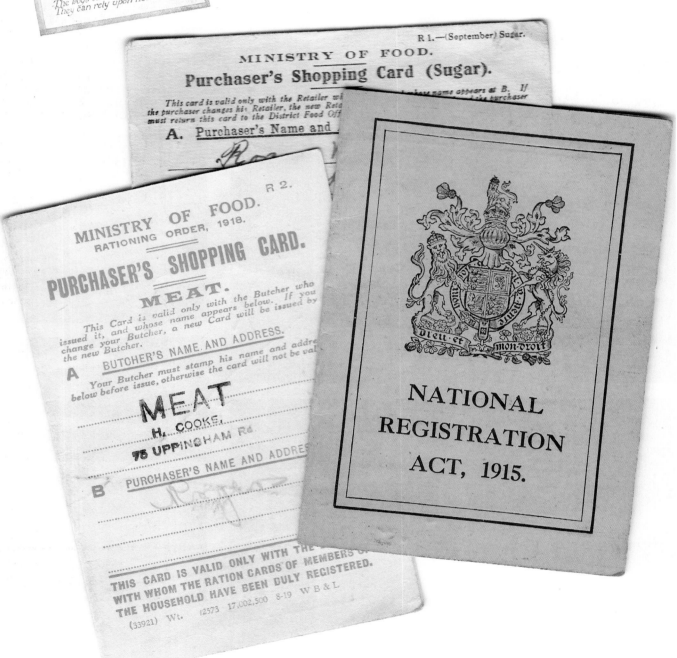

War Savings

While on leave, Tommy would be aware of many changes since his departure, not least the growth in war savings advertising. Prosecuting a world war was costly, and ensuring that there were sufficient funds in the coffers led the government to appeal for war savings from the public. Purchase of National War Bonds and War Savings Certificates was portrayed as a patriotic duty, contributing to the development and construction of the materiel of war. Some of the advertising appealed directly to women; this poster by Bert Thomas likens the investment in war savings to the actions of Joan of Arc in 'Saving her Country' many centuries before. As in the Second World War, many novel approaches were used to promote, including the 'Tank Banks', which toured Britain in 1917. Following the debut of two Mark IV tanks at the Lord Mayor's Show in London during November 1917, the Government mobilized examples of these new 'wonder machines' to raise money and support from the sale of War Bonds and War Savings Certificates. Six Mark IV male tanks – Egbert (No 141), Nelson (No 130), Julian (No 113), Old Bill (No 119), Drake (No 137) and Iron Rations (No 142) – toured Britain in 1918, raising millions of pounds through 'Tank Bank Weeks'. Each tank became the focal point for donation, and each donor received a souvenir tissue like that illustrated (below left); this is a rare survivor today. Postcards, tank money-boxes and other memorabilia similar to those illustrated were produced in commemoration. With the war's end, those boroughs that had raised the most money received a full-sized tank, which was usually displayed in a park or town square – the last survivor now stands in Ashford, Kent.

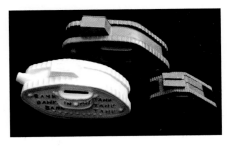

Newspapers

In the days before radio, newspapers offered one of the best ways of obtaining information on the battle front and Tommy would pore over papers sent from home to understand 'his bit' in the wider war. Illustrated newspapers such as The Daily Mirror *and the* Daily Mail *were particularly important in this respect, but the broadsheets were also avidly read, with many compiling scrapbooks of war news. These examples from early in 1914 and 1917 capture the arrival of the BEF in France and the dismissal of the 'contemptible little army'. The illustrated papers, particularly the* Daily Mail, *were able to use the services of the official photographers. The* Mail *produced a series of postcards in colour, sepia and black and white editions based on these pictures, and there were many devoted collectors of these cards. The* Daily Mirror *offered the equally stunning Canadian Official War cards.*

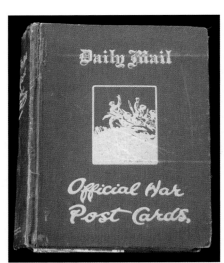

Following the War

Tommy was often the last person to be able to say how the war was progressing, and for many men on leave discovering how his little piece of front fitted into the bigger picture must have been a revelation. Maps for armchair generals have always been of interest. Despite the static nature of many of the fronts, the purchase of war situation maps, published by newspapers and map companies, remained a popular pursuit, particularly as the fronts spread out from Europe, into the Middle East and Africa. The examples illustrated are typical, including the innovative 'Bird's-Eye Map of the Front', which gave a bird's-eye view of the main geographical features, providing more depth to the newspaper reports. Partworks, such as Wilson's The Great War, *were also to proliferate, and the bound editions of the many different examples produced during the war are still common in booksellers today.*

Games

Board games and other pastimes typically reflect the times. One example is Recruiting for Kitchener's Army (*illustrated in Chapter 2*), which represents the early-war push for men. As the war dragged on, other board games would be evolved, with an entirely different aim: getting to Berlin and finishing the job. The Old Bill's Race *game, dating from 1917 and depicting Bairnsfather's creation, was again based on snakes and ladders, and provoked reaction through squares such as 'Killed – go to base' or 'Gassed – go to ambulance'. Laudably, peace is its final goal. Other games that reflect the developing war were extensions of the traditional maze games of the late nineteenth century, the object of which is to guide balls (or even beads of mercury) around a maze.* The Silver Bullet (*also known as* The Road to Berlin) *is an early-war example, encased in glass, and using a small metal ball that had to be guided past 'entrenchments' and other obstacles before reaching Berlin.* Trench Football, *by the same manufacturer, reflects the development of the 'maze of trenches' on the Western Front; here, the ball had to be guided past German commanders in footballing positions, before reaching the ultimate goal – the Kaiser's gaping mouth. Both types are illustrated.*

Crested China

Collecting crested or branded china was a craze that developed in the late nineteenth century, when the British public began increasingly to go on holiday and looked for inexpensive souvenirs to bring home. William Henry Goss developed the concept of small china models of cottages, animals and the like, bearing the arms of the town or village in which they were bought. Some authorities have suggested that 90 per cent of households in the United Kingdom owned at least one piece. Crested china was manufactured by a large number of companies in the Stoke-on-Trent region, including Goss, Arcadian, Shelley, Willow Art. There was considerable rivalry regarding the designs, with legal battles often taking place over copies of popular pieces. By the time of the First World War, the craze was on the wane, yet the opportunity to reproduce models of war materiel as diverse as incendiary bombs and Dreadnought battleships proved too much for the crested china manufacturers. A huge number of different models depicting Tommy's war were produced – what the average soldier thought of them on his return from the front is not recorded. Some typical examples are illustrated: helmets, hats and, bizarrely, legs with puttees; artillery pieces (field gun and howitzer); tanks (Marks I and IV); and Bruce Bairnsfather's everyman soldier, 'Old Bill'. Despite this brief revival, the popularity of crested china was to nose-dive in the post-war world.

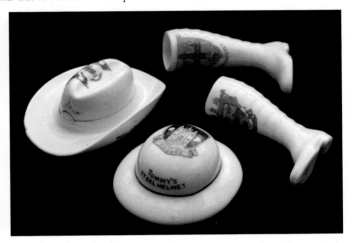

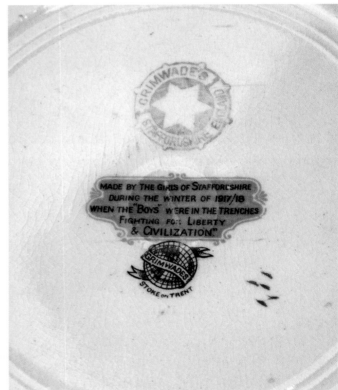

'Bairnsfatherware'

Bruce Bairnsfather's cartoons, published almost exclusively by the magazine The Bystander *from early in the war, were a hit with almost everyone – except some in high positions who deplored the 'base language' and scruffiness of the front-line soldier depicted. Bairnsfather's character 'Old Bill' encompassed the stoic attitude of the average old soldier towards the difficult conditions experienced at the front. His cartoons were reproduced in collected* Fragments from France *books and postcards, and were very soon to appear as transfer prints on china manufactured by Grimwades of Stoke-on-Trent. The sheer variety of pieces, produced from 1917 'By the Girls of Staffordshire when the boys were fighting in the Trenches', is bewildering – a few examples are illustrated. Other memorable objects included bronze car mascots, an example of which sits on the 'Old Bill Bus', a veteran of the Great War, in the Imperial War Museum. 'Bairnsfatherware' would continue to be manufactured into the 1920s, until the popularity of war souvenirs waned.*

6 Aftermath

At home, enthusiasm for the war began to diminish as the years rolled on. Nineteenth-century images of the gallant Thin Red Line in the Crimea, the Relief of Mafeking and the defence of Rorke's Drift must have in part fuelled the initial fervour for the war, and contributed to the rush to the colours of August 1914. However, by 1917–18, with the reality of conscription, the daily news of casualties on all fronts, and life on the Home Front becoming an experience of shortages, air raids, rationing, and the 'dilution' of engineering trades (among others) by the acceptance of women workers, the 'new adventure' of the Great War had become mired in the mud of Flanders.

When the war ended, the British Empire had lost over 947,000 men killed, while 2,121,906 men had been wounded. For Tommy, returning home was often an alienating experience, and for those who survived to be discharged to a 'Brave New World', life was often hard and unrewarding. The cost had been inconceivably high and, in many cases, soldiers who had served their country well were left without work or a stable home, forced to see out their days selling matchboxes or scraping a living in some other way. Medals were issued, but they were of low intrinsic value – in some cases only the silver war medal could be pawned to keep body and soul together. The post-war era saw the development of mass tourism as people made the pilgrimage back to the battle zones. Bereaved mothers and wives, and old soldiers all showed an interest in taking a trip to the sites of war, and new organizations emerged to look after their needs.

THE END OF THE WAR

For many, the end of the war came abruptly. The Central Powers had been crumbling during the autumn of 1918. Bulgaria was first to capitulate, on 29 September; the Ottoman Empire followed on 30 October, Austria-Hungary on 3 November, and, finally, Germany on 11 November. The terms of the Armistice with Germany required the cessation of hostilities at 11am on 11 November, the evacuation of occupied territory, the surrender of large quantities of arms and equipment, and the disarming and internment of the High Seas Fleet. German soil was to be occupied west of the Rhine. For those troops not instructed to take on occupation duties, demobilization could not come soon enough. Many men had been discharged unfit, entitled to wear the silver war badge, but, for able-bodied men, there was nothing for it but to bide their time. Interspersed with the enforced military discipline there were moments of light relief, with concert parties, sports days and the like. It would take many months to return Britain's citizen army back to its peacetime occupations.

The Armistice

The war officially ended with the Armistice of 11 November 1918, after a succession of hammer blows that had fallen on the German Army since the opening of the Battle of Amiens on 8 August 1918 – the beginning of one hundred days of continuous advance. During this advance, the Allied armies pushed the Germans back to a line that was broadly similar to the one where it had first met the British 'Old Contemptibles', four years before. With the Armistice agreed, the war on the Western Front was to end abruptly, and the British Fourth and Second armies commenced their advance into Germany as an occupying power on 17 November. The news of the end of the war was received in many ways – for the soldiers, its occurrence was almost a matter of fact, as illustrated by the entry in Pte Frederick Walker's diary: 'Armistice signed with Germany.' The popular newspapers, such as The Daily Mirror, *were to make more of the occasion.*

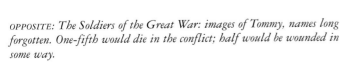

OPPOSITE: *The Soldiers of the Great War: images of Tommy, names long forgotten. One-fifth would die in the conflict; half would be wounded in some way.*

Disablement

Serious wounding or disability would lead to soldiers being discharged from service, receiving a war pension (the scale of which varied according to the severity of the injury) and a silver war badge intended to distinguish the ex-soldier from the civilian. Some 2,414,000 men were to be entitled to a war pension, the maximum they could hope to receive being twenty-five shillings a week. The silver war badge was the visible evidence that a service-man had served his country honourably and had been discharged from service through sickness or wounding. It was first initiated in September 1916, awarded to all who had been honourably discharged from the start of the war. The badge, in sterling silver, was numbered uniquely to the man to whom it was issued (like that awarded to Gunner Shellis, illustrated with its award letter opposite, bottom), and was to be worn on the right breast of civilian clothes. In addition to the badge, discharged soldiers also received a handsome scroll, like the example illustrated below, which was issued to Pte William Chisnell of the Northamptonshire Regiment, discharged on 25 January 1918. Disabled and discharged soldiers were issued a wallet that would also contain discharge papers and pension certificate. Pte Muckle of the Northumberland Fusiliers was to receive a pension of twelve shillings a week for life, following the fracture of his tibia and fibia on war service (opposite).

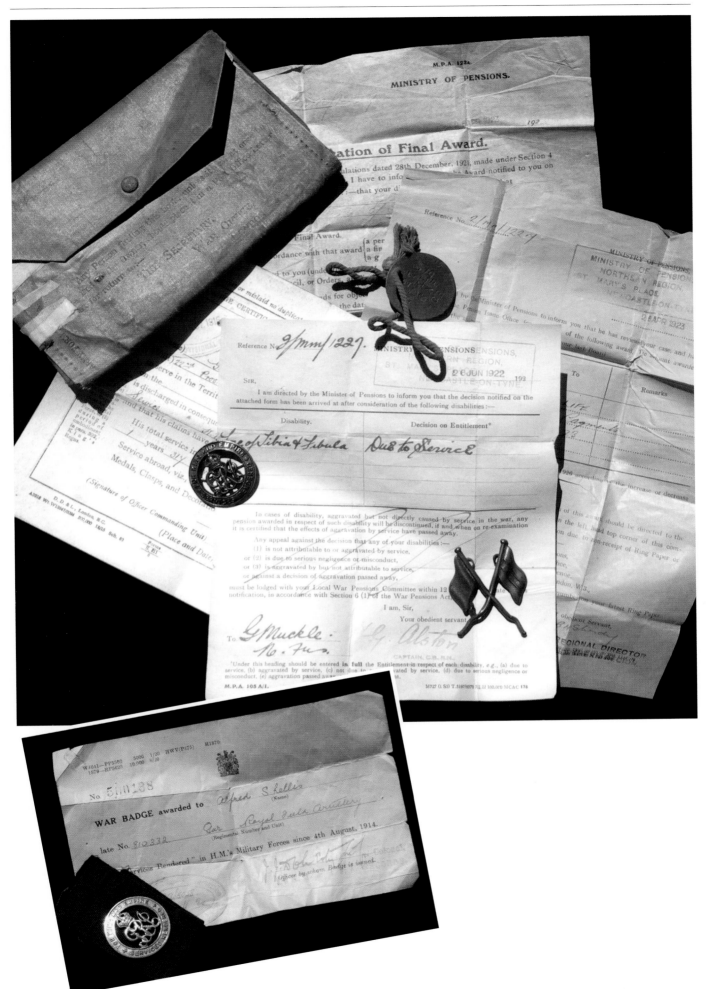

Demobilization

Demobilization was available for some men from the end of November 1918, but many more would have to wait some time for their 'ticket'. Tradesmen deemed vital for the rebuilding of Britain's peacetime industry were released first, with the rest following later. Around 2,750,00 men had been processed by August 1919, but demobilization was not formally complete until 1922. Men leaving the army overseas were sent to one of the many dispersal centres, where their paperwork would be processed. Allowed to keep their greatcoat and boots, and often their uniform as well, soldiers were also issued either with an allowance for new clothes or with a 'demob' suit. The issue of several official forms completed the process; the examples illustrated, from Driver Charles Pitman of the Royal Field Artillery (top) and Pte Frederick Walker (bottom), are typical. Any arrears owed were paid (itemized on the Soldier's Demobilization Account form), and a travel pass was issued, along with a guarantee of unemployment benefit of up to twenty-four shillings a week, the allowance to last twelve months (as indicated on the Protection Certificate). The Certificate of Employment was intended to act as a bald statement of what the soldier had been doing in the army; whether it was of any value to potential employers remained to be seen. Finally, despite demobilization, the army was at pains to point out that each soldier was transferred to a reserve, and that the nation could still call upon him again in time of need.

Homecoming

Depending on which town he came from, a returning soldier might receive recognition of his service through the local issue of certificates, commemorative medals or books. Pte Robinson of Northumberland received one such certificate from his town's Soldiers' Comforts Committee, in thanks for his loyal service on the Somme. Some good employers had guaranteed jobs for those returning, but many others were in no position to make such a grand gesture. In such cases, the unemployment allowance provided by the army would be vital. The London County Council, a huge employer, was to commission a special record of every one of its employees who served in the armed forces, a book that was given and inscribed to each employee who had served. Presumably, they were also offered employment; many others were not so fortunate.

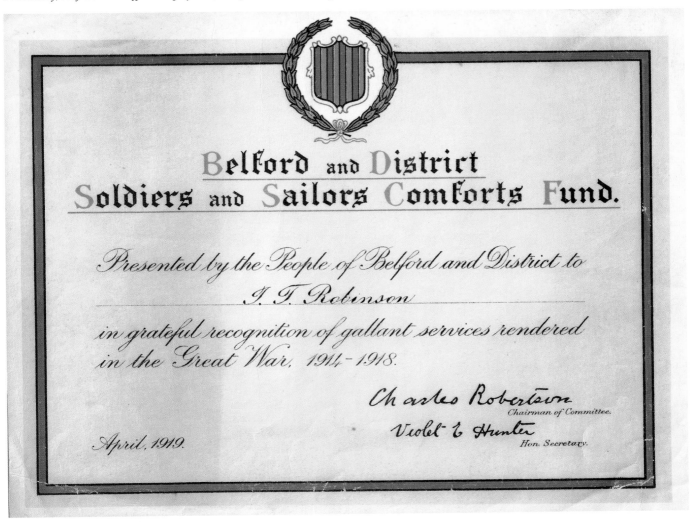

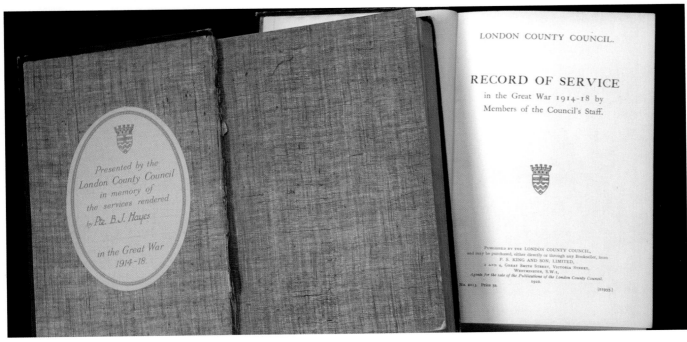

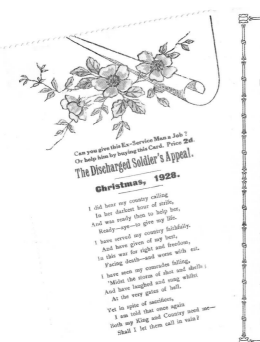

Can you give this Ex-Service Man a Job?
Or help him by buying this Card. Price 2d.

The Discharged Soldier's Appeal.

Christmas, 1928.

I did hear my country calling
In her darkest hour of strife,
And was ready then to help her,
Ready—aye—to give my life.

I have served my country faithfully,
And have given of my best,
In this war for right and freedom,
Facing death—and worse with est.

I have seen my comrades falling,
'Midst the storm of shot and shells ;
And have laughed and sung whilst
At the very gates of hell.

Yet in spite of sacrifices,
I am told that once again
Both my King and Country need me—
Shall I let them call in vain?

By buying this Bill you are helping
an unemployed ex-Service Man.

**THE MEN WHO MANNED
THE GUNS.**

Where are the lads of the village to-day,
The heroes of the war :
Why—many in rags—drawing no pay
Wondering what they fought for.

While risking their lives in Khaki,
Fighting their Country's foes,
What were their thoughts of the future ?
Not starvation and misery ; God knows.

They were promised a better England
Comfort after strife,
What a rude awakening—
To come back to this miserable life.

When standing knee deep in water—
Facing the treacherous "Huns,"
They moulded their Country's future
As they calmly manned their guns.

Now, in justice give them something,
A bit of what they fought for ;
If it's only a tumble-down cottage
With a good old oaken door.

'A Land Fit for Heroes'

It is a cliché that soldiers returned from the war expecting a 'land fit for heroes'. In fact, with so many men demobilized, and the country in the depth of a post-war slump following its gearing up for 'total war', finding employment was a nightmare task. For those who had been left with disabilities, there were few choices. Saint Dunstans, set up in 1915 by Arthur Pearson, proprietor of the Evening Standard, *was one charity that provided a lifeline. Pearson was himself blind, and believed that, given training, servicemen who had lost their sight during the war could go on to lead an independent life. His organization, based first in Regent's Park in London, helped give hope to those who had been disabled, funded through donations or via the sale of cards (like those illustrated below). Other ex-soldiers, such as George Eames, 'the soldier baritone', who was blinded on the Somme (below left), would find their own way. For many others, charity, and the sale of small goods such as matches or cards like those illustrated (left), would be the only way of scratching a living in the 'land fit for heroes'.*

GEORGE EAMES, THE SOLDIER BARITONE.
Totally Blinded on the Somme, July 1916.

"BLINDED FOR YOU !"
From the painting by R. Caton Woodville

"WHEN NIGHT SETS IN
THE SUN IS DOWN."
From the painting by R. Caton Woodville

REMEMBRANCE

During the war, soldiers and other servicemen fought for a cause they believed in, trusting that, when they returned home, their country would reward them. Although Lloyd George had spoken of 'homes fit for heroes', in the early 1920s a new battle had to be fought for social justice for all, with concerns over homes and the right to work for ex-servicemen. This echoed the injustices of the nineteenth century, when it was common to see old soldiers who had served their country well living on the streets. Riots and mass demonstrations by ex-servicemen formed part of this background of dissatisfaction and unrest. In the wake of this, national organizations such as the Comrades of the Great War, the Memorable Order of the Tin Hats (MOTHS), and several others, were formed to provide a support mechanism for their members. The British Legion, formed in 1921, was to supplant these organizations in power and influence, providing a nationwide support organization for ex-servicemen and their families. It continues to fulfil this role today. The first pilgrimages to the battlefields were to start not long after the guns had fallen silent; these pilgrimages also continue today.

The 'Old Contemptibles'

The Old Contemptibles Association was a group of old soldiers who had served in the regular British Army that became the British Expeditionary Force of late 1914. They were that select band who served in France and Flanders between 5 August and 22 November 1914 and received the 1914 Star. The term 'Old Contemptible' comes from the 'Order of the Day' given by the Kaiser, Wilhelm II, at his headquarters at Aix-la-Chappelle, on 19 August, 1914: 'It is my Royal and Imperial Command that you concentrate your energies, for the immediate present upon one single purpose, and that is that you address all your skill and all the valour of my soldiers, to exterminate first, the treacherous English, walk over General French's contemptible little Army.' The British soldiers involved inevitably took this as a reverse compliment, and adopted it as their nickname. The Old Contemptibles Association was founded on 25 June 1925. The last Old Contemptible, Alfred Anderson of the Black Watch, died in November 2005. Illustrated is the record book of the West London Branch of the Old Contemptibles Association, whose members were referred to as 'chums'; its members each had a separately numbered badge.

Ypres. **Hell Fire Corner** British Demarcation Stone.

The Ypres League

The Ypres League was formed on 28 October 1920 as an organization open to 'all who had served in the Great War', but with specific reference to those who had served in the Ypres Salient. Its president was none other than Field Marshal Lord Plumer of Messines and both Earl Haig and Viscount Allenby were vice-presidents, and it was to have considerable clout. It was responsible for the erection of the granite 'pylons' (demarcation stones) that denote the maximum limit of the German advance in the Ypres Salient, including the famous example at Hellfire Corner on the Menin Road. Perhaps its most important mission, however, was to help widows, family and other pilgrims visit the graves and battle sites of their loved ones. It adopted the motto 'Lest we forget', had an official song called Tramping Along, and published a guidebook entitled The Immortal Salient, with an accompanying map, which is still much sought after today. It is illustrated with its equivalent, The Pilgrim's Guide to the Ypres Salient, produced by Toc H, an organization born out of the famous 'everyman's club' in Poperinge.

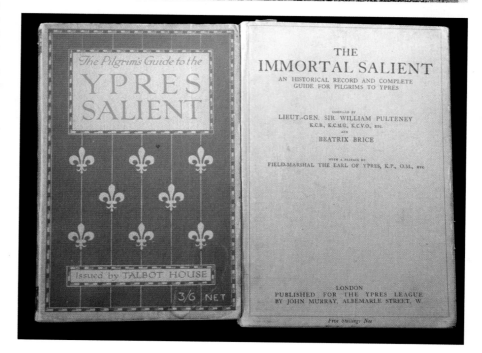

The British Legion

The British Legion was formed in 1921, bringing together four of the main old soldiers' organizations (including the Comrades of the Great War), with Field Marshal Earl Haig as the first president. A special employment committee was set up and employers were encouraged to take on at least 5 per cent war-disabled men. By 1925, the British Legion had formed 2,500 branches and had 145,000 members. Like many of the ex-servicemen's organizations, the Legion was to instigate travel to gravesides and battle fronts for relatives and old soldiers, notably the 1928 mass pilgrimage. A Legion lapel badge, individually numbered to its owner, is illustrated, together with that of the Legion's predecessor, the Comrades of the Great War. The British Legion was to become closely associated with the poppy, with artificial poppies and poppy emblems being sold for the purposes of fundraising. In fact, the emblem had first been used by American Moina Michael, who, inspired by John McCrae's poem In Flanders Fields, conceived the idea of wearing an artificial poppy in 1918 as a tribute to US veterans and to raise funds for disabled veterans. On 11 November 1921, the first British Poppy Day was held on the third anniversary of the end of the Great War; the appeal, known as the Haig Fund, raised £106,000. In 1922, Major George Howson formed the Disabled Society in a bid to aid disabled servicemen. Through Howson's suggestion, a Poppy Factory was founded in Richmond in 1922, with the poppy being designed so that disabled workers could easily assemble it. More complex wreaths and arrangements were also available being marketed in the catalogue illustrated. Haig is pictured visiting the factory in the 1920s.

THE LATE EARL HAIG AT BRITISH LEGION POPPY FACTORY.

Pilgrimages

For those whose husbands, sons and loved ones had been killed overseas, making a pilgrimage to the graveside or battle site was a long-held desire – a desire that would often be unfulfilled, particularly if that grave was in the Middle East or Africa. In the aftermath of war, the Imperial War Graves Commission (now Commonwealth War Graves Commission) was established to ensure that those who fell were given an individual grave or place of commemoration. Soldiers' bodies were not to be repatriated; they were to lie as close as possible to where they fell, with no preference shown to rank or position. The Commission carried on the work of the Graves Registration Service, founded by Sir Fabian Ware, which scoured the battlefields for soldiers' remains and recorded the locations of battlefield burials. The IWGC was to supply photographs of graves to those who applied for them; the photograph showing the grave of Second Aircraftsman Henry Lucas of the Royal Flying Corps, who died in 1917 and is buried at Hadra Cemetery, Alexandria in Egypt, is typical. Henry Lucas was one of many friends to be lost to Win Dellow of Enfield.

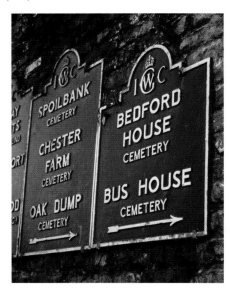

Into the 1920s and 1930s, the crosses erected over soldiers' graves were replaced with the familiar Portland stone headstones or, in Gallipoli and elsewhere in the Middle East, stone markers, and the cemeteries became the 'silent cities' they remain today. In Ypres, some original signs from the IWGC are preserved; elsewhere, the modern green signs of the Commonwealth War Graves Commission are encountered, worldwide. Organizations such as the Ypres League and the British Legion, among many others, were also able to assist pilgrims to visit the graves of their loved ones in the 1920s, with financial and practical help. In The Ship of Remembrance *and* The Tracks they Trod, *the 1926 St Barnabas Society pilgrimages to Gallipoli, Salonika and other theatres in the Middle East are described. Other books record individual journeys to Flanders. For others less fortunate, the Cenotaph in London was to become the focal point for remembrance, as it is today.*

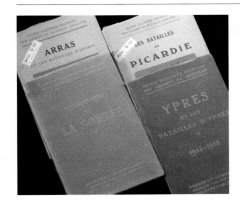

Battlefield Tourism

The rise of personal visitors to the battlefields of the Great War in the post-war world is a phenomenon of mass tourism, with numerous visitors to the Ypres Salient, French Flanders and the downland of Artois and Picardy easily accessible by steamer and road or rail from Britain. Ex-soldiers advertised their services as guides, and larger companies, such as Thomas Cook and American Express, ran tours. It was not long before specialist guidebooks started to appear, those produced by the Michelin Company being most celebrated. Contemporary Ward Lock, Baedeker and Blue guides all make reference to the battlefields, with pointers of where to stay and what to see. Maps and guides to the 'Western battlefields' proliferated; similar levels of support are available to today's battlefield tourist or pilgrim. Also popular were books of postcards depicting the ruins of shattered towns and villages along the line of the old front; some from Ypres and Arras are illustrated overleaf.

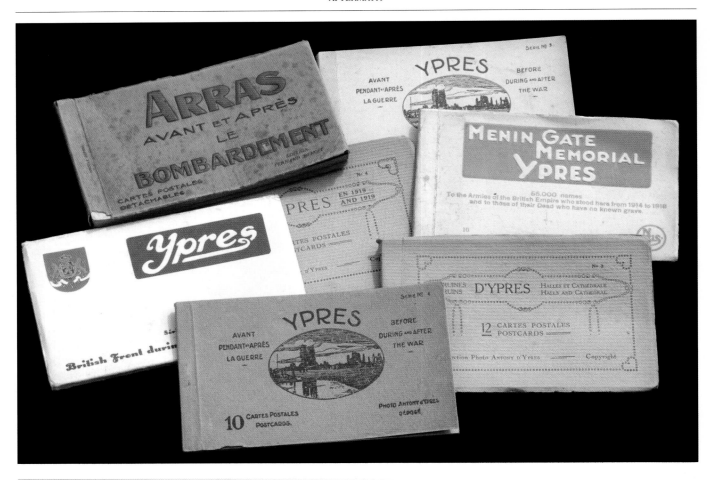

Books of postcards of the devasted zone of France and Flanders were popular during and after the war. Win Dellow visited Ypres in the 1920s – her souvenir then and now booklet and photo of the ruins of the Cloth Hall in Ypres are illustrated. Her brother Percy survived the war, but other soldier correspondents were less fortunate. Win would undoubtedly have visited cemeteries such as Tyne Cott, the biggest Commonwealth War Graves Commission cemetery in the world.

Armistice Day

The anniversary of Armistice Day was to become the focus for remembrance in Great Britain, and was first marked on 11 November 1919 with two minutes' silence solemnly observed across the country. In London, a wooden structure known as the Cenotaph – literally 'empty tomb' – designed by Sir Edwin Lutyens, was first erected in Whitehall on 19 July 1919 as part of the Victory Celebrations. Its sombre form representing the fallen soldiers spontaneously became a focal point for mourning, and there were growing demands for a more permanent structure. It was agreed at the end of the month that a stone version would be built on the same site, and work began in January 1920 on a version in Portland stone. It was ready for 11 November 1920 and has remained the focal point for the nation's remembrance service ever since. In a symbolic gesture of remembrance, the 'Unknown Soldier' was also to be buried in Westminster Abbey as part of the commemoration. The image of the Cenotaph as a symbolic condemnation of the futility of war is plain.

Anzac Day

In Australia and New Zealand, 25 April is a significant date: the anniversary of the 1915 landings at Gallipoli. (The taking of Vimy Ridge on 9 April 1917 is remembered in the same way by the Canadians.) Although the largest force deployed at Gallipoli was British, 25 April passes largely unnoticed in Britain, except in Bury, the regimental home of the Lancashire Fusiliers, whose first battalion was to land at Cape Helles and earn itself 'six Victoria Crosses before breakfast'. Adopted by Australians and New Zealanders as a day of national significance soon after the withdrawal from the Peninsula, ANZAC Day (named from an acronym for the Australian and New Zealand Army Corps) has become symbolic of the birth of nationhood of these two countries. The photograph shows two returned Australian soldiers with their families on what might be assumed is ANZAC Day in Sydney – the pin badges are typical of those sold in aid of less fortunate comrades across Australia and New Zealand.

'In Memoriam' Frames

With so many men killed or wounded, it was understandable that loved ones would wish to cherish the photographs of their men, particularly in uniform. Manufacturers produced a great many picture frames to cater for this market, often with a regimental or military theme. Illustrated are a simple frame from the New Zealand Expeditionary Force (NZEF) and a metal 'theatre of war' frame indicating in raised motif pattern the map of the theatre in which the soldier served. This version is of the Middle and Near East theatre; other examples are known to depict the UK and the Western Front. Finally, perhaps echoing the female figure of the memorial disc, is a circular brass frame with an Art Nouveau *female figure holding a laurel wreath over the picture of the soldier. These were displayed in homes across Britain, in this case, in memory of Pte Albert Howard of The King's (Liverpool) Regiment, who died of wounds in September 1918 at Le Bac du Sud Casualty Clearing Station near Arras. His grave at the cemetery is illustrated on page 192, above.*

MEDALS AND COMMEMORATION

At the end of the Great War, old soldiers had little to show for their efforts. The medals of the Great War, mean in comparison with the galaxy of campaign stars issued for the Second World War, fall into just two categories: stars for early participants – the Old Contemptibles of 1914, and the men who followed in 1914–15. From then on, for the men who served from 1916 onwards there were just two simple awards: the War Medal and Victory Medal. The silver War Medal has been described by some experts as 'uninspiring', and the Victory Medal 'like some of the cheap coronation medals handed out to children'. Nevertheless, many old soldiers would wear them with pride (although others would never take them out of their boxes of issue). In the hard times of the 1920s and 1930s, old soldiers down on their luck would find that these hard-won items would have little intrinsic value, and were difficult to pawn. Gallantry medals had greater value, and two new ones, the Military Cross and Military Medal, were awarded for acts of bravery not warranting the award of the existing Victoria Cross (VC), Distinguished Service Order (DSO) or Distinguished Conduct Medal (DCM). Today, despite their relative uniformity, Great War medals are sought after. In addition, as each campaign medal is individually named, they have become the starting point for many family historians in tracing the actions of their forebears. Those families who had lost a loved one would receive a named bronze plaque and certificate in addition to the campaign medals – rightly cherished to this day.

The 'Mons Star'
The first of the campaign medals to be issued was the 1914 Star, sometimes known erroneously as the 'Mons Star'. Not all its recipients would have experienced the retreat. The star came about from a suggestion by King George V that some distinction was warranted for those men (and women of the nursing services) who had served overseas in 1914. Finally initiated in November, the star was awarded to those who had served in France and Flanders with an active unit between 5 August (the day the BEF landed) and 22 November 1914 (a date during the First Battle of Ypres, when the BEF was relieved by the French). The ribbon of this campaign medal was awarded while the war was in progress, and was worn by some survivors in the closing months of the war. In October 1919, a further distinction was made; if the recipient of the 1914 Star had been under fire, he was entitled to attach a bar to the medal ribbon bearing the dates of entitlement, and a rosette when the ribbon bar alone was worn. However, not all those entitled to the bar claimed it. The example illustrated, awarded to Gunner (later Corporal) H. Cuthbert, of the RFA, has no bar. The star itself would not normally be worn on its own, as it would often be accompanied by War and Victory medals.

'Pip, Squeak and Wilfred'

In researching the later campaign medals of the Great War, just two variations are commonly encountered for the soldiers, sailors and airmen of Britain (and its Empire): 'Pip, Squeak and Wilfred' or, in other words, the 1914–15 Star, War Medal and Victory Medal; or 'Mutt and Jeff', the War Medal and Victory Medal alone. Both combinations were nicknamed after cartoon strips, indicating their common currency at the time. Illustrated is a trio ('Pip, Squeak and Wilfred') awarded to Pte Thomas Brenan of the 1st Battalion Lancashire Fusiliers, one of the first to land at 'W Beach', at Cape Helles on 25 April 1915. Six of his comrades received the Victoria Cross for gallantry that day, as depicted in the famous engraving 'The Lancashire Landing'.

From the original in the possession of Major Richard Raymond Willis, V.C., to whom it was presented by Sir Lees Knowles, Bart., C.V.O.

THE "LANCASHIRE LANDING"

The 1914–15 Star ('Pip') was awarded for service after the qualifying dates for the 1914 Star, up to the end of 1915. Similar in design to the 1914 Star, with the same ribbon, 2,350,000 were awarded to the men who served in the actions of late 1914–15, including Ypres and Gallipoli. The British War Medal ('Squeak'), minted in silver, has been criticized for its design, which depicts a man on horseback trampling a shield bearing the Imperial German Eagle. The figure and horse represent the symbolism of man controlling a force of great strength, a skull and crossbones stand for the casualties of the war, and the rising sun, peace. Some 6,500,000 of these medals were issued, including service in 1919–20, involving mine clearance in the North Sea and service in Russia. An additional 110,000 were awarded in bronze to foreign labour battalions drafted in to assist with the heavy work in the rear areas. Finally, the Victory Medal ('Wilfred') was one of the many that were issued to all Allied nations, bearing the same ribbon – limiting the need to issue the British medal to other nationalities, for example. British, French, Belgian, Italian and US versions are illustrated; there are many more. The British medal bears an Art Nouveau-inspired female figure of Victory, with the inscription 'The Great War for Civilisation' on the reverse. A bilingual version was issued for South African troops, like this one, awarded to Pte J. Mingus of the 9th South African Infantry. A total of 5,725,000 Victory Medals were awarded, fewer than the War Medal, as the qualifying period for this extended into 1920. For those who had been Mentioned in Dispatches (MID), the right was granted to wear a bronze oak leaf on the ribbon of the Victory Medal.

For some men, the award of medals would not be significant; this was perhaps the case for Pte J. T. Robinson of the Northumberland Fusiliers, who served overseas from 1916, received only 'Mutt and Jeff' and never removed them from their box of issue. Others would never have the chance to wear their medals, which were also sent, by registered mail, to the next of kin of killed in the war. Supplied with a certificate like this one issued to the family of Pte Jordan of the South Staffordshire Regiment, they were small compensation for a family's sacrifice.

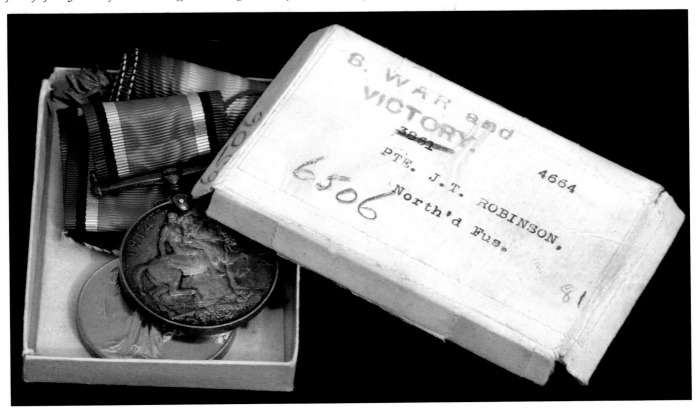

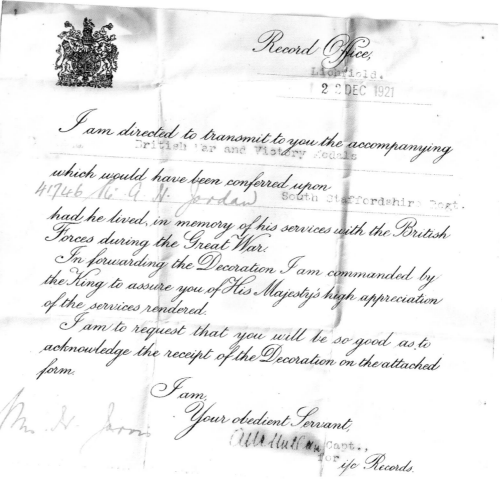

The 'Death Penny'

Officially termed the Memorial Plaque, this large bronze plaque was issued to the next of kin of those who had given their lives as servicemen (and women) in the First World War. Resembling an oversized penny, it soon earned the nicknames of the 'death penny' or 'dead-man's penny'. The idea of the plaque, given by the Government in honour of the fallen, was mooted in 1916, and by November a committee had been formed to consider making the idea a reality. By August 1917, the committee (comprising peers, MPs, and representatives from the Commonwealth) had decided that the commemoration was to be in the form of a bronze plaque bearing the words 'He died for Freedom and Honour'. A competition was announced to find the best and most appropriate design to adorn the plaque and over 800 entries had been received by the end of 1917. The winner, announced in March 1918, was Edward Carter Preston of Liverpool, whose design depicted a figure of Britannia with trident, holding a laurel wreath crown over a space intended for the name of the individual commemorated. A lion 'striding forward' and dolphin represented the armed forces; at the lowest part of the plaque, the exergue, a design was placed loaded with symbolism: the lion of the Empire pouncing on a German eagle. The name of the serviceman or

woman was worked in relief on the tablet left for the purpose, without noting rank or regiment, which causes identification difficulties today. Mass production of the plaques commenced in December 1918, originally in the Memorial Plaque Factory (a disused laundry) in Acton, in west London, and then finally at the Woolwich Arsenal. A total number of around 1,150,000 individually named plaques were produced for all those who had died during the war or from war-related causes between 4 August 1914 and 30 April 1920. Each plaque was sent out in a stiff card wrapper, and was accompanied by a letter from King George V – 'I join with my grateful people in sending you this memorial of a brave life given for others in the Great War' – bearing his signature in facsimile. In addition, relatives would receive a scroll that gave more details, including the rank and regiment/service of the individual, as well as the lines, 'Let those who come after see to it that his name be not forgotten.' Manufacturers were not slow in producing frames to hold the plaques, much to the disdain of the designer. An example is illustrated.

The Gallantry Medals

The Great War saw the award of an unprecedented number of medals for gallantry, a fact that was not without controversy at the time, with awards of medals for distinguished service in the rear areas. Most were hard-won, however. Joining the Victoria Cross (VC, for all ranks), Distinguished Service Order (DSO, for higher-ranking officers) and Distinguished Conduct Medal (DCM, for NCOs and men), were the Military Cross (MC, for junior officers), initiated on 31 December 1914, and the Military Medal (MM, for NCOs and men), instigated in March 1916. The Military Cross was awarded 'in recognition of distinguished and meritorious services in time of war', and could therefore be awarded to those not in the thick of action; over 37,000 awards were made, with 3,155 bars (additional awards of the same medal) also granted. The cross was refined, minted in silver in an 'upright' Art Nouveau style. Famously, Captain Siegfried Sassoon cast his MC ribbon bar into the River Mersey as an act of defiance against the prosecution of the war. The MC is illustrated here with the three campaign medals and a DCM to 2nd Lt Douglas Wharram of the Leeds Pals. The Military Medal was awarded for 'bravery in the field'; 115,000 awards were made, including some to nurses, with an additional 5,977 bars; Pte Joe Clark's MM and trio is illustrated; he would later be promoted to 2nd Lt, also in the Leeds Pals, and his Commission is illustrated in Chapter 3. Justly, the most illustrious award for gallantry was the Victoria Cross, with 613 being awarded in the Great War, including two bars, both to RAMC men.

Victory

With the signing of the Peace Treaty at Versailles in 1919 came the Victory Parade through London in July 1919; the Cenotaph was erected to represent the dead of the Empire at this march-past. The war was over, and the inevitable commemoratives would be made to mark the occasion, but the terms of the Treaty of Versailles would ensure that there was another world war in living memory.

Disillusionment

The losses and conditions of the Great War were so awful that, when a generation of literary soldiers, mostly junior officers, put pen to paper to record their experiences, it was towards the end of the 1920s. From this fertile period came the memoirs of Siegfried Sassoon, Robert Graves and Edmund Blunden, and the best-selling 1929 anti-war novel, All Quiet on the Western Front. *Few accounts would come from the pen of the private soldier – those that did, like Stephen Graham's* A Private in the Guards *and Frederic Mannings'* Her Privates We, *stemmed from their more privileged background. These have laid down such a reference point, that much subsequent interpretation of the war derives from their prose, so much so, that for some historians, the idea of the futility of this war has gone too far. Post-war books written by the ordinary soldier, such as Pte F. Hodges who wrote* Men of 18 in 1918, *and Rifleman G. Dennis who was the author of* A Kitchener Man's Bit *(both locally published), redress this balance, giving a simple, honest account of service.*

Suggested Reading

Chapter 1:
The British Soldier: Barnes (1968), Bet-El (1999), Brown (1978), Bull (1998), Chappell (2003, 2005), Corrigan (2003), Green (1968), Holmes (2004), Liddle (1988), Messenger (2005), Rawson (2006), Westlake (1991, 2004), Winter (1978).
Trench Warfare: Anon (1916), Ashworth (1980), Brown (1993), Bull (2002, 2003), Corrigan (2003), Ellis (1976), Griffiths (1996, 2004), Haythornwaite (1992), Houlihan (1974), Lloyd (1976), Saunders (1999, 2000).

Chapter 2:
Joining Up: Beckett (2006), Brown (1978), Corrigan (2003), Darracott (1974), Holmes (2004), Messenger (2005), Middlebrook (2000), Rawson (2006), Simkins (1988), Tulloch-Marshall (2001), Winter (1978).
Regulars, Territorials, Kitchener's Army: Brown (1978), Cox (1983), Gaylor (1977), Green (1968), Holmes (2004), Kipling & King (2006), Maddocks (1996), Messenger (2005), Milner (1998), Simkins (1988), Westlake (1991, 1996, 2004).

Chapter 3:
Uniforms: Bull (1998), Chambers (2006), Chappell (1986, 1987, 2003, 2005), Funken (1974), Laffin & Chappell (1982), Mollo (1977), Pegler (1996), Simkins (1988), War Office (1914).
Equipment: Brayley (2004, 2005), Bull (1998), Chambers (2006), Chappell (1989, 2000), Pegler (1996), Petrillo (1992), Simkins (1988), Skennerton (1982), Westlake (1996), Williamson (2003).

Chapter 4:
Trenches: Anon (1916), Bull (2002, 2003), Chasseaud (2005), Griffiths (1996, 2004), War Office (1914).
Trench Equipment: Baert (1999), Brayley (2004), Bull (1998, 2002), Chambers (2006), Chasseaud (1986), Dixey (1915), Ellis (1976), Haselgrove & Radovic (2000, 2006), Holmes (2004), Messenger (2005), Pegler (1996), Saunders (1999, 2000), Winter (1978).
Industrial Warfare: Brown (1993), Bull (2002), Fletcher (2007), Griffiths (1996, 2004), Jones (2007), Haythornwaite (1992), Hogg (1998), Nash (1977), Rawson (2006), Saunders (1999, 2000).

Chapter 5:
On Rest: Anon (1916), Brown (1978), Currie (1988), Hot & Holt (1978), Messenger (2005), Holmes (2004), Winter (1978).
At Home: Baert (1999), Beckett (2006), Bishop (1982), Caunt (1994–2001), Currie (1988), Derracott (1974), Holt & Holt (1977, 1985), Jarmin (1981), Jones & Howell (1972), Kennedy & Crabb (1977), Laffin (1988), Nettlingham (1917), Opie (2000), Saunders (2001, 2003), Southall (1982), Walsh (1975).

Chapter 6:
General: Holmes (2004), Jones & Howell (1972), Lloyd (1998), Messenger (2005), Opie (2000), Southall (1982).
Medals and Awards: Messenger (2005), Purves (1989), Taprell Darling (1941).

Bibliography

The books and articles listed here are the most important in terms of fact, but many others have been consulted, including personal accounts. Some of these, containing significant details of the everyday life of the British Tommy at war, and whose examples have been used in this book, are marked with as asterisk.

*'A Rifleman' [A. Smith] *Four Years on the Western Front* (Odhams, 1922)

Anon [Second in Command] *Notes on Trench Routine & Discipline* (Forster Groom & Co, 1916)

Anon [General Staff] *Notes on Trench Warfare for Infantry Officers* (HMSO, 1916)

Ashworth, T. *Trench Warfare 1914–1918. The Live and Let Live System* (Macmillan, 1980)

Baert, K. *In Flanders Fields: Catalogue of the Objects* (In Flanders Fields Museum, 1999)

Barnes, Major R. M. *The British Army of 1914* (Seeley, Service & Co., 1968)

Barton, P., Doyle, P. & Vandewalle, J. *Beneath Flander's Fields. The Tunneller's War, 1914–1918* (Spellmount, 2005)

Beckett, I. *Home Front 1914–1918. How Britain Survived the Great War* (National Archives, 2006)

Bet-El, I. R. *Conscripts, Lost Legions of the Great War* (Sutton, 1999)

Bishop, J. *The Illustrated London News Social History of the First World War* (Angus & Robertson, 1982)

Brayley, M. J. *Bayonets: An Illustrated History* (David & Charles, 2004)

Brayley, M. J. *British Web Equipment of the Two World Wars* (Crowood, 2005)

Brown, M. *Tommy Goes to War* (J.M. Dent, 1978)

Brown, M. *The Imperial War Museum Book of the Western Front* (Sidgwick & Jackson, 1993)

Bull, S. *World War One British Army* (Brasseys, 1998)

Bull, S. *World War I Trench Warfare, I: 1914–1916* (Osprey, 2002)

Bull, S. *World War I Trench Warfare, II: 1916–1918* (Osprey, 2002)

Bull, S. *Trench Warfare* (PRC, 2003)

Caunt, P. *Military Sweetheart Jewellery. A Guide for Collectors, I–III* (ARBRAS, 1994–2001)

Cecil, H. & Liddle, P. *Facing Armageddon: The First World War Experience* (Pen & Sword, 2003)

Chambers, S. J. *Uniforms & Equipment of the British Army in World War 1. A Study in Period Photographs* (Schiffer, 2006)

Chappell, M. *British Battle Insignia 1: 1914–18* (Osprey, 1986)

Chappell, M. *The British Soldier in the 20th Century 1: Service Dress 1902–1940* (Wessex Military Publishing, 1987)

Chappell, M. *The British Soldier in the 20th Century 2: Field Service Head Dress 1902 to the Present Day* (Wessex Military Publishing, 1987)

Chappell, M. *The British Soldier in the 20th Century 7: Personal Equipment 1903–1937* (Wessex Military Publishing, 1989)

Chappell, M. *The Guards Divisions 1914–45* (Osprey, 1995)

Chappell, M. *British Infantry Equipments (2) 1908–2000* (Osprey, 2000)

Chappell, M. *The British Army in World War 1 (1) The Western Front 1914–16* (Osprey, 2003)

Chappell, M. *The British Army in World War 1 (2) The Western Front 1916–18* (Osprey, 2005)

Chappell, M. *The British Army in World War 1 (3) The Eastern Fronts* (Osprey, 2005)

Chasseaud, P. *Trench Maps – A Collector's Guide: British Regular Series 1:10,000 trench Maps (GSGS 3062)* (Mapbooks, 1986)

Chasseaud, P. *Topography of Armageddon. A British Trench Map Atlas of the Western Front 1914–1918* (Mapbooks, 1991)

Chasseaud, P. *Rat's Alley: Trench Names of the Western Front, 1914–1918* (Spellmount, 2005)

Chasseaud, P. & Doyle, P. *Grasping Gallipoli, Terrain, Maps and Failure at the Dardanelles, 1915* (Spellmount, 2005)

Coppard, G. *With a Machine Gun to Cambrai* (Imperial War Museum, 1980)

Corrigan, G. *Mud, Blood and Poppycock* (Cassell, 2003)

Cox, R. H. W. *Military Badges of the British Empire 1914–18* (The Standard Art Book Co., 1983)

Currie, B. *The First World War in Old Picture Postcards* (European Library, 1988)

Darracott, J. *The First World War in Posters* (Dover Publications, 1974)

*Dennis, G. V. *A Kitchener Man's Bit. An Account of the Great War 1914–18* (MERH Books, 1994)

Dixey, W. A. On the design, details of construction, and use of trench periscopes *Transactions of the Optical Society*, vol.15, 78–98 (1915)

Doyle, P. *Geology of the Western Front 1914–1918* (Geologists' Association, 1998)

*Dunn, J. C. *The War the Infantry Knew, 1914–1919* (Abacus, 1994)

Edmonds, C. [Carrington, C.E.] *A Subaltern's War* (Peter Davies, 1929)

Ellis, J. *Eye-deep in Hell. The Western Front 1914–18* (Croom Helm, 1976)

Fletcher, D. *British Mark IV Tank* (Osprey, 2007)

Funcken, L. & F. *Arms and Uniforms. The First World War Part 1* (Ward Lock, 1974)

Gaylor, J. *Military Badge Collecting* (Seeley Service, 1977)

General Staff, War Office *Field Service Pocket Book 1914* (HMSO, 1914)

*Graham, S. *A Private in the Guards* (Macmillan, 1919)

Green, H. *The British Army in the First World War. The Regulars, the Territorials and Kitchener's Army* (Privately published, 1968)

Griffiths, P. *Battle Tactics of the Western Front: The British Army's Art of Attack, 1916–18* (Cass, 1996)

Griffiths, P. *Fortifications of the Western Front 1914–1918* (Osprey, 2004)

*Groom, W. H. A. *Poor Bloody Infantry* (William Kimber, 1976)

Haselgrove, M. J. & Radovic, B. *Helmets of the First World War, Germany, Britain and their Allies* (Schiffer, 2000)

Haselgrove, M. J. & Radovic, B. *The History of the Steel Helmet in the First World War. Volume One, Austro-Hungary, Belgium, Bulgaria, Czechoslovakia, France, Germany* (Schiffer, 2006)

Haselgrove, M. J. & Radovic, B. *The History of the Steel Helmet in the First World War. Volume Two, Great Britain, Greece, Holland, Italy, Japan, Poland, Portugal, Romania, Russia, Serbia, Turkey, United States* (Schiffer, 2006)

Haythornwaite, P. J. *The World War One Source Book* (Arms & Armour Press, 1992)

*Hitchcock, Captain F. C. *'Stand To' A Diary of the Trenches* (Naval and Military Press, n.d.; original edition, 1936)

*Hodges, F.J. *Men of 18 in 1918* (Arthur Stockwell Ltd, 1988)

Hogg, I.V. *Allied Artillery of World War One* (Crowood, 1998)

Holmes, R. *Tommy. The British Soldier on the Western Front 1914–1918* (Harper Collins, 2004)

Holt, T. & Holt, V. *Till the Boys Come Home. The Picture Postcards of the First World War* (Macdonald and Jane's, 1977)

Holt, T. & Holt, V. *In Search of the Better 'Ole. The Life, The Works and The Collectables of Bruce Bairnsfather* (Milestone, 1985)

Houlihan, M. *World War 1 Trench Warfare* (Ward Lock, 1974)

*Jackson, J. *Private 12768, Memoir of a Tommy* (Tempus, 2005)

James, E. A. *British Regiments 1914–18* (Naval & Military Press, 1998)

Jarmin, K. W. *Military 'Sweetheart' Brooches* (Lavenham Press, 1981)

Jones, B. & Howell, B. *Popular Arts of the First World War* (Studio Vista, 1972)

Jones, S. *World War I Gas Warfare Tactics and Equipment.* (Osprey, 2007)

Kennedy, A. & Crabb, G. *The Postal History of the British Army in World War I* (George Crabb, 1977)

Kipling, A. L. & King, H. L. *Head-dress Badges of the British Army. Volume One, Up To The End of the Great War* (Naval and Military Press, 2006)

Laffin, J. *World War I in Picture Postcards* (Alan Sutton, 1988)

Laffin, J. & Chappell, M. *The Australian Army at War 1899–1975* (Osprey, 1982)

Liddle, P. *Soldiers' War, 1914–18* (Blandford, 1988)

Lloyd, A. *The War in the Trenches* (Granada, 1976)

Lloyd, D. W. *Battlefield Tourism. Pilgrimage and the Commemoration of the Great War in Britain, Australia and Canada, 1919–1939* (Berg, 1998)

MacGill, P. *The Great Push* (Herbert Jenkins, 1916)

Maddocks, G. *Liverpool Pals. 17th, 18th, 19th & 20th Battalions The King's (Liverpool Regiment)* (Pen & Sword, 1996)

*Martin, B. *Poor Bloody Infantry* (John Murray, 1986)

Messenger, C. *Call to Arms. The British Army 1914–18* (Wiedenfield & Nicholson, 2005)

Middlebrook, M. *Your Country Needs You. Expansion of the British Army Divisions 1914-1918* (Leo Cooper, 2000)

Milner, L. *Leeds Pals. A History of the 15th (Service) Battalion (1st Leeds) The Prince of Wales's Own (West Yorkshire Regiment) 1914–1918* (Pen & Sword, 1998)

Mollo, A. *Army Uniforms of World War I* (Blandford Press, 1977)

Nash, D. *German Army Handbook, April 1918* (Arms & Armour Press, 1977)

Nettlingham, F. T. *Tommy's Tunes* (Erskine-Macdonald, 1917)

O'Neill, H. C. *The Royal Fusiliers in the Great War* (Naval & Military Press, n.d.)

'Opener, T. I. N.' *The Rubáiyát of a Maconochie Ration* (Gay and Hancock, 1919)

Opie, R. *The 1910s Scrapbook. The Decade of The Great War* (New Cavendish, 2000)

*Patch, H. & Van Emden, R. *The Last Fighting Tommy. The Life of Harry Patch, The Only Surviving Veteran of the Trenches* (Bloomsbury, 2007)

*Paton, A. W. *Occasional Gunfire. Private War Diary of a Siege Gunner* (Bishop-Laggett, 1998)

Pegler, M. *British Tommy 1914–18* (Osprey, 1996)

Petrillo, A. M. *The British Lee Enfield Number 1 Rifles* (Excalibur, 1992)

Purves, A. A. *The Medals, Decorations & Orders of the Great War, 1914–1918* (Hayward, 1989)

Rawson, A. *British Army Handbook 1914–1918* (Sutton, 2006)

Ripley, H. *Buttons of the British Army, 1855–1970* (Arms & Armour Press, 1979)

*Rogerson, S. *Twelve Days on the Somme. A Memoir of the Trenches, 1916* (Greenhill, 2006)

Saunders, A. *Weapons of the Trench War 1914–18* (Sutton, 1999)

Saunders, A. *Dominating the Enemy, War in the Trenches 1914–1918* (Sutton, 2000)

Saunders, N. J. *Trench Art: A Brief History and Guide 1914–1939* (Pen & Sword, 2001)

Saunders, N. J. *Trench Art: Materialities and Memories of War* (Berg, 2003)

Shipley, A. E. *The Minor Horrors of War* (Smith, Elder & Co., 1915)

Simkins, P. *Kitchener's Army. The Raising of the New Armies, 1914–1916* (Univeristy of Manchester Press, 1988)

Skennerton, I. *The British Service Lee* (Arms & Armour Press, 1982)

Southall, R. *Take Me Back to Dear Old Blighty. The First World War Through the Eyes of the Heraldic China Manufacturers* (Milestone, 1982)

Taprell Dorling, H. (Taffrail) *Ribbons and Medals* (George Philip & Son, 1941)

*Tennant, N. *A Saturday Night Soldier's War 1913–1918* (Kylin Press, 1983)

Tulloch-Marshall, T. On War Service Badges 1914–1919, the official issues. *Armourer Magazine,* 45, 46 (2001)

Walsh, C. *Mud, Songs and Blighty. A Scrapbook of the First World War* (Hutchinson, 1975)

War Office *Regulations for the Clothing of the Army. Part I: Regular Forces* (HMSO, 1914)

Westlake, R. *British Territorial Units 1914–18* (Osprey, 1991)

Westlake, R. *Collecting Metal Shoulder Titles* (Leo Cooper, 1996)

Westlake, R. *Kitchener's Army* (Spellmount, 2004)

Williamson, H. *The Collector and Researchers Guide to the Great War. II Small Arms, Munitions, Militaria* (Anne Williamson, 2003)

Wilkinson, R. *Pals on the Somme 1916* (Pen & Sword Military, 2006)

Winter, D. *Death's Men: Soldiers of the Great War* (Penguin, 1978)

WEBSITES

http://collections.iwm.org.uk (a good reference source)

firstworldwar.com (useful site)

kaisersbunker.com (excellent resource for German and Canadian uniforms)

trenchart.org (describes many pieces)

1914-1918.net (excellent and comprehensive)

Index